Transition to Common Work

The Six Virtues

The six virtues on which The Working Centre is based are celebrated in this illustration by Kitchener artist Andy Macpherson. The illustration is structured as a spiral derived from the Fibonacci sequence, in which each number is the sum of the previous two: 1, 1, 2, 3, 5, 8, and so on. In this illustration, the spiral—built on an underlying grid of squares based on the Fibonacci sequence—seemed a fitting metaphor for the story of The Working Centre: the story of an ever-evolving way of working and thinking, a story built on the stories of those who have gone before, a story that reflects a natural equilibrium, a sort of golden ratio.

Transition to Common Work

BUILDING COMMUNITY AT THE WORKING CENTRE

Joseph and Stephanie Mancini

WILFRID LAURIER
UNIVERSITY PRESS

Wilfrid Laurier University Press acknowledges the financial support of the Government of Canada through the Canada Book Fund for our publishing activities.

LIBRARY AND ARCHIVES CANADA CATALOGUING IN PUBLICATION

Mancini, Joseph, 1958–, author
Transition to common work : building community at the Working Centre / Joseph Mancini and Stephanie Mancini.

Includes bibliographical references.
Issued in print and electronic formats.
ISBN 978-1-77112-160-6 (pbk.).—ISBN 978-1-77112-162-0 (epub).—
ISBN 978-1-77112-161-3 (pdf)

1. Working Centre (Kitchener, Ont.). 2. Community development—Ontario—Waterloo (Regional municipality). 3. Unemployed—Services for—Ontario— Waterloo (Regional municipality). 4. Social work with the unemployed— Ontario—Waterloo (Regional municipality). 5. Poor—Services for—Ontario—Waterloo (Regional municipality). I. Mancini, Stephanie, 1959–, author II. Title.

HV110.K57M35 2015   362.5'80971344   C2014-908359-9
                                                    C2014-908360-2

Front-cover image by Andy Macpherson. Cover design by Sandra Friesen. Text design by Sandra Friesen.

Waterloo, Ontario, Canada

www.wlupress.wlu.ca

This book is printed on FSC® certified paper and is certified Ecologo. It contains post-consumer fibre, is processed chlorine free, and is manufactured using biogas energy.

Printed in Canada

Every reasonable effort has been made to acquire permission for copyright material used in this text, and to acknowledge all such indebtedness accurately. Any errors and omissions called to the publisher's attention will be corrected in future printings.

RECYCLED
Paper made from
recycled material
FSC
www.fsc.org   FSC® C103567

Contents

CONTENTS

Foreword

Within days of my arrival in Kitchener in 2007 to join the University of Waterloo and to establish the Waterloo Institute for Social Innovation and Resilience, I was introduced to The Working Centre and to Joe and Stephanie Mancini. The Working Centre was synonymous with social innovation in the minds of those concerned with social justice and positive change in Kitchener/Waterloo region, and was viewed with pride as a homegrown example of successful transformation.

Over the next few months I became familiar with many of the places described in this book. I had meals and meetings in the Queen Street Commons, visited the bicycle repair shop, the Job Search Resource Centre, shopped at Worth a Second Look, and had the pleasure of many conversations with Joe and Stephanie Mancini. What I saw puzzled me: it was clear that something unusual was going on, but it was not clear *how*. How could these two gentle, kind, responsive, and unassuming people have produced what felt like an empire of innovation—including multiple renovated buildings and interlocking initiatives—from the restaurant to the gardens to the St. John's Kitchen, to the outreach program. How all this was resourced—how had they found the funds to do this—to build so much, to feed so many, to support even more? It felt like the biblical story of the loaves and fishes. Direct enquiries produced vague answers about this small government grant, that small donor, this initiative, but somehow these answers did not add up to an explanation, did not relieve my curiosity. I was looking for the magic formula that has allowed The Working Centre to create the transformation of downtown Kitchener, a transformation impossible to miss. Lastly, it puzzled me that, given their success, the Mancinis weren't out selling this "formula." They seem to have found the secret to addressing so many of the problems facing the downtown core of small cities—and doing it while reclaiming and restoring old buildings into beautiful community spaces—all with no visible show of resources. Why weren't they trumpeting their story to the world?

Our research in social innovation indicates that those who want to change the world come in many shapes and forms, as do the movements and the projects they espouse. When we think of successful change, particularly that associated with social innovation, we often think of those changes that transform our culture or our economy at a very high level—creating a sea change, if you will, in the way we as a society think, care, and behave. We see many small and local innovations that never have a broad impact, or those that add tremendous value by providing a service or relieving the immediate difficulties of a vulnerable group, but do nothing to address the attitudes or institutions that increased the problem in the first place.

Joe and Stephanie Mancini seemed to have little preoccupation with taking on the regional or provincial governments, on challenging the private-property laws that produced homelessness as a by-product, or the deinstitutionalization of the mentally ill that accounted for many of the homeless people they dealt with. It wasn't the broader *why* that captured their interest and their energies; rather, it was the personal, specific why—the circumstances of those they encountered in their work. They remained focused on Kitchener, on this community, on making change happen here, and were resistant to efforts to suggest that they had invented or created a process that should be replicated on the one hand, or to divert their attention to broader structural change on the other.

At the time, convinced as I was that only broad institutional change could ensure the success or long-term impact of social innovation, I felt that this decision to stay focused on local efforts was a pity. Nonetheless, the radical nature of the organization and of the process by which its activities multiplied over time felt huge and far-reaching.

So it was with great eagerness that I opened this book and began to read. What this book contains cannot be described as a formula, but it does describe the alchemy that a selfless and dedicated few can ignite and therefore holds lessons worth learning for all those who are unhappy with the world as it is and who believe that change is possible. For me those insights occurred at three levels: that of the individual, that of the community relationships, and that of the broader institutions shaping our world.

The story starts at the level of the individual. Joe and Stephanie are without doubt an extraordinary couple with many gifts. But the gift with which the story begins is that of commitment. "We committed to The Working Centre," they write, "by declining our acceptance into teachers' college. We knew this decision was not a path to riches, so we learned the skills of keeping a frugal household. Our commitment was strengthened by the relationships that were growing from the work of the centre." As a young couple the Mancinis made a choice—to live in a way that was consistent with the community and innovation they wanted to create, and to find strength through the relationships they were building. Later we see that this was translated very directly into the decision that The Working Centre would be a flat structure in which everyone would be paid approximately the same living wage. It is hard to imagine that this innovation would be successful if it had not had the full commitment of its founders, not just the commitment to build an innovative approach to work and to community but to *be the change we want to see."*

But equally strong as this personal commitment to a simple and dedicated life is the commitment to drawing strength from relationships. This book is full of tributes to the individuals who inspired and strengthened The Working Centre. From the local individuals who helped to shape their thinking in the early days, such as Margaret Nally, Hulene Montgomery, Ted Jackson, Ken Westhues, Theresa Houton, and others to the social activists and intellectuals such as Dorothy Day, Ivan Illich, Schumacher, Gandhi, Martin Luther King, Leopold Kohr, Paul Goodman, John Maynard Keynes, and John Galbraith whose writings shaped their broader philosophy, the Mancinis spread the credit widely and generously. And then there were the myriad individuals whose stories make up this book and who, quite clearly, *are* the resource that made the loaves and fishes multiply. They helped with the design of each project and each building in which it unfolded, they added their expertise, their work, and their dedication. As many successful social innovators have noted, there is a kind of flow when the time is right for a project and when the project is right for the time. When that happens there is no shortage of resources of the most important kind—human energy, expertise, and freely given labour. The energy is so plentiful that it just needs to be directed, appreciated, harnessed. And the loaves and fishes multiply.

Of course there were mistakes—projects that proved too difficult or circumstances that defeated their efforts. But each of these were treated as a learning opportunity, because the core of the initiative was not a single project but rather a "set of virtues," a way of living and engaging others, an exchange of labour and of caring. This was the essence that could fill numerous project vessels, and when any single vessel was cracked, that was how learning got in. A new vessel could be created.

So that answered my first question: how such unassuming, gentle individuals could inspire so much change—it was in fact their receptive and unassuming approach that allowed others to step up, to connect their own visions and energies. And that answered the second question, how so much could be made from so little. It was so little money, perhaps, but so much of a more precious resource—the dedication of time, attention, passion caring, and, above all, work.

Which brings me to the third question: Why weren't Joe and Stephanie promoting their innovation—taking it to other communities and trying to provoke institutional change? It was in this dimension that I learned the most from this book. For while so much of our work in social innovation has pointed to the need to create institutional change in order to sustain an innovation over time, our studies of social innovation also suggest that resilient systems (and systems where innovation is a way of life) are those where hierarchy does not become too rigidly fixed, where values of equality prevail, where there is ongoing learning, and where the wisdom of elders is respected as holding the keys to contemporary challenges. What the Mancinis, and the many, many individuals who joined them in the creative enterprise that is The Working Centre, have done is to perpetuate a way of being, a way espoused by Gandhi, Dorothy Day, Ivan Illich. They have brought these themes into their work in Kitchener, and in so doing they have strengthened a thread that runs through our Western democracies. The virtues they espouse in this book may not characterize our dominant institutions, but they do characterize resilient organizations and resilient communities. The real innovation is to enact these virtues once again, in a new time and a new place, and through succeeding, keep alive this candle flame—a viable alternative for another generation. As the poet Wallace Stevens said:

> Out of this same light, out of the central mind,
> We make a dwelling in the evening air,
> In which being there together is enough.

Frances Westley
J.W. McConnell Chair in Social Innovation.
Waterloo Institute for Social Innovation and Resilience
Waterloo, February 2015

KENNETH WESTHUES

Foreword

Since its founding in 1982, the Working Centre has won broad recognition and respect in Waterloo Region, Ontario, a city of half a million two hours west of Toronto. Yet few people there or anywhere appreciate what an extraordinary, seminal institution it is. This eye-opening book by its founders corrects superficial impressions. It will awaken fresh, hopeful, practical thinking in anybody worried about today's economic trends and the people left behind.

Probably most residents of Kitchener-Waterloo imagine that the Working Centre is an ordinary charity, the same kind of non-profit organization as exists in most cities, for providing food, clothing, and shelter to the poor. At St. John's Kitchen on Victoria Avenue, the Working Centre invites all comers to share a noontime meal at no charge. In the same building, Worth a Second Look is a thrift store selling low-cost used furniture, books, and housewares. The Green Door on Market Lane sells used clothing. In renovated houses and storefronts throughout the downtown, the Working Centre rents apartments at below-market rates. Its original and oldest project is the unemployment help centre on Queen Street in the Kitchener core.

The Working Centre is indeed a charity, legally chartered and frugally run. That it is known as such is a good thing. Close to a thousand people show up every spring for the centre's main fundraising event, the Mayors' Dinner. Thousands more make tax-deductible donations throughout the year, especially at Christmas, and drop off surplus bikes, home furnishings, and clothes. Hundreds volunteer their time. This generous community support, along with grants from foundations and all levels of government, keeps the centre financially afloat.

Whoever visits the Working Centre in person or pages through its quarterly newsletter, *Good Work News,* gets hints that the Working Centre is not just your average dispenser of handouts and alms. It offers personal counselling and psychiatric help. It includes a variety of social enterprises: a thriving restaurant called Queen Street Commons, which also sells books and crafts, and where folk music, jazz, and poetry are sometimes on offer; the Speak English Café for immigrants; Computer Recycling; Recycle Cycles; Hacienda Sarria Market Garden; Community Access Bikeshare; GROW Herbal Gardens; the Commons Studio for digital media. Also part of the Working Centre is the Waterloo School for Community Development, which offers an annual Diploma Program in Local Democracy, now in its seventh year. The centre has long hosted courses of the University of Waterloo and Wilfrid Laurier University. Its groundbreaking joint initiative with WLU, the Community Engagement Option for undergraduates, enrolled its first class in 2014.

Beyond this multiplicity of programs and services, visitors to the Working Centre notice also a distinct feel or atmosphere, a culture that is hard to put one's finger on: at once friendly and serious, bustling and calm, laid-back and purposeful, bohemian and businesslike. The Working Centre is a place where work gets done with the least possible bureaucracy. There is lots of listening, with every effort made *not* to give anyone the runaround. Visitors have trouble telling paid staff from volunteers, or volunteers from people who might be called *clients* if that word were used—which it is not.

The Working Centre is more than the full list of its projects, more than the sum of its parts. This book tells what that "more" is. Here Joe and Stephanie Mancini, who created the centre and embraced it as their life's work when they were fresh out of university, trace its history, its growth from conversation around a kitchen table to the present network of myriad activities, with scores of employees, a dozen properties, and a seven-figure budget.

Most important, the Mancinis set forth in this book the thinking behind the Working Centre, the traditions and philosophies, the values and virtues that have inspired it and guided the evolution of its priorities, policies, and practices. These authors may sound utopian. You may doubt that their lofty plans could ever work. In fact, those plans have been working for thirty-two years, while hundreds of other social-change initiatives have failed. Theirs is a daring venture that began with no capital at all but has grown, prospered, and woven itself securely into the fabric of its host city. How has this been possible? This book tells how—in fluent, straightforward, factual, readable, unaffected prose.

Without trying to summarize this book, what can I say to whet your appetite for it?

For a start, I can tell you that the Working Centre has captured my own interest, time, and work for the greater part of my adult life. In 1987, when Joe asked me to join the Board of Directors, I would not have agreed had I not detected in our conversation the prospect of something fresh and decent, an experiment in social change that promised to bring out the best in all concerned, in particular people treated as chaff in the mainstream economy.

I would not have continued on the board all these years had I not witnessed Joe and Stephanie's fidelity to that promise, even when the coffers were dry and the outlook grim. What I saw over time was the blossoming of an institution that recalled in some ways the Hull House that Jane Addams and Ellen Starr created in Chicago in 1889, and the Catholic Worker House that Dorothy Day and Peter Maurin founded in New York in 1933. Making the Working Centre part of my academic and personal life these past twenty-eight years has been a pleasure and privilege.

Material abundance unimaginable in times past is a hallmark of our time. The free capitalist economy has spawned so much technical invention and such mass production of consumer goods that in the Western World only octogenarians can remember when the essentials of life were scarce. To be sure, some citizens are left out. A small proportion of the population lives in absolute poverty. As a society, nonetheless, we have a surfeit of food, clothes, housing, and much else. The question is how to respond to this glut of stuff.

The mainstream response is to keep finding new things to spend money on. This is the ethic of consumerism that the Barenaked Ladies poked fun at. "If I had a million dollars," Steven Page and Ed Robertson sang in 1989, "we wouldn't have to eat Kraft Dinner"—adding that they'd eat it anyway because they like it, so they'd eat more of it, with "really expensive ketchups." They would also buy a house, car, furniture, fur coat, Picasso, an emu or some other exotic pet ("Haven't you always wanted a monkey?"), and a tree fort with pre-wrapped sausages and things in a tiny fridge. And on top of everything else, the money would "buy your love."

The song was such a hit that at the band's concerts in the 1990s, fans would pelt the stage with boxes of Kraft Dinner. This became so disruptive the Ladies eventually asked that the KD be donated to food banks instead. Bins for this purpose were provided at the entrance to performances.

The Working Centre pointedly rejects the materialist ethic the band parodied. "Simple living" is a watchword in all its projects and programs. This is not out of ascetic self-denial. The Mancinis are not St. Joe and St. Stephanie. They simply recognized from the start that beyond a certain level, accumulating things does not make people happier, instead sadder and needier, feeling envy that some other people have more. The Working Centre rejects consumerism in favour of producerism—the ethic of finding joy in the work of mak-

ing things (conceiving, designing, building, assembling, painting, decorating, repairing, renovating, and, maybe best of all, growing and cooking) in relations of care and reciprocity. "Work as gift" is a Working Centre shibboleth. So is "community tools," the precious instruments for producing mutually valued goods.

An emphasis on doing rather than having pervades all facets of the Working Centre. St. John's Kitchen invites people not just to eat nutritious meals but to help make them, serve them, and clean up afterwards. Goods and services are provided not as ends in themselves but as means for people to develop their skills and get on top of life. Even in a society saturated with ads for things beyond financial reach, this orientation draws thousands through the Working Centre's doors, and not only the unemployed, marginalized, and poor. Over the years, the centre has attracted as staff members and volunteers hundreds of refugees from consumer capitalism: lawyers, doctors, teachers, nurses, professors, holders of all kinds of advanced degrees, who are fed up with climbing the consumption ladder and choose instead to find meaning in work.

At the same time, the Working Centre's *homo faber* philosophy has deterred it from a scornful stance of moral superiority toward the consumerist mainstream. In 2014, an Ottawa soup kitchen made headlines by announcing it would henceforth refuse donations of Kraft Dinner, deeming its nutritional value too low. KD joined canned stew, potato chips, pop, candy and hot dogs on the agency's list of unwelcome foods.

Folks at the Working Centre might sympathize with a ban on KD, on grounds of bland taste if not poor nutrition. The menu at Queen Street Commons Café is vegetarian with zing, heavy on whole grains, vegetables, and herbs. St. John's Kitchen avoids junk food and serves balanced meals. Yet the Working Centre shies away from politically correct rules, preferring to accept people as they are, warts and all, and to try to respond to them humbly, constructively. The centre shows few signs of a self-conception as an ethical elite.

"If I had a million dollars," Joe Mancini began a speech in January 2015, "we would buy a six-plex, a four-plex, and 256 King St., and create nineteen more units of affordable supportive housing." The audience laughed and cheered, knowing that the Working Centre had just received its largest single grant to date, a million dollars for low-rent apartments. Whether Joe had the Barenaked Ladies's song in mind or not, his line gives insight into the centre's priority: not on conventional consumption, neither on moral virtuosity, instead on providing all with the prerequisites for a decent life and good work.

You will notice lots of names in these pages. It is one way the Mancinis show their awareness that while the Working Centre started out as their baby, it has grown up under the care and guidance of thousands of other people, too. It is a product of collaborative good work, and a stimulus to more.

Kenneth Westhues
Professor Emeritus, University of Waterloo

Acknowledgements

Transition to Common Work reflects the remarkable work that is accomplished by The Working Centre community. It is evidence that integrated communities can build new civic cultures that engage citizens in solving problems with simple work that brings people together.

In retrospect we are pleased that it has taken us thirty years to write this history of The Working Centre. The shape of this distributed network is clearer, and the projects are more mature than they were in our twentieth year.

We have supported the vision of The Working Centre by dividing our labour in complimentary ways, applying our skills and abilities to do the work that needed to be accomplished. There is no project, word, report, idea that we probably have not argued, debated, or looked at from completely different perspectives, while enjoying the growth around us.

We start by acknowledging our children Christina, Rebecca, and Thomas, and all the ways they have contributed to our community. When we started homeschooling they became immersed in a co-operative work culture. They got involved by choosing projects that matched their interests. Christina showed up on the construction crew at 43 Queen, leading crafts, working at St. John's Kitchen and helped start the thrift store that grew into Worth a Second Look. Rebecca was doing construction, bookkeeping, fundraising, and organizing before she was a teenager. Thomas learned thrift store work, fixed bikes, held café shifts, cooked in Maurita's Kitchen, and worked on construction projects.

Rebecca has chosen to commit to The Working Centre community and continues to offer her long-term clarity, hard work, and insights toward the common good. We are grateful that our children continue to seek work that builds community. They have patiently shared their lives as they grew up in the context of this work.

ACKNOWLEDGEMENTS

Ken Westhues has been more than a friend and board member. Ken's practice of sociology matches perfectly with the culture of The Working Centre. He taught us critical thinking about organizations, structures, and how to avoid bureaucracy and hierarchy. He understood and supported our fragile yet dynamic nature. As a professor emeritus of sociology and legal studies at the University of Waterloo, Ken acted as our agent to help get this book published.

The Macpherson family has played a large role since 1987 when Arleen joined as coordinator of St. John's Kitchen. Arleen retired in 1999 but a few years later joined the board and is now president, translating her deep knowledge of our culture into our monthly meetings. Arleen's son Andy is the talented artist who has developed a unique art form that helps to illustrate Working Centre culture, primarily in the pages of *Good Work News*. The cover art for this book is another skillful example of weaving commitment through illustrating spirit and community.

Over thirty years we have had long-serving board members who have come to understand the challenges of doing community development without bureaucracy. These board members have taken their responsibility seriously and have watched with pride as the organization has evolved its leadership without internal strife. We would like to thank our present board members and those who have served for long periods including Gordon Crosby, Jim Crawford, Mike D'Silva, Rob Donelson, Roman Dubinski, Dennis Eaton, Mary Graham, Rita Levato, Arleen Macpherson, Maurita McCrystal, Margaret Motz, Linda Nagel, Margaret Nally, Bob Nally, Patrice Reitzel, Wayne Samuelson, Mike Shimpo, Carol Taylor, Andrew Telegdi, Ken Westhues, and John Wintermeyer.

The coordinators of The Working Centre have contributed in extraordinary ways to the building of our co-operative culture. We have all grown together, sometimes bewildered by the community growing around us. We would like to acknowledge the work of Arleen Macpherson, Jennifer Mains, Beth Greco, Don Gingerich, Darol Seigmiller, Michael Bernhard, Dave Bright, Jason Spencer, Chris Mockler, and Val Girodat, all of whom have offered tremendous energy that reflects their commitment to the common good.

The work described in this book is carried out every day by many people who have helped to shape the community of The Working Centre. The daily practice of compassion and intentionality makes the ideas in this book a reality. The principles shared here have been forged and developed in practical action, the discussion of ideas and the daily work contributed in significant ways.

ACKNOWLEDGEMENTS

Finally, we want to thank two people who edited drafts of this manuscript. Nicole Langois offered her editing talents to focus the manuscript and teach us book writing from an editor's perspective. Jim Lotz, our friend from Nova Scotia, is Canada's most insightful community development writer. He has been urging us to write our story since the 1990s. On a visit, we gave him a draft manuscript and it came back in a series of letters, expertly edited and filled with helpful comments. It has been a pleasure to work with Brian Henderson, Clare Hitchens, Blaire Comacchio, Rob Kohlmeier, and the other resourceful and devoted staffers of Wilfrid Laurier University Press.

Lastly, we thank our parents, Joe and Phyllis Mancini and Ron and Vicki MacDonald for giving us the opportunity to grow up with faith and optimism for a better world.

Joe and Stephanie Mancini
Kitchener

PART ONE

The Working Centre Takes Root

Illustration by Andy Macpherson

CHAPTER ONE

Introduction: Beyond Us and Them

A Community Takes Root

The Working Centre was a new idea, a freshly planted seed, in 1982. It found a nourishing, cultivated soil on Queen Street South in downtown Kitchener. Friendship, hospitality, and problem solving helped the centre take root as a useful place. From its beginnings, it fostered a world view that was less materialistic than the dominant culture. The Working Centre was founded on the values of living simply and nurturing dialogue, inclusion, and openness to the other. Practical and communal services around employment, housing, and other human services were organized in ways that people could shape together. The projects grew from the frustrations and waste of human potential that result from unemployment, poverty, and dependency.

Sir Albert Howard describes "the maintenance of the fertility of the soil as the first condition of any permanent system of agriculture."[1] Equally true is that the maintenance of the virtues[2] are the primary condition for sustainable living, understood as changing civic culture through opening ourselves to greater compassion, inclusiveness and hope. Authentic community development is rooted in norms of generosity.[3] On Queen Street, over the years, we have cultivated the soil so that The Working Centre could grow and flourish.

The Working Centre consists of 67,000 square feet of community space in various locations in downtown Kitchener. We provide the buildings, leaders who act like servants, tools to make the projects function, a base of community-development knowledge and design, and a commitment to support individuals through their stories and pain.

We chose to write The Working Centre story in one voice. We name ourselves in stories where we are directly involved, but the majority of the time we used "we" and "our" to describe our role. The "we" and "our" includes Stephanie and Joe Mancini and many others whose thoughts and actions

3

have been crucial and decisive. The Working Centre has been a communal effort involving thousands of people. Names of the many people who make up the Working Centre story are sprinkled throughout the book. Where possible, we have gained permission to use real names. In other cases we have changed the names to protect the privacy of the individual. The back of the book contains a section dedicated to naming those crucial to our work.

Out of Your Car

It is now more than thirty years since The Working Centre took root. To see how this community has branched out and followed its lofty ideals, we will do what Wendell Berry suggests is the best way to learn what is going on around you: get off your horse and out of your car.[4] The Working Centre is best experienced with your feet on the ground, feeling the vibrancy of its spaces and places, watching how ideas and practices live in the midst of a community doing its work.

On a Friday afternoon in mid-June 2013, after a hot humid week, a torrential rainstorm clears the streets. Joe parks and runs from the borrowed van to St. John's Kitchen at 97 Victoria St. N., where Margaret Nally is leading a memorial service for Kate. The service has started and Frank waves Joe over to sit beside him. "Did you hear about the flood downstairs?" he asks in his mischievous way. Joe rolls his eyes, hoping it is not as bad as Frank implies.

When Margaret invites people to share their stories, memories reveal complex layers of relationships. Kate had an addiction to alcohol and drugs that she could not break. She died of complications from a life lived hard and full, a life of accidents and disappointments, the life of a woman we came to know and love.

Chris tells about Kate taking loads of food from the market distribution project and delivering it by handcart to people who couldn't get out their apartments. Barb tells how Kate had an eye for making interesting displays at Worth a Second Look (WASL), while Ruthi remembers Kate as a sous chef at Maurita's Kitchen, proudly offering her culinary skills. Kate used to mix flowers and art at the greenhouse and art space, and she was always available to scrape and clean dishes at St. John's Kitchen. What everyone remembers was her endearing way of making friends, always asking forgiveness while staunchly doing her own thing.

For five years, Kate has been helping us hand deliver our yearly fundraising letter to Kitchener-Waterloo neighbourhoods. Some years she could handle multiple routes and other years only one or two. This past December she was earning money toward tickets to a Led Zeppelin tribute concert at Centre in the Square. Kate could pack a great deal of determination in her tiny frame. She was living in an unsafe rooming house, just surviving through the evening and getting up to deliver flyers for 8:00 a.m. After the service, everyone gathers to share more stories, snacking on pizza and dessert squares made lovingly in Kate's honour from Maurita's Kitchen.

Downstairs at Worth a Second Look, the flood is as bad as Frank had implied. A crew of people are cleaning up the water using shop vacuums and squeegees. The torrential rainstorm has overwhelmed our roof drains, causing the water to bubble up from the drain, threatening the stockpiled furniture, bags, and boxes. Our daughter Rebecca had stopped into the store before Kate's memorial and called Greg to bring some shop vacuums over to combat the water. They are just starting to win as the rain subsides. Rebecca, in her thin sandals continues working a shop vacuum as a well-dressed young man approaches Joe to do some court-ordered community hours. Joe's first thought is one of exasperation: "Why don't you come back tomorrow?" But he quickly changes tack: "Sure let's get started right now—here is a Shop-Vac. You can take over from Rebecca!"

When we renovated 97 Victoria eight years ago, there were questions about the storm drains. As Joe and Greg discuss the plumbing conundrums and decisions made during the construction, the WASL folks know they need a plan to clean out the back. Eunice offers to work an extra shift while Art plans to spend Saturday trucking damaged goods and furniture to the dump. By the next evening the storeroom is clean and almost shiny.

At the main buildings on Queen Street, the story has been Cal, a short stocky man with menacing-looking grey hair despite his age of less than fifty. Cal is quiet unless he starts arguing with you. We have known him for years, but recently he decided to take up residence on Queen Street. He has lost his housing and is using a homemade walker to hobble around. It is no wonder he's angry, living on concrete. Business owners call the police who simply escort him to another location—it is too costly to put a man in jail for being homeless. Except for a couple of yelling episodes, people on Queen Street have been generous to Cal: he always has a coffee, and people buy him sandwiches and wraps from the Queen Street Commons Café. Twice he has been taken away by ambulance, only to be released with the suggestion that he may have suffered small strokes. Outreach workers offer support, but he is often not fully coherent.

In early July, Kitchener Mayor Carl Zehr called, responding to business complaints about homeless people loitering on Queen Street. Joe tells him that we have helped Cal to sleep outside at 97 Victoria, where he can get his meals at St. John's Kitchen, and that medical tests are scheduled for the end of July. Joe emphasizes how busy our Queen Street location is, implying the benefit to the community. On that day, over two hundred people used our job search resource centre, and our café served 360 customers. Queen Street has come a long way since the early 1990s when the Walper Hotel was closed, many store fronts were empty, and most of the second and third floor flats were vacant.

This past month, it has been hard to know where to turn. In the last week of June we held graduation for the latest Waterloo Region ASSETS+ Project (WRAP) graduates, who proudly described their planned small businesses in painting, technical writing, interior decorating, ice cream sales, therapeutic touch, gardening, and computer services. Maureen Brosnahan, a CBC Sunday Morning radio journalist, spent a couple of days interviewing older workers for a radio show exploring how they are being left out of the labour market.[5] The next day, the CSA (Community Shared Agriculture) pickup at the Queen Street Commons Café felt like a celebration. We have been coordinating CSA projects for over ten years, and now our two-acre market garden at the Hacienda Sarria is producing our own abundant harvest for fifty members.

The Working Centre helps people solve problems. Lately the number of seniors who navigate the downtown without supports seems to be growing. One woman with mental health issues is losing her apartment but is convinced she can look after herself. Another woman just sits in the resource centre smiling and making small conversation, seemingly with no place to go; another homeless women comes in to use the phone and then is back on the street. A retired new Canadian is harassed by her manic son in the resource centre and calls the police for protection.

This spring, Job Café[6] undertook a major repainting of the exterior of 97 Victoria; now we are planning with our plumber how to repair the storm sewer. It is a major operation to cut out 80 square feet of concrete. The Job Café workers line up to participate in the work. Mike lets Joe know he has all the skills needed to complete the job. Joe rents the quick-cut saw and jackhammer, the area is tarped over, and the operation begins. When Joe comes back on Sunday afternoon, he notices Ron sleeping on a skid in the sun beside a neatly covered pile of dirt and concrete. He has been hospitalized for the last six months but it looks like he has been released. Cal is on the other side of the building entertaining some friends. Inside 97 Victoria, a large trench over twelve feet long has been dug out, revealing the storm pipe eight feet below the concrete floor. Mike and his crew, all without steady work, are more than capable of hard work and are grateful for the opportunity. Jennifer lets Joe know she has been at the hospital all weekend with Sandra and Jay, both of whom are suffering the effects of long-term drug use.

The Working Centre Story

Transition to Common Work is the story of The Working Centre's beginnings almost thirty years ago, about lessons learned, and about the myriad ways in which its strategies and innovations can be understood and adapted by the many groups that share The Working Centre's goals. It is the story of co-operation, of moving beyond us and them—beyond institutional responses—into creating grassroots cultures of support.

For activists and bureaucrats and those in between, this book describes, in terms both practical and inspiring, a method for individuals and third-sector organizations (NGOs, charities, not-for-profits, and co-operatives) to move beyond the doldrums of "poverty relief" into the exciting world of community building.

The community space in downtown Kitchener was for the most part purchased, renovated and paid off without government support. From modest beginnings we have grown in size and scope over the years and organize our projects into six areas.

- *The Job Search Resource Centre* offers a wide range of supports for both job searchers and employers; we walk alongside over two hundred people a day looking to find a place in the labour market and navigate the many stresses that come from living on a limited income and often without work.
- *St. John's Kitchen* has been serving a free community meal in downtown Kitchener since 1985. With limited staff, it operates with the work of approximately one hundred volunteers, 80 per cent of whom are also patrons. It is a community that redistributes surplus food with spirit and generosity. St. John's Kitchen also serves as the base for an extensive network of outreach activities such as Downtown Street Outreach and the Psychiatric Outreach Project.
- *Community Tools* projects are designed to put productive tools into the hands of people seeking to make daily living more affordable and co-operative. Examples of Community Tool projects include Recycle Cycles (a bicycle repair shop), Worth a Second Look Furniture and Housewares, Barterworks, Hacienda Sarria Market Garden, Green Door Clothing and Arts Space, Multicultural Cinema Club, Maurita's Kitchen, and the Queen Street Commons Café.

- *Access to Technology* helps make technology more affordable and accessible and includes the computer recycling/refurbishing workshop, public access computers, community voice mail, and computer training that is self-directed and affordable.
- *Integrated Supportive Housing* provides transitional housing for up to forty women and men who are between jobs, leaving a difficult relationship, in recovery from addictions, or otherwise needing a temporary place to live. The Hospitality House is for individuals with significant medical issues who are without a stable home.
- *The Waterloo School for Community Development* is the name given to the many educational initiatives undertaken at The Working Centre, including training, research, publishing, mini-courses, the Diploma in Local Democracy, the publishing of *Good Work News*, and the sharing of new ideas on work and community.

The Working Centre as Model of Community Development

As The Working Centre branched out, it became a widely recognized model of community development. It is a vast network of practical supports for the unemployed, the underemployed, the temporarily employed, the homeless, and many others who don't fit into the regular labour market. The Working Centre method of incubating community enterprises is unorthodox but effective. We start from a lived philosophy of "small is beautiful." Our work is anchored by the writings and ideas of Dorothy Day and Peter Maurin, Ivan Illich, E. F. Schumacher, Christopher Lasch, Jane Jacobs, Jean Vanier, Wendell Berry, Moses Coady, Ken Westhues, Jim Lotz, Jane Adams, and Thomas Berry.[7] The ideas of these authors and how they relate to The Working Centre are described throughout this book.

- We work to dissolve the boundary between those who serve and are served—the boundary between "us" (those with power) and "them" (the disadvantaged). By walking with others through the experience of unemployment (or underemployment), addiction, family breakdown, and so on, we have gained insight into the nature of work and community, and into what enhances people's lives.
- We value producerism in contrast to consumerism. Producerism is the ability of people to produce things for themselves or in community that formerly they paid for. It gives people a way to weave through the cycle of poverty, to overcome the deadening effects of consumerism, and it enhances dignity by re-enlivening the ability to do and make.[8]

- Community Tools projects are more than social enterprise as they emphasize access to tools, skill development, public spaces, and a philosophy of community service. We have seen the infectious growth of projects that foster community and self-help opportunities for creative livelihood.
- We have integrated six virtues into our culture: *work as gift, living simply, serving others, rejecting status, building community,* and *creating community tools.* These virtues are practical and crucial ways of acting.
- We have engaged in large-scale revitalizations of six old buildings (committing to do this without debt), honouring heritage, fulfilling a vision for open public space, embracing the craft of construction work, and facilitating volunteer involvement. This has contributed to downtown Kitchener's rejuvenation and our own model of inclusive, integrated communities.
- We try to maintain a balance of about 50 per cent government funding while also earning social enterprise income and accepting charitable donations. We have attempted to minimize the encroaching power of bureaucracy while emphasizing frugality, personal responsibility, and hospitality.
- We believe that people can rise above materialism when co-operation and responsibility are integrated into the intrinsic structure of work. This is evident in our salary policy, which is radically flat, ensuring that our scarce resources are used for building solidarity and common infrastructure.
- We have slowly demonstrated that decentralized projects can generate solidarity and reciprocal relationships by involving people in the sharing of skills and tools. This approach builds local democracy and social inclusion. It bypasses bureaucratic responses with on-the-ground community effort.
- We believe each person is important, and we work to act intentionally and thoughtfully, walking alongside people, building inclusive spaces, and being open to each other.

When we started in 1982, we realized that work had been turned into a competition. Incentives, layoffs, and disappearing social income served to treat workers as merely cogs in the wheel. Consumerism, the engine of the economy, functions best when people are disconnected from community.[9] The unemployed, the losers in this game, were often depressed and stripped of their self-worth. It seemed to us a poor way to build a workforce, and it was no way to build a society, in the language of The Catholic Worker, "where it is easier for people to be good." We were intent on creating a community with a new direction, one that could inspire a new world view on the meaning and dignity of work that serves community.

The spirit of co-operation allowed the seed of The Working Centre to take root on Queen Street South in downtown Kitchener, and the soil into which we put down roots over thirty years ago continues to be nourished. We were fortunate to inherit and extend the values we found around us in downtown Kitchener. Fostering sharing was paramount in our early days, an ethic that became rooted in the fabric of the centre, an ethic that helped to develop a wide network of informal and formal co-operative supports. This book looks back and describes the philosophies and practices that have helped to build The Working Centre into a thriving community. It looks forward by emphasizing that the potential for the transition to common work starts by creating community structures that give people agency to develop cultural supports that extend solidarity and that consciously increase the social bond between people and their environment.

Building Community:
The Working Centre's Roots

In the Fall of 1982, a German immigrant named Victor could often be found knitting toques and scarfs at The Working Centre's upstairs Queen Street office. "You work thirty-six years, teach others your skill, and then you get into this depressing situation," he often said. "You can't save or plan and, when the income is not secure you believe you're useless. You feel as if you have no tomorrow." Victor was a skilled weaver who thought that people should work together, be less materialistic, and share their skills to help each other.

Victor was caught in the North American economic crisis of 1980. Interest rates for bank loans hovered at 21 per cent, and government policies put in place to purge inflation resulted in an unemployment rate of 12 per cent, with manufacturing plants closing or reducing production.[1] The Working Centre was established during this crisis to create a non-judgmental place that offered hospitality and support for the unemployed.

A group of people, many of whom were unemployed and displaced, were attracted to our work of building a helpful community. Jim was a drifter who came by the centre every day and soon brought his friends. Maria, a volunteer, started offering sandwiches at lunch. Jim was our first connection with people who lived in shelters. Despair described this group's relationship to work, and drinking with friends at different rooming houses was considered a meaningful activity. Jim taught us what was behind this, telling stories that emphasized how rejection and loneliness drove people into an underground world of alcohol.

Stephanie started teaching an introductory ESL class for refugees from Laos and Vietnam, which gave us some understanding of their difficult journey to Canada. On arrival, the refugees faced the daunting challenge of learning English, a language completely at odds with their own.

Alex would limp up the stairs to our office, seeking help for his many battles with authorities. He was always making plans that never worked out, and he struggled to make sense of Canadian society. His factory job ended suddenly when he was hit by a car, the accident causing major damage to his hip and legs. He spent a year in rehabilitation and received $100,000 in insurance compensation. Thinking he was making a wise decision, he purchased a condominium and went back to university to complete a master's course in Russian literature. Four years later, he could not get a job, the condominium board was demanding increased fees, he had no money to pay for a flood in his condo, and he was trying to sue an insurance company. Without any money in the bank, his situation seemed hopeless. Alex wanted us to help him get the attention of politicians, who he believed would help him.

John was a graduate from St. Jerome's College at the University of Waterloo, who Stephanie and Joe had met while studying. He was from a small town in the Ottawa valley and did not want to go back, but he was completely frustrated by the lack of opportunity he experienced. His natural optimism often collided with that anger. Allan had a disability and lived on welfare. He started finding small cleaning jobs, which soon enabled him to live independently in his own apartment. Bob had developmental barriers and wrote a letter telling us he was disappointed that we had not helped him. We were learning about an economy that had limited work slots for people who did not fit in, even if they fully desired to contribute.

These story snippets illustrate how in our first months we learned that the unemployed were all individuals with hopes and dreams no matter how depressed the lack of money and work made them. They experienced the double frustration of feeling that work was withheld from them and that their empty pockets limited their participation in society. Each unemployed individual felt that working people judged them for shirking their duty. Poverty meant a struggle to find a room and a meal each day, and many lived with despair.

The Working Centre was established in May 1982 as a summer project. We had expected to pursue work in developing countries, but as the summer progressed, we saw the importance of integrating our social justice ideas with social service work. Soon we were committed to bringing the two together, and the doors stayed open. It has always been that way, taking one step at a time, learning and growing while trying to build community in downtown Kitchener.

Building Community Ujamaa Style

We grew up during a time of prosperity and optimism in the 1960s and '70s. Stephanie's parents were attracted to the opportunities Hamilton offered when they left PEI and Cape Breton in the early 1950s. Joe's parents grew up in a working class Italian neighbourhood in Hamilton, where his grandparents already owned their own houses, reaping the benefits of Hamilton's prosperous steel factories. Stephanie grew up on the west mountain while Joe's family settled on the east side. Both families had Catholic roots connected to an active parish culture—Regina Mundi on the west mountain and St. Margaret Mary on the east mountain were the schools and parishes we attended. Our families marked the seasons in unison with the church calendar, a rhythm of family, church, and community that became central to our way of thinking.

In 1972, we both were enrolled at St. Thomas More High School on the west mountain. It was a small, experimental, open-concept high school that did not have walls. We became friends in grade 10, sitting together in open classes and co-operating on assignments. St. Thomas More emphasized independent learning, and we both adapted easily to the environment.

By university we were going in separate directions. Stephanie was at McMaster University in Hamilton studying kinesiology; Joe was studying philosophy at St. Jerome's College and living at Resurrection College at the University of Waterloo. During the summer of 1977, Joe told Stephanie about C.PP.S. Mission Projects, a group led by the Society for the Precious Blood, that was building windmills in Tanzania. This sparked Stephanie's interest, and in October we went together to a meeting in Toronto at St. Alphonsus Church to learn more.

In March 1978, we were invited to join with ten others to build seven windmills to pump clean water in central Tanzania. The windmills, imported from Italy, were like big Meccano sets, reaching up more than twenty feet. They needed four large concrete foundations for the structure to sit on, providing for us an early example of understanding the importance of a good foundation for community work. The project included a training school to teach local mechanics windmill maintenance. When the windmills pumped clean water, the village celebration demonstrated practical development.

In the mid-1970s, Tanzanian president Julius Nyerere implemented a "villagization" policy, known as *Ujamaa*, that moved scattered settlements into larger villages with the goal of sharing scarce resources like fertilizer and agricultural training.[2] The windmill project was extending clean water to some of these new Ujamaa villages. When we went with the mobile medical unit, we assisted the sisters who attended to the long lines of villagers who came for the cleaning and wrapping of festering sores. We wondered how Tanzanians could accept their poverty; they had no possessions but were kind and generous. While working on the windmills they offered us celebratory meals of *ugali* and chicken. We felt uncomfortable, feeling as though we were depriving them of their minimal food. We sensed that the Ujamaa villages were successfully creating a culture of co-operation.

During our time there we saw the challenges on the ground, where both nomadic and agricultural people were living in scattered, small villages, struggling to eke out a living. We learned that having too little was not soul destroying, but we saw first-hand the ravages of poverty. The average life span in Manyoni District, where we worked, was only forty-two. We were welcomed in these new villages with official ceremonies and traditional dances. The integration of state and culture was seamless: there was no difference between the political party and the delivery and representation of government services. When we arrived TANU (Tanzanian African National Union), the political party that had brought Tanzania to independence, had been dissolved and had renamed itself Chama Cha Mapinduzi (CCM), which translates as The Revolutionary Party. CCM, from our limited perspective, seemed to be encouraging grassroots, rural revolution using small scale technology that people could maintain.

President Nyerere described an Ujamaa village as "a voluntary association of people who decide of their own free will to live together and work together for their common good....They, and no one else, will make all the decisions about their working and living arrangements."[3]

Before we left, we were invited to meet Nyerere at his house in Dar es Salaam. It was a hot day, and we met in an open-air reception area. He asked us about our experiences, thanked us for our efforts, and encouraged our group to do more. We were amazed that *Mwalimu* (teacher)—as he was known—had time for us. We were learning that development in Tanzania had a different formula. The president led by example: he practised a humble lifestyle, he cared about relationships, and he was known to get directly involved with the issues of his people.

Tanzania continues to be known as a peaceful country. Despite early problems with Ujamaa, the policy supported the conditions for a national identity. Nyerere made Kiswahili the official language, he instituted education in the new villages, and he infused the country with a co-operative development approach. The success of the Tanzanian experiment has been linked to Nyerere's thoughtful vision of human justice, a philosophy that he preached to the country while embedding it in practical action.

During our time together in Tanzania, we became the best of friends. We relied on each other to interpret what was going on around us. We tried to understand the missionary work of Fr. Francesco and the nuns. We learned about the world of the Tanzanians who were employed at the mission compound. We talked together in the early morning as we walked from the compound to the church among crowing roosters, offering a greeting of jambo ("hello" in Swahili) to passersby. The time spent together trying to understand this mind-changing experience bonded us in ways we had not yet realized. When Stephanie registered in religious studies at McMaster University and Joe returned to St. Jerome's, we realized how much we missed each other. Three months later, during a November mission group retreat weekend at Mount Mary in Ancaster, we stayed up all night talking. We started planning a life together. We saw that we could meaningfully express our discontent with materialism while engaging in creative work.

We became actively involved in C.PP.S. Mission Projects through fundraising, sending shipments of food and clothing to Tanzania, organizing the student group, and conducting retreats and "starvathons." We made over a hundred presentations at high schools, churches, and community groups throughout Kitchener-Waterloo and Hamilton. We both studied international development and environmental issues in new ways. Simple living became important to us. Our interests brought us to the doorstep of Global Community Centre, which was located in downtown Kitchener on Queen Street South. We were asking deeper questions about the society in which we had grown up.

Global Community Centre

In the early 1980s, Global Community Centre was responding to the escalating human rights abuses associated with the El Salvador civil war. The Latin American Support Group, with many Chilean refugees as members, organized letter-writing campaigns and community education on the documented evidence of terror by the paramilitary death squads. When Archbishop Romero was assassinated in March 1980, we helped organize a memorial service in solidarity with the poor he had defended in El Salvador. The rape and murder of four US church workers nine months later brought more international attention. At the same time, Nicaragua's Sandinista government was under attack for literacy, participatory democracy, and self-sufficient-agriculture initiatives. Freedoms we took for granted in Kitchener were under siege in Central America.[4]

Margaret Nally connected us to the Kitchener-Waterloo social justice community in her job as church animator at Global Community Centre. Her main role was to work with parish-based social justice committees to educate and develop local action that matched the initiatives of ecumenical coalitions like 10 Days for World Development, Taskforce on Church and Corporate Responsibility, and the InterChurch Committee on Refugees. She and her husband Bob had emigrated from Ireland just ten years earlier and were busy raising their two young daughters. They helped start the local chapter of Amnesty International while Bob completed his masters in engineering. They offered an open door at their home. Soon we helped Margaret organize a full day Lenten fast at Forest Hill United Church to bring attention to the Salvadoran death squads and then a day-long teaching event against Nestle's baby formula marketing campaign that convinced poor women to buy expensive baby formula.[5] Building local awareness for international justice became integral to our thoughts and actions.

In March 1982 we attended the annual Global Community Centre Dinner in the St. Louis Catholic Church gymnasium, and politics was in the air. The protesters were a group of pro-Albanian communists who had formerly controlled the University of Waterloo student newspaper *The Chevron*. They had set up pickets to denounce the Chinese Communists as opportunists. The speaker, United Church missionary James Endicott, had lived in China before the 1948 revolution. This elderly gentleman gave a rousing defence of the non-aggressive strategy of Chinese foreign policy. He emphasized his family's satisfaction that the Chinese Communist Party was dedicated to building a better society.

When the dinner ended, the organizing group stacked chairs, washed dishes, and swept the floor. We went back to the Nallys' house to continue the discussion. There was one aspect of the conversation that made everyone uncomfortable. How could we understand poverty in Chile, Nicaragua, El Salvador, and China when we knew so little about poverty in Kitchener-Waterloo? Once identified, this nagging question was hard to ignore. The example of James Endicott stood large. He was a major proponent of the social gospel and a leader in the worldwide Ban the Bomb movement. The United Church of Canada had just offered a full apology for denouncing him three decades earlier, even as these pro-Albanian communists were attacking him from another direction. How could we stand for justice in a rooted way in Kitchener-Waterloo? What was the reality of poverty locally? What did we know about the ongoing auto industry layoffs at Budd Automotive and Lear? These were questions and challenges.

We left the Nally house to walk home, promising Margaret that we would think seriously about bringing social justice analysis to local poverty issues. This was not the first time we had talked about these ideas.

A Centre to Understand Unemployment and Poverty

Margaret Nally had a special influence on our development. We saw in her a practising spiritual director who understood the gospel message of justice. She asked questions such as "Is this the way things should be?" "Is there not a higher calling to love of others?" She invited us to help her with projects that she always integrated with relationship, discussion, warmth, and tea. We would go to St. Michael's Church to listen to Margaret's lyrical and spiritually moving social justice reflections. It was natural for us to assist her work, and she welcomed our effort. A few days later as we discussed this new project, Margaret went into the basement of Global Community Centre and dug up a pamphlet from the Canadian Conference of Catholic Bishops' Social Affairs Commission entitled *Unemployment: The Human Cost.*

The back page had a section called "Study and Action Guidelines." The first step was to become aware of "the local realities and experiences of unemployment. This includes being present with unemployed workers, listening to their problems." It continued by analyzing the basic causes of unemployment, making ethical judgments about the realities of the meaning of human labour, supporting specific struggles of unemployed workers, and developing alternative strategies.

A plan started coming together. Margaret already had contact with PLURA,[6] which funded projects that were "grassroots, self-help, and low income in nature," not about services or individual support but related to "the redistribution of power, knowledge, and resources."

It was decided that Patrice Reitzel (now Thorn), Stephanie, and Joe would meet with Margaret at her kitchen table to plan out a project based on these guidelines. Patrice was invaluable to this process. A lawyer who had become disaffected by the adversarial nature of the law, she had taken a sabbatical and become interested in the spiritual exercises of St. Ignatius. Patrice and Margaret shared the animator's job at Global and were subtle but highly energetic workers for justice. Patrice had recently studied praxis as it related to spiritual development. She had insights into the meaning of the pastoral circle, the most important theoretical concept with which we started our work.[7]

As we sat around the table, the words and ideas that we used to describe this new kind of social justice work were in the air. All four of us were studying the nature of social justice movements, and we wanted to incorporate authentic community practice. We envisioned a place of hospitality from which practical action could develop. The application came together easily. Stephanie and I drafted an original version; Margaret talked with PLURA, commented on the draft, and sent it to Patrice, whose insightful and practical mind critiqued it, rearranged sections, and added new ideas. We were proud of the application we submitted, asking for $6,000 to further our work.

The ideas in that application are as relevant today as they were when we wrote them thirty years ago:

- A broad focus is needed to allow the unemployed to define their own needs. Once these needs have been specified, the centre will act as a facilitator for co-operative self-help.
- The centre will bring people together to begin to discuss their problems in a way that will lead them to discover causes of poverty and unemployment, and to recognize similar obstacles that marginalize many other groups of peoples. It is from sharing their experiences that the centre will facilitate the analysis of the experiences of the unemployed. Action-oriented responses will be a method of promoting solutions.
- The centre will evolve as a social justice education/action centre. It will provide resources that analyze the situation within our economic system.
- The Alternative Employment Feasibility Study will recommend projects that the centre may be able to incorporate into its basic co-operative structure. It is thought that such alternative employment ventures such as a craft co-operative, gardening co-operative, etc., could generate operating revenues in the near future.
- The centre's self-help philosophy will encourage the unemployed to seek solutions through sharing experiences, social analysis, and education.

The Working Centre Takes Shape

On Tuesday April 28, 1982, even before hearing about the status of our application, we met Margaret at the house of some friends from the Latin American Support Group. On the front porch we started thinking about different names. We liked how the name Global Community Centre spoke to its mission as a place for reflection and action on international issues. We ruled out associations with unemployment and poverty as too pejorative. John Paul II's recent encyclical *On Human Labour* had phrased the issue positively. The meaning of human labour is found in the wide sharing of benefits: people work in order to fulfill their dignity and their creative spirit. Society should find ways to ensure that all can engage in human labour that distributes the benefits of society fairly.[8] We could easily have settled on The Catholic Worker, but we already had in mind a different model and were reluctant to opt for a sectarian description. Instead we started thinking about "work" and settled on The Working Centre. It would be a centre that reflected and acted on the meaning of human labour.

We started the project on May 3, and by mid-week we heard that the PLURA grant had been approved. We met with Hulene Montgomery, the local coordinator of a project that involved working with church groups to resettle Vietnamese refugees, commonly called at the time "boat people." She informed us about federal government funding available through the Industrial Labour Adjustment Program (ILAP) and the Employment Development Branch (EDB). She reminded us that that immigrants engage in self-blame when they can't get a job and advised us to explain the reasons for the current high unemployment and emphasize that Canadian workers were in the same situation. She pointed out that at that time only a small fraction of Canadians volunteered in community service organizations and generally the unemployed did not volunteer at all. If we wanted our volunteer projects to be successful, therefore, we would need to first offer practical assistance.

Hulene was mostly interested in projects that developed long-term viability, stressing that communities are left no further ahead when intrusive projects fail to establish meaningful roots. She handed us *Neighbourhood Economic Enterprises*, an American publication that described how small economic projects can develop and grow. It was helpful to learn about this newly developing field of social enterprise right from the beginning.

On May 11, we traveled to Welland to learn about All People's United Church. Here we saw a church dedicated to creating a community for its people with co-operative housing, daycare, and moving service. They had recently rebuilt the church using the labour of its members. When we arrived they were cleaning up the daily free lunch served by the church. On the way home to Kitchener, we stopped in Hamilton for a barbecue for Joe's mother's birthday. Joe's father had questions about our project: "What kind of job was this? How can you earn a living from this work?" We didn't have many answers, but we spoke glowingly of the community we had seen at All People's United.

We registered ourselves for the Creative Job Search Techniques workshop at the Canada Employment Centre (CEC). We expected it to be condescending because of the workshop pamphlet that featured cartoon beavers looking disappointed at the "no opening" sign. We were surprised by the open-ended nature of the group facilitation method and the detailed job search information that they offered. This did not change the message though. The CEC had a fixed answer for the unemployed: Unemployment could be beaten by an organized and meticulous job search. The jobs are out there, the system works, and it's up to the unemployed to work hard to find them. What else could the government say? This was the same service that was paying out Unemployment Insurance claims. The CEC service was designed with carrots and sticks. Part of its mandate was to help the unemployed find work, but it could also suspend benefits if the job search was not up to undisclosed standards.

On May 18 at the Nallys' kitchen table we had our first informal organizational meeting, and we announced that we had a location.[9] It was at 94A Queen Street South above Global Community Centre, and we decided to open in late June. Ideas for projects included ESL training, self-help job searching, an alternative phone-message service, recreation projects, solutions for daycare, and educational sessions. The Working Centre would be a gathering place for critical thinking around work.

Strengthening Our Ideas

We registered for a five-day course called Democratic Management School for Public Interest Groups, and when we stepped off the train in Kingston we searched the downtown with new eyes. Kingston seemed to be thriving compared to Kitchener. On Sunday morning we made our way to Big Rideau Lake, where a boat taxi took us to Grindstone Island.[10] The sessions on management theories, democratic structures, and fundraising were new and enlightening and addressed problems that we were already confronting. We had a great deal of learning to do. The conference organizers served home-cooked vegetarian meals, reinforcing our growing interest in simple living. The discussion during the cleanup was as interesting as the sessions.

Ted Jackson, a leading co-operative thinker, taught us about the pitfalls and potentials of co-operative development, and Stephanie was just waiting for someone like Marianne Moershel to teach her basic accounting and budgeting, a skill that became fundamental to ensuring the sustainability of The Working Centre. It was a week of new friendships along with cold rainy weather. As we left the island, people from Kingston told us we had to meet Theresa Houston, a labour union organizer who had established the Kingston Unemployed Help Centre.

Theresa welcomed us and then proceeded to kindly lecture us for the next two hours in a gruff Scottish accent. Theresa was the real thing. No stone would be left unturned to support an unemployed worker's UI (Unemployment Insurance) or welfare benefit. She hardly took a breath as she described all we needed to learn. As we edged forward, struggling to understand her accent, she went on about teaching people the UI rules and her dislike for UI administrators who didn't respect the unemployed. She distrusted the inaccurate labour market data that she claimed Statistics Canada produced because lower unemployment statistics saved the government money on UI claims. She talked about job-search courses, clothing swaps, meal services, recipes for cheap meals—including her own liver casserole recipe, which she described in detail—organizational development, how to apply to United Way, and how to connect with labour. Theresa was nothing like the people we had met at Grindstone Island. She had no use for process, only action—and she embodied it. Theresa *was* the Kingston Unemployment Help Centre, and it was a labour of love for her. We only met Theresa one other time before she died in the late 1990s, but we never forgot that first meeting and her total commitment to unemployed workers.

The following weekend we participated in one of the largest political demonstrations ever. On June 12, 1982, during the United Nations Second Special Session on Disarmament, we were with one million people in New York City demonstrating against the Reagan administration's nuclear weapons buildup. The bus from Kitchener pulled up to an eight-storey hotel where, with sleeping bags, we would share the floor with ten other people. We joined the protest at the NGO disarmament pavilion near the UN Headquarters. Although we worried that it would be impossible to line up one million people for the demonstration, it was a moving, friendly, and peaceful walk, surrounded by thousands of people and groups from all around the United States.[11]

After the protest we strolled through Central Park and went off exploring New York. We met Margaret and a few others at Washington Square late in the afternoon. Less than two blocks over, we wandered into what could have been a movie set from *The Godfather*; it was the New York version of the June 12 Feast of St. Anthony of Padua. Sullivan Street was chock-full of red and green booths, tinsel and lights strung across posts, barbequed sausages, fish, colourful peppers, a Ferris Wheel, peaches and wine, games of chance, stuffed animals, bands, dancing, a street carnival like we had never seen. It was a religious festival in name only. It seemed like the morning protest with one million people had never happened.

We were told that The Catholic Worker was celebrating the disarmament march with a drop-in for visitors. We took the subway to the Lower East Side, where we walked down empty and dark streets, opening the front door we entered what, to us, were hallowed grounds. We were welcomed into St. Joseph House by a soft-spoken woman who showed us into the large room used for chapel and the Friday night discussions. People were talking in groups as our greeter described the daily work of the house. We stayed long enough to breathe in the atmosphere. It had a mystical quality, this place where Dorothy Day, founder of The Catholic Worker movement and newspaper, had recently died. It was enough to have just been there to inspire us to learn more. In the cab on the way back to our hotel, a gregarious New York woman told us of her friendship with Dorothy and how much she missed her.

Unemployed Worker Centres and Ethical Reflections

When we returned from New York, we had renewed enthusiasm for building a community response to unemployment. We committed to The Working Centre by declining our acceptance into teachers' college. We knew this decision was not a path to riches, so we learned the skills of keeping a frugal household. Our commitment was strengthened by the relationships that were growing from the work of the centre.

We were creating a place that was useful. We found a corkboard to display job leads and made a telephone, phone books, and a daily newspaper available—the *K-W Record* offered to deliver a free paper each morning and continues that tradition thirty years later. We wanted to make it easy for people to help each other while job searching. We worked with volunteer job counsellors to assist people informally, practising interviews and helping organize their job search.

The Alternative Phone Message Service, in the years before answering machines, created a co-operative service, with people taking turns answering the phone. When we opened the storefront in mid-June, ten people had already signed up. Today, a hand-crafted message board continues our vital message services along with community voice mail, faxes, and mail. Our public computers provide access to emails and social media.

Over the summer, we had gained the trust of Wayne Samuelson, the President of the K-W Labour Council.[12] He was also co-chair of the Industrial Labour Adjustment Program (ILAP) committee established to retrain laid-off auto workers. We worked with Wayne on a proposal to the ILAP committee to establish three temporary Unemployed Worker Centres (UWC).

The ILAP committee was a federal Liberal response to the bleak jobs situation. Two years earlier, Budd Automotive, the region's largest auto parts manufacturer, had laid off 2,500 workers. ILAP was designed for income maintenance and retraining. Unemployed workers who exhausted their UI after a year could work for twenty weeks on an ILAP project and re-qualify for another year of benefits. Local industry owners supported our proposal as a complement to other retraining initiatives, and the Federal EDB supervised the grant. The project lasted for twenty months and employed fifty-six people on a twenty-week rotation.

ILAP was a major learning experience. The people we hired were primarily long-term unemployed workers, most on social assistance. We negotiated three locations at churches and a community centre. These places became neighbourhood job search drop-in centres, providing, in the words of one manager, "a great benefit to unemployed people to help them through a difficult time." Another talked about how she and her husband had been without work for over a year and that ILAP had changed her situation, giving her social connections and job-ready skills. Managers described how the centres assisted people with UI claims, social service benefits, job placements, a forum to air their views, and someone to listen to their problems. They talked about experiencing the highs of someone finding work and the lows of someone without hope slowly giving up, describing the project as offering them the opportunity to understand unemployment from a human perspective.

The ILAP centres recorded fifteen thousand visits in their final ten months.[13] The St. John's UWC in downtown Kitchener was our busiest location with two to three hundred visits a week, mainly from people living in downtown shelters and rooming houses. People came to St. John's looking for an inexpensive way to spend their day away from the cold, rain, and heat. We came to understand the struggles of the street population, and when the ILAP funding ended, we converted our experience into St. John's Kitchen.

We received a Canadian Community Development Project (CCDP) Grant to expand the job search resource centre at 94A Queen Street South. A report by Janet Wilson, *Working with the Unemployed: Towards a Helping Framework*, emphasized that people dropped in to The Working Centre looking for different kinds of assistance. They came in looking to talk about job searching, job leads, and developing a resume. Each deserved support whether it was the twenty-four-year-old who quit his job because it was boring, the desperate young father who was caught stealing food from a grocery store, or the man whose family was breaking apart because of his lack of work. Between September 1983 and August 1984 about 1,139 people used the Job Search Resource Centre.

We received a major boost in confidence when on December 31, 1982, the Canadian Conference of Catholic Bishops released its groundbreaking statement, *Ethical Reflections on the Economic Crisis*. The CCCB Social Affairs Commission had been using the ethical framework of the Preferential Option for the Poor and the Value and Dignity of Human Labour to question Canadian economic direction.[14] The *Toronto Star* picked up on the document's radical critique and dedicated a full page to it, with the headline "Unemployment Immoral, Bishops Charge." People started talking about Catholic Social Teachings. Wayne Samuelson, now elected to Kitchener City Council, asked Joe to invite Fr. Norm Choate, president of St. Jerome's College to speak at a council meeting to defend the Bishop's statement. A sociologist with a labour bias, Fr. Choate addressed the meaning of labour, agreeing that unemployment was immoral. CBC's The National featured a news report from the Kitchener Labour Hall's public forum on *Ethical Reflections*. City councils, labour halls, and the House of Commons alike were debating the ethics of high unemployment.

The Social Affairs Commission printed 200,000 copies of *Ethical Reflections on the Economic Crisis*, but few probably read the back page where the commission reprinted the study and action guidelines from *Unemployment: The Human Cost*. These were the guidelines Margaret Nally had passed on to us and we used for establishing The Working Centre. The model we started with had strong theological and pastoral grounds.

Ethical Reflections helped influence the local United Auto Workers (UAW) to establish a union of unemployed workers. The first public meeting was in June 1983 at the St. John's Unemployed Worker Centre. Bishop Proulx, one of the authors of *Ethical Reflections*, was the guest speaker. On a hot afternoon, his compassionate voice rang clear to the hundred unemployed workers: "Unemployment breaks human dignity, human pride and self-reliance. It sows fears of all kinds in the hearts of those plagued by unemployment."

Ron Eade, wrote a positive review in the *K-W Record*, quoting Proulx's hope for "more groups coming forth so we can have a voice in the affairs of the nation ... we should have something to say and we should be allowed to say it." Despite a promising beginning, by the fall of 1983, the Union of Unemployed Workers had failed to catch on, the UAW's four thousand dollars had run out, and the project was shut down. We were learning that the unemployed could not be classified and that their reality defied cohesiveness. They were labourers, millwrights, office workers, and more. Their desire for work was matched by their pessimism, fed by the lack of job opportunities. The constant competition for jobs wore them down. The Union of Unemployed Workers was not effective at breaking this cycle.

The Founding of St. John's Kitchen

In July 1982, when Working Centre volunteers presented to the Downtown Ministerial Committee to ask their support for establishing a soup kitchen in downtown Kitchener, they deferred the request to the newly formed Core Area Ministry Committee (CAMC).[15] The new committee also deferred a decision as they were still developing their terms and membership. In the meantime, two other developments took place. The St. John's UWC demonstrated the importance of a gathering place even serving just coffee and doughnuts in the Kitchener downtown. For a couple of months in 1984, Fr. Andrew Naud, a priest of the Old Catholic Church, opened up a house for street people that offered a daily meal. Fr. Andrew brought significant media attention to the issue along with a new understanding of the importance of a community meal service.[16]

In October 1984, after the Unemployed Worker Centres had closed and Fr. Naud had moved away, the provincial government announced the Emergency Shelter and Food Program. The provincial Conservative party recognized that hostels were stretched to their limits and that the effects of the recession were straining social services. The Tories were proposing to fund inner-city food programs to respond to growing hunger issues.

The CAMC was now functioning and they convened a meeting to discuss the need for a meal service downtown. Martin Buhr, executive director of the House of Friendship, a men's hostel, made a strong intervention in support of the idea. He suggested that The Working Centre should take the lead in developing the project. Martin's support was crucial, and a motion was made for The Working Centre to send a proposal to the Emergency Shelter and Food Program. The CAMC committed to support the soup kitchen by helping to find a church to host the project and pledging to recruit volunteers and financial resources from the downtown churches.

A meeting was set up with Rev. Cy Ladds at St. John the Evangelist Church to suggest extending St. John's UWC into a soup kitchen. Rev. Ladds was supportive of the social gospel and he was able to convince the wardens to back the project. The name St. John's Kitchen was settled on early. Many thought this was a temporary project, but the past two years had taught us that the need for a community kitchen was not likely to go away.

The first-year grant totaled $74,000, with 80 per cent coming from the province. It was used to help pay for the startup renovations and a portion of the cost for providing the daily meal. We immediately started fundraising and learned to scavenge for food. The first meal was served on January 15, 1985, to about forty people. The volunteers prepared and served soup, sandwiches coffee and dessert. We hired the former manager of the Chicopee UWC, giving her full-time work doing what she loved to do. The first volunteer labour force was recruited from retired members of First Mennonite Church. By the end of the month we were serving a hundred meals a day, storing food in seven chest freezers scattered throughout the church.

We soon found ourselves straddling the line between justice and charity. With the help of the downtown churches, we ensured that a hot meal would be served each weekday. Justice would mean giving people a voice to ensure the meal was served with dignity. Should people be able to raise their bowl to ask for more or to ask deeper questions about food distribution? The long-term goal was a place of hospitality and friendship where the patrons would be an integral part of the daily work.

The Ontario Help Centre Program

Politics were changing in Ontario. The forty-two-year Progressive Conservative dynasty in Ontario ended with the May 1985 provincial election, the Liberal and NDP leaders signing an accord on May 28, to give their parties a combined majority over the Conservatives in the Ontario Legislature. David Peterson and Bob Rae were intent on pursuing legislation for social housing, environmental protection, and labour law reform. That same day our daughter Rebecca was born. Christina, our two-year-old, was glad to have a sister to go to meetings with. St. John's Kitchen had quickly developed into a going concern, while The Working Centre was just hanging on. It was a vital job search centre but it had no funds and operated with volunteer resources.

In September 1985, Ted Schmitt, a bureaucrat from the new Ministry of Skills Development, walked into our feeble offices, exuding confidence.[17] His goal was to change adult unemployment services in Ontario. The last Conservative budget had set up a new ministry and allocated money primarily to labour-council–supported Unemployed Help Centres across Ontario. Provincial bureaucrats were frustrated that Ontario had youth employment services, but ignored the much larger group of adult unemployed. Schmitt's assignment was to establish a network of Adult Help Centres. He was working from a list, visiting centres that were just hanging on using local resources.

Since 1983, the Ontario Federation of Labour had helped the network of help centres by holding weekend conferences to discuss services and strategies for funding. Wayne Samuelson had included The Working Centre with this group even though as a church, community, and labour help centre we had a broader focus.[18] These were the original centres that Schmitt was priming to start offering a full spectrum of job search and training services. Schmitt followed the best tradition of government bureaucrats who learn by observing what was happening on the ground. He immediately took a liking to us. We were operating with minimal resources yet we were gamely committed. As we walked to St. John's Kitchen for lunch, Ted looked in the window of the empty store front at 58 Queen Street South and stated that this was going to be The Working Centre's new location and he was going to help make it happen.

Another opportunity was opening up. We had slogged for three years to create an independent place for adult unemployed workers to make phone calls, type resumes, meet others, and share job leads. Schmitt was offering support from the new Ontario Help Centre program. It would provide seventy thousand dollars a year in core expenses if we matched that amount with in-kind donations. We immediately arranged a tour of 58 Queen. The owners were anxious to rent their empty building after selling their family business, which left 58 Queen without tenants. One wondered what services we would offer: "You are not going to let people sleep here are you?" He reminded us that this was serious business and the rent cheques were his retirement income. The other became interested in our work, teaching us about the building and introducing us to his business friends.

In November and December 1985, we worked day and night painting and renovating this new 2,500-square-foot location at 58 Queen. Our first renovation project opened up the large main floor employment area, and we extended the space by drywalling the basement and adding carpet. On Monday January 6, 1986, we were overwhelmed by the number of job searchers who walked into our new resource centre. Schmitt was true to his word. We had a grand open house in June 1986 with John Sweeney, the Minister of Community and Social Services, cutting the ribbon announcing the era of Ontario Help Centre funding.

Everything we had learned was due to the gifts of generosity offered by people who were our elders, people who went out of their way to teach us the meaning of community. Over four years, we learned the spirit of self-giving at a time when we were hungry to learn and had the means to put into practice these ideas. By creating The Working Centre, we opted to not just study unemployment and poverty but to create projects that offered communal supports. After four years, St. John's Kitchen and the Help Centre were projects that were focused on issues we increasingly understood. We were reacting against a system that treated labour as an afterthought. We knew from our own upbringing and as we watched the carefree spirits of our two growing daughters, the importance of the dignity of each individual. The potential for a community taking root around The Working Centre seemed possible.

Liberation from Overdevelopment

During the summer of 2011, a man was given a room at Hospitality House, located beside 97 Victoria North. Joe Mancini immediately remembered Alex as a troublesome but fun loving nineteen-year-old who for six months combined community service hours with baling cardboard at Tri-Tech Recycling, one of the Working Centre's early projects. Now Alex had been diagnosed with multiple sclerosis and used a wheelchair. He had few family members to turn to and recognized that he had not developed many close relationships. When Joe went to visit him, Alex, the proud worker, wished for a chance to escape his disability and do any kind of work.

During The Working Centre's first years we learned of the frustration unemployed workers experienced trying to find their way into the labour market. Dimitri bumped against the system because he could barely commit to any work schedule. Adriana enrolled in our office re-entry program to find work to support her growing family, while her husband failed to find work as an agricultural technician, a position he had trained for in Eastern Europe. At St. John's Kitchen, older men with outdated skills had little hope of finding work.

With St. John's Kitchen and the Help Centre, we wanted to explore the link between unemployment, poverty, and the environment, considering that skills and lives of the unemployed were being wasted in the same way as cardboard, paper, and glass. We were determined that the project should protect the environment and involve people in meaningful ways.

By 1988, Tri-Tech Recycling was launched as a social enterprise and would ultimately give us a lesson in the recycling business. Our depot accepted all kinds of recyclable items that we baled and prepared to sell to markets downstream. We started with altruistic notions about recycling and sought companies and individuals eager to recycle their waste. We learned that the paper mills had no loyalty and treated us like second-class citizens and that the equipment salespeople had their own agenda that barely coincided with ours. You cannot plan for this kind of practical learning.

Our analysis was sharpened by our on-the-ground education about the recycling industry. This experiential learning gave us insights into the ethics that were driving the environmental crisis and became invaluable as we thought about new ways of recycling. By operating the recycling depot we came to identify overdevelopment as the prime generator of the environmental crisis. We learned that the structure of the recycling industry was dependent, like all other industries, on convincing consumers to purchase more products that could then be recycled. It was a business that had a growing need for more resources. Rather than devising a strategy to use fewer resources, recycling was now fixed as an additional step. Overdevelopment, according to Leopold Kohr, is the fierce appetite, almost like that of an addict, of both the private and public sector dependent on injections of resources and money. By labelling a system as overdeveloped, it helps recognize the continuous circle that needs to be broken in order for structural change to happen.[1] When Tri-Tech Recycling closed after almost three years in operation, the hard lessons we learned were integrated into our critical thinking as we developed an alternative approach to project development.

A Theory of Liberation

E.F. Schumacher's *Small Is Beautiful* documented the astronomical increase in consumption of non-renewable natural resources that took place in the 1950s and 1960s.[2] Schumacher asked questions about why so little thought was given to what happens when these resources are gone or what happens to the environment when they are used to fuel expanding production. These questions matched The Working Centre's interest in developing models of work that were gentle on the environment.

The Working Centre became enmeshed in environmental issues through following a model of liberation theory. When we started operating the recycling company, it gave us a perspective to analyze and reflect on the social context of overdevelopment and it led to projects that utilized new ideas for building community.[3]

Ken Westhues, a professor of sociology at the University of Waterloo, taught us to think practically about following a liberation model. He helped us define liberation as a way of acting on minute details that made a difference in the practical day-to-day work. As a new board member of The Working Centre, he questioned why our organizational structure used a standard hierarchical chart. "Why don't we find a way to describe this process as a circle?" Ken asked, pointing out the contradictions that can develop between ideals, process, and structure.

In *First Sociology*, Westhues describes the starting point for the sociological method toward liberation: "To speak of Liberation is to affirm that the status quo is not forever, that people have power to make change and history."[4] Westhues's book is designed to help the reader recognize that before we can respond to the angst and stresses of living, we must be comfortable to walk from where we stand. When we opened The Working Centre it was important to acknowledge that we did not have all the answers, but we did have a clear sense of who we were and what we were seeking to accomplish. Our first attempts at social change involved a commitment to learn the experience of unemployed workers and to support their situations by offering hospitality and friendship. We accepted the uncertainty of living in history while taking personal responsibility for the direction.

In *First Sociology*, Westhues lays out the conditions for liberation. "A new idea does not strike quite like a bolt of lightning from a clear blue sky. It happens along only after one's very self has been jostled by incongruous experiences."[5] The process is in no way a straight line and is seldom influenced by material circumstances. If poverty could create change, the world would be rid of hunger by now.

> No revolution ever stirred anywhere because people did not have enough to eat. It is not material circumstances that give rise to dissidence but rather the relationship between material circumstance and what is going on in people's minds. The basic proposition can be formulated as follows: what arouses people's urge to break with convention and innovate is the clash between what they have been taught and what they find in their experience.[6]

The process of liberation unfolds through steps, starting with learning the experience, listening to stories, and knowing the source of one's judgments. New ways of doing things do not just arise because a group of people have gathered together to support an issue they believe in. Liberation, the search for freedom, is a more complex, interactive process. The second step toward liberation is the recognition of dissonance, the realization that the experiences of daily living no longer match the values and ideals that one has learned to expect.

By the time we established The Working Centre we were taking steps toward recognizing new ways of extending freedom, by developing new ways for work to serve the common good. We started to understand the lack of purpose that we observed, the feeling that the meaning of work and the dignity of workers were being compromised by consumerism. This critique, and underlying tension, was the necessary ingredient for both creativity and change. Westhues emphasizes the need for discontent and restlessness, and that one must be ready "to exercise the freedom that is theirs."[7] Liberation is a step-by-step process, never spontaneous, building on connections already in place. It depends on openness to others, or it stalls and relationships break down.

Change also happens through identifying the dissonance that others feel. Experiencing daily life at The Working Centre helped us to offer support to people searching for work. We learned of the dislocation unemployed workers felt and their frustrations at not being able to use their skills. The unemployed were frustrated by the economy that had denied them work. They did not dare speak the truth about their frustrations to family and friends but were expected to search for another job. Even those who recognized the contradictions of the system accepted the cultural imperative that their role was to look for work.

We learned how unbendable systems can stimulate change—Tri-Tech Recycling provided an excellent example of that. Despite its many successes, it could not survive the imperatives of the competitive market that granted no leeway for altruism. The closing of Tri-Tech resulted in dissonance and frustration, but over time, we developed a model of Community Tools[8] that visualized for us how to bypass the competitive market and to put those ideas into action. These projects demonstrated new ways of recycling, community building, and the generation of new work, and so the final result was more satisfying and more liberating than the original idea.

The first step of liberation is the effort to learn where you stand. The second step is identifying the dissonance that you feel. The third step is the ability to implement practical projects. In the song "Democracy," Leonard Cohen describes how there must be "the machinery for change" and "a deep spiritual thirst." Change happens when new light is thrown on an old problem, coupled with a commitment to deal with the complexities and the competence to see the project through. Ideas must be nurtured. They need help to find roots among people willing to support them. Liberation combines knowing where you stand, listening to and acting on dissonance, and the practical ability to effectuate change. Together, all these processes turn mere notions into full-fledged ideas, blending philosophy and action toward the creation of new liberating concepts.

Establishing the Tri-Tech Recycling depot to address environmental issues taught us lessons that changed our organization in surprising ways. Our learning reflected a model of liberation that echoed the spirit that Westhues was helping to teach us, "If we put our minds and hands to the task, we will find a way of organizing ourselves that gives all and each of us the chance to become more than we are."[9]

Tri-Tech Recycling

The Tri-Tech Recycling years began in June 1988 with a commitment to purchase or start a recycling company. It ended when the operation was shuttered in June 1991. In those three years of intensive learning, what is most memorable is the effort of a group of workers committed to making a recycling enterprise viable for the sake of the environment. In addition, the workers knew that together we were pursuing a common purpose of creating a workplace that was fair and co-operatively run.

A typical day at Tri-Tech Recycling started with the delivery from Big Bear Waste Management of a forty-foot compactor load of cardboard. Often two of these loads would come at once and a trail of cardboard would run more than fifty metres into the driveway. Don, our fearless skid steer operator, would push the cardboard toward our two upright cardboard and paper balers that could compact one-thousand-pound bales. Workers were paid a penny a pound for each bale. Tri-Tech operated with three shifts baling ten to twenty tons per day. The cardboard had to be processed first, while the more lucrative fine paper and computer printout paper was baled later. Baling was a physical job that demanded continuous attention and speed.

Meanwhile, other material kept coming in, demanding to be sorted and stored. We needed people like Janice who could receive and move material while keeping the pop-can separator operating. A friendly engineer had converted an old machine so that we could easily recover the value of the new aluminum pop cans. We continually had to clear space around the scale. Lines of people came each day with their glass, plastics, paper, tins, copper, aluminum, and car batteries. We had to avoid the paralysis of clogged lanes as schools, individuals, companies, scrappies, and waste haulers delivered their recycling.[10] One of Tri-Tech's successes was helping people imagine how to increase their recycling.

Dave, our shop manager, had been laid off from a plant closing and was keen to learn the recycling industry from the bottom up. He knew how to organize and schedule. Bill, who had started in this role was an old-hand recycler and part hippie. He was skilled at moving materials and scouting opportunities, but the details of constant pickups and deliveries eluded him. Donna, the friendly office worker, kept track of the baler schedules and recycling payouts. She knew more about what was going on than anyone else. Alex, who twenty years later found his way to our Hospitality House, was a hard-working baler who came to us after trouble with the law.

Our goal was to develop an alternative economic model that would include the skills of those left out of the labour market. We were optimistic that we could recycle the paper that was going to landfill but less sure how to make this a productive enterprise. We were limited by a lack of capital and the reality that large and small businesses use their highly developed capabilities to pounce on market niches, often long before community groups can even get organized. We got directly involved in the recycling market in order to identify the possibilities.

Tri-Tech Recycling began from a simple question, "What enterprise opportunities could we pursue that would bring people together to solve problems?" To facilitate this process we helped to establish the Community Economic Development Resource Centre (CEDRC), which sought working capital to start an economic venture. It was our good fortune in the long run that this separate corporation sheltered The Working Centre from the enterprise we were creating. Our first decision was to purchase outright an existing shredding and recycling company—the owner was ready to retire and was sympathetic to our ideas. We negotiated terms, but at the last minute he opted to sell to someone else. When that deal fell through, we established Tri-Tech Recycling, a multi-purpose, multi-material recycling depot built from scratch. We took delivery of three balers in late October and were operating by November 1988. Within weeks of opening, the industrial space on Dotzert Court in Waterloo proved too small. Material dropped off for recycling overflowed in the long driveway to the drop-off door.

Three members of the CEDRC Board each loaned Tri-Tech Recycling five thousand dollars, to be paid back with interest, as a personal investment in community recycling. There were no strings on this personal contribution, just an expectation that we would work to make this venture successful. The Canadian Alternative Investment Cooperative, an organization that invests endowment money from religious orders in social development projects, also contributed capital for the purchase of the balers needed to produce the bales of cardboard and fine paper that we sold to the mills. Generous individuals and groups offered financial support to help get this project off the ground.

At its peak, every week Joe spent two long night shifts, often into the early morning, loading trucks for delivery the next day. We had no choice but to make our deliveries in order to have money in the bank for payroll and rent. We spent a memorable all-nighter one steamy summer evening, our kids staying with their grandparents, cleaning, sorting, and trying to create some order. But we were not alone. During the Tri-Tech years, there were at least four all-night cleanups that required all hands on deck. Reorganization of material was as constant as the new material that kept arriving at our door.

Tri-Tech Recycling was a project that was constantly on a knife's edge. Our offshore German landlord once toured our project with his environmentalist daughter. She convinced him that he should build us a flow-through recycling facility to allow us to operate more efficiently, but we could not prove to him that we had the financial backing to expand our social enterprise. The fast pace of these three years showed us how much knowledge and support is necessary to properly hold an enterprise together.

A local entrepreneur on The Working Centre Board heard in our second year how financially stretched we were. He lent us five thousand dollars for Tri-Tech with the condition that we repay it in instalments of four hundred dollars over one year. That kind of social trust is a constituent part of community building.

We survived for almost three years by being a low cost-operator, but the market for paper and cardboard was historically low. Everyone worked as hard as possible over three shifts, six days a week, baling the materials, weighing them, and loading forty-foot trailers. We collected large amounts of scrap aluminum to go along with the aluminum cans we were sorting, which gave us a better price when we sold it. We also ran a car battery drive to recycle lead. In another attempt to generate increased income, our paper broker got us contracts to rebale rejected truckloads of paper that had come all the way from Chicago.

We were confident that our volume of recycled materials would get us through, and then the recession hit in the spring of 1991, resigning us to the fate of many enterprises at the bottom of the food chain. When the recession reduced the demand for paper, the mills cut us off without warning, refusing delivery. Our cash position dwindled as our bales of cardboard and fine paper piled up.

We knew that the game was coming to an end when one morning we found our truck cab on blocks with the wheels removed. The bill for the tires had not been paid and so they were removed by the vendor during the night. We would have closed our doors, but they were too damaged and we didn't have the money to get them fixed, much to the dismay of our landlord! Adding to the insult, our mechanic showed up with his trailer and stole our skid steer because he was also owed money. Westhues described this at the time as the vultures of capitalism descending on our project, picking it apart.

After three years, we realized that despite all our efforts to create jobs and a depot to recycle mixed materials, the initiative had no value in itself. At its peak we recycled up to four hundred tons per month and employed twelve workers on three shifts, generating up to twenty thousand dollars per month in revenue. We had minimal government support. Hard work, thrift, and progress on an environmental issue were proved irrelevant. Enterprise development is only viable if there is money in the bank to pay for workers, rent, and services. It did not matter that board members contributed personal loans toward the start-up. Our personal bank account was drained many times to pay Tri-Tech bills. Eventually we learned that failure is not the end but a step along the path that teaches us to maximize creativity.

We had made our share of mistakes at Tri-Tech, but we knew that our customers loved the work we did. There were many community-minded people who assisted us with finances, marketing, compost barrel distribution, car battery collection, establishing the Waterloo Recycling Depot, and business recycling drives. Tri-Tech Recycling enjoyed widespread community support for its efforts. Many Sunday afternoons or holiday Mondays we found ourselves trying to contain the piles of recycling material that people left at our doors even when we were closed. People were not just dumping their garbage on us—they wanted to be good stewards of the environment and to curb waste.

The failure of Tri-Tech did not quench our thirst for community recycling. Over time, we continued to ask questions about the recycling work that is ignored, that is not considered economically viable, or is too cumbersome. Tri-Tech taught us valuable skills about how to move tons of material, how market commodities are priced, and how to read a recycling market. Over time we applied these lessons in new circumstances.

The closing of Tri-Tech Recycling was a shock to The Working Centre. Tri-Tech never filed for bankruptcy. We spend the next year selling off the assets, begging mills to take our remnant bales, and courting companies that appeared out of nowhere who proposed to help us. After all the excitement, cleaning out the abandoned warehouse was disheartening. Ending the project early and selling our assets meant that we had dollars to offer our creditors, however. Our original CEDRC board members, CAIC, and the banks took proportional losses. There was a collective understanding that Tri-Tech had been a hard-working enterprise that used its minimal resources gamely for three years. The Working Centre Board, especially Ken Westhues and Gord Crosby, actively negotiated the final steps to close the enterprise.

The Third Sector: Creating New Ways of Acting

The main factor that led to Tri-Tech's closing, the recession of 1990, resulted in increased numbers of unemployed people at the Job Search Resource Centre and more coming for lunch at St. John's Kitchen. There was no denying that The Working Centre's world had changed, and as we moved into our tenth year we reappraised where we stood. We had learned that the brutal efficiency of market economics demands "single-minded fixation on the bottom line."[11] We started looking in a different direction. We questioned our own assumptions, needing to understand why we felt trapped by large institutions. Despite Tri-Tech's closure, how could we practically influence local environmental thinking and action?

In the early summer of 1992, Joe picked up a copy of David Cayley's *Conversations with Ivan Illich.*[12] The back jacket description of this freshly published book spoke to The Working Centre's experience. Illich had an uncompromising critique of Western institutions, which he saw as dulling the senses and dispossessing people of tools and their ability to do and make. Illich had a mystical quality, and this book of interviews promised to bring some clarity to his critical and alternative ways of thinking. The questions we had been asking ourselves allowed us to hear the ideas of Ivan Illich in new ways.

The book was jam packed with ideas, concepts, and experiences. Illich had established the Intercultural Documentation Centre (CIDOC) in 1960, a school that combined enterprise, language training, scholarly inquiry, and advocacy that critiqued growing institutional and technological power. His ideas on education, access to tools, professions, the virtues, and technology all had implications for the way The Working Centre was organized. We took time to reflect on the implications of Illich's ideas. Slowly, The Working Centre started adapting these ideas in practical ways.

Illich had moulded CIDOC into a centre for cross-cultural studies that combined a language school, a publishing house, a research centre, and an educational institute, attracting prominent activist scholars such as Paul Goodman, Paulo Freire, Leopold Kohr, John McKnight, Wolfgang Sachs, Dom Helder Camara, Eric Fromm, Joseph Fitzpatrick, S.J., and John Holt. At the centre in an old hotel in Cuernavaca, Mexico, students were challenged to understand the cultural assumptions they brought to international development. CIDOC's work reverberated widely, demonstrating how independent organizations can shift public perceptions by challenging hardened institutional monopolies with critiques and alternatives.[13]

Illich questioned the direction of our era of abundance, which was overwhelmed by counterproductive institutions. What was the purpose of organizations that modelled cultural domination and dehumanizing systems? Why were missionaries eager to accept the division between the privileged and underprivileged? CIDOC offered an unambiguous social critique of the present reality while encouraging debate and discussion on new possibilities. Illich had larger goals in mind; he wanted people to see for themselves a new era of "self-chosen work and the freedom to follow the drum of one's own heart."[14]

Illich's CIDOC created a public organization that was rich in new ideas, grassroots energy, and problem-solving methods, but we heard from Ken Westhues about the tensions at CIDOC. Westhues's mentor at Fordham University had been Joseph Fitzpatrick, S.J., a regular teacher at CIDOC and a dear friend of Illich.[15] Fitzpatrick had talked about the disagreements between the language school and the activist publishing/education project. As The Working Centre started to promote some of Illich's ideas, Westhues warned us that individuals born into and committed to Western values might not understand complicated critiques that shake the foundation of their culture. It was important that we move slowly and develop small successful examples of what we were aiming to develop.

We used Illich's book, *Tools for Conviviality*, as a guide for the philosophy behind creating projects that elevated people so that they were not "accessories of bureaucracies and machines" but rather producers and makers of tools and culture.[16] We started calling projects with this approach *community tools*. As these projects started developing, we researched institutions counterproductive to our vision, "access to tools," and producerism.[17] The experience of Tri-Tech Recycling had jarred us into learning about alternative perspectives on development in Western society.

The Extra Equipment We Carry Around

The stark lesson we learned from Tri-Tech Recycling was that competition in work feeds consumerism and bureaucracy rather than creating an economy that could look after pressing social problems. Commentators such as Illich, Leopold Kohr, John Kenneth Galbraith, and John Maynard Keynes all envisioned human communities that could attain a sustainable standard of living, which would allow craft, art, and teaching to flourish. Eric Fromm called this the art of living and said that "to live well was an art that had to be learned; that the learning of this art required effort, devotion, understanding and patience; that it was the most important art to learn."[18] The art of living rises beyond the emptiness of acquisitive materialism and embraces the subtle arts of sharing, giving, and sacrifice. Community builds as human potential to move beyond isolation is unlocked.

In Paul Goodman's 1959 classic, *Growing Up Absurd*,[19] the author speculates that the same level of production of food and goods could be maintained if the work week was cut in half to 20 hours. Goodman backs up his analysis with a critique of the wasteful, bureaucratic mentality that had invaded the work process in the mid-twentieth century. Workers were becoming mere cogs in a growing production machine. Fifty years later, most workers in industrialized economies are less than cogs, they are on the periphery of the actual work process. Advanced computer and production technologies ensure that most workers are employed in busy work designed to enhance the profitability of corporations, expand government projects, and elaborate the techniques of selling, advertising, and marketing.

John Maynard Keynes envisioned three-hour shifts and fifteen-hour work weeks as he recognized that "humanity was beginning to solve its central economic problem, the struggle for subsistence."[20] He was no doubt familiar with philosopher Bertrand Russell's assertion in his 1932 essay "In Praise of Idleness" that the First World War had "shown conclusively that, by the scientific organization of production, it is possible to keep modern populations in fair comfort on a small part of working capacity of the modern world."[21]

John Kenneth Galbraith concluded *The Affluent Society* with a prescient reminder that industrial capitalism was no longer furnishing barren rooms. He reminded the reader that the problem of producing goods had been solved. Galbraith saw the main problem as squeezing furniture into crowded rooms, buckling the foundations. He thought that ignoring our growing overconsumption while not moving on to "the next task would be fully tragic."[22] All evidence points to our world becoming a crowded room where the foundation is buckling.

By the 1950s, Western societies had learned how to solve the problem of production, how to ensure that all had access to food, clothing, and shelter. Despite a standard of living in North America beyond what was once thought possible, there is a constant fear that it is declining, leading to an all-out effort to create jobs.[23] Nonetheless, food, clothing, and housing are abundant. The main problem is not the declining standard of living but that the economy is eating into our wealth. We have lost the flexibility to share the abundance we have created. Increasingly, the way we make economic decisions leads to diminishing returns no matter how hard we work.[24]

Our level of subsistence keeps rising, best described not as a rising tide that lifts all boats but as an excess of water that makes swimming increasingly difficult. The consumer junk—gadgets and cars, for example—weigh us down. We think we cannot survive without them, but Leopold Kohr contends that swimming with all this equipment in deeper waters is inefficient.[25]

Leopold Kohr and Overdevelopment

The failure of Tri-Tech Recycling forced us to look more closely at the systems we were interacting with. We concluded that private and public bureaucracies expend vast sums of money administering systems that are often second rate or unimaginative and that governments tie up tax money in highly counterproductive activities. The Working Centre had a front row seat watching bureaucratic experiments exert power over community projects with declining results.

We have seen both the provincial and federal government bureaucrats and politicians attempt to control costs by imposing amalgamations and centralization on community services. They believe they can save money by creating large service organizations, with funds allocated through one big budget. The result is that community groups are weakened, while powerful groups keep their seat at the table. The system is increasingly designed to take away the voice of the small group, and bureaucrats fulfill the roles they are assigned, even against their better judgment.[26]

Leopold Kohr had no time for bureaucracy, describing Western society as overdeveloped before he fled the German annexation of Austria in 1938. In his first book, *The Breakdown of Nations*, he wrote, "There seems only one cause behind all forms of social misery: bigness. Oversimplified as this may seem, we shall find the idea more easily acceptable if we consider that bigness, or oversize, is really much more than just a social problem. It appears to be the one and only problem permeating all of creation. Wherever something is wrong, something is too big."[27]

Kohr understood why small organizations, small cities, and small states can practically solve problems with imagination and efficiency. It is not a coincidence that E.F. Schumacher and Ivan Illich,[28] popular critics of centralized institutions, sharpened their ideas on proportionality through discussions with Kohr. He stated that when any social organism becomes bigger than needed to fulfill its intended purpose, then decay can be observed, whether physically, socially, or economically. Jim Lotz also describes how moral and spiritual decay are at issue as organizations get bigger.[29] Too much baggage obstructs the organization's purpose. Kohr called this mechanism overdevelopment.

Overdevelopment describes the application of bureaucratic techniques in organizations. Most formal paid work is now controlled through centralized systems in government, private corporations, and other large entities. Workers navigate this culture by learning that the work day involves refusing personal responsibility. Ethics are separated from work by simply accepting that these relationships should not affect you too much. Christopher Hedges despairs at the proliferation of unimaginative work controlled by university graduates who become "system managers trained to serve the corporate state."[30] Overdeveloped systems dispense with doing the right thing guided by conscience. Bureaucracy demands workers who follow the rules designed to serve the system.

The opposite of overdeveloped systems is paid or unpaid work that serves the community. The Working Centre calls this *work as gift*, creating meaningful relationships that foster practical problem solving. We ask whether the work is respectful of relationships, whether it builds friendships, whether the environment is better because of it. We find people adding to the story of The Working Centre when their desire for connectedness and honest work are respected. It is a cascading effect and it is contagious. This is how work and community are linked, and it is only possible from the bottom up. It falters when imposed from the top down.

Work as gift reflects the essence of Kohr's insights on proportionality. Overdevelopment in public or private bureaucracies results in the neglect of social virtues necessary for common life. Dialogue is limited in bureaucracies through the exercise of power. In the rush to execute plans, a bureaucracy confuses form with beauty. Authority and status is given licence over discussion. The results are second-rate utilitarian accomplishments. The opposite is recognizing that people relate to each other through friendship and relationship. Common tasks completed in non-bureaucratic settings such as organizing a concert, a community bike shop, or launching a business often result in satisfying contributions from all involved. Work as gift is the art of co-operating toward a shared horizon, a vision to which each of the parties can relate and for the beauty of the accomplishment.

Kohr wondered about the logic of ever-expanding organizations. He agreed, like all economists, that wealth is created from specialization. This emphasized his main point that specialization is an act of division and therefore organizations are more efficient in their smaller components. Grassroots creativity happens when people experiment with new ideas. Kohr lamented that creativity is discouraged in large organizations that demand loyalty to the corporation over experimentation. Technology makes ever-larger organizations possible, and impairs the art of judgment—knowing when enough is enough. Kohr lamented overdevelopment's assault against nature and argued for a civic life that was primarily concerned with friendship and art.[31]

The Idea of Community Tools Starts to Grow

In the early 1990s, The Working Centre found itself trapped by large organizations that barely noticed our existence. In the recycling industry we had been defeated by highly capitalized companies pursuing the profit motive. St. John's Kitchen had its emergency food program funding curtailed by the Ministry of Community and Social Services, and bureaucrats at the Ministry of Labour were attempting to professionalize grassroots job search centres like The Working Centre. We were concerned about how to hold our core premise of supporting the dignity of those rejected by the labour market.

The writings of Illich, Kohr, Westhues, and Wendell Berry brimmed with ideas about following the path of local development. Their writings prodded us to create access to tools through small, intentional services that gave people opportunities to express their skills. We wanted to build a work ethic for the common good. We wanted to echo the stories of the unemployed, who yearned for ways to meaningfully contribute through their work.

Our first ten years had ingrained in our organization support for two groups who felt little connection to the formal economy. The first group was made up of those rejected by the economy and the second group of those who rejected the economy. While both groups were unemployed and searching for work, the first group was discouraged like victims while the second group avoided contributing to overdevelopment. Both groups could relate to the experiences of the Tri-Tech workers whose work was environmentally meaningful but who were now disheartened by how easily they had been cast aside. Both groups asked the same questions to describe their dissonance, "Who is the economy organized for and what are the alternatives?"

It was crucial to The Working Centre to listen to these questions. Even as Tri-Tech was closing, we had the opportunity to secure contracts to provide job search services to laid-off workers from a string of plant closings.[32] Our work supporting the unemployed kept us busy, but we knew we had to put the same energy into new projects that could demonstrate grassroots, sustainable models of community development. We started Tools for Living[33] groups to explore these ideas in a wider forum. We sought to build on the positive aspect of the Tri-Tech experience, the demonstration of the benefit of using tools for building community. We started working on the possibilities of developing small community tool projects. The practical starting point was our Job Search Resource Centre.

From Public Access Computers to a Philosophy of Community Tools

We credit one of our first tenants with establishing the goal of building ten public computers for typing resumes and correspondence. At the same time, The Working Centre became the keeper of thousands of resumes. Public computers would give people opportunities to create their own resumes and cover letters. The basement at 58 Queen became the base for a burgeoning recycling project. A collection of computers started to grow from cannibalizing old computers to make others work. Soon the computer lab generated volunteer roles such as computer maintenance and hosting. Over time, more computers were networked together and the Internet added. Refurbished computers were added to a self-directed training lab for teaching basic and advanced computer skills at affordable prices. The software of an existing voice mail system was altered and community voice mail became another community tool offering public access.

These projects made computer technology accessible to those who could not afford it and offered the benefit of creating public spaces for teaching, repairing, and experimenting with changing computer technology. By 2005, in the basement of 66 Queen, the computer recycling project had a four-thousand-square-foot home with the capacity to refurbish computers, train people in computer hardware and software applications, and a lab for repairs. The project provides a unique convivial public space for those without work to explore technology with the help of volunteers, many of whom are also learning.

We found that public access computers created informal rules for co-operation that can also be found in the computer recycling lab, self-directed computer training, and community voice mail. We learned how community tools projects encourage collaboration between people, who work as equals to serve the idea of public access.

During the 1990s, we experimented and developed infrastructure to build new community tools such as the Recycle Cycles Community Bike Shop, the Barterworks network, the Sewing Space, and community gardens. The Working Centre grew as we purchased our main office at 58 Queen and the three-storey 43 Queen building across the street. We added housing in both buildings and purchased 79 Lancaster as a community house. The renovations of these buildings along with the integration of housing and the development of the tools projects created a new foundation. This work was supported by the art of Andy Macpherson,[34] the writings in our newsletter, *Good Work News*, and the publication by Ken Westhues of *The Working Centre: Experiment in Social Change*.[35] At the same time, St. John's Kitchen and the Job

Search Resource Centre changed their structure to reflect a community tools approach.

Each venture filled the spaces of The Working Centre with a new enthusiasm for community projects that allowed people to shape their work. We learned that the opposite of overdevelopment was the creation of useful public services that emphasized participation and inclusion. These projects generated meaningful work through practical services. We moved on from Tri-Tech Recycling, remembering it only for the lessons it taught us.

The first step we took to avoid an atmosphere of bureaucracy was to ensure that the cultivation of hospitality was a common occurrence at The Working Centre and St. John's Kitchen. We rekindled our original spirit while integrating an access-to-tools philosophy. This meant that friendships were more important than the actual projects. It was from the graces of serving others that the projects took root. Community grows by accepting our weaknesses in order to accept those of others and by encouraging a spirit of co-operation.

Conclusion

The Working Centre could easily have turned into a social service bureaucracy, meeting needs defined by government planners. Instead we honed our critical thinking skills. We sought to avoid the dulling societal malaise by acting on the dissonance that people were experiencing. While well-paying factory jobs were disappearing there was a growing competition for forests, fisheries, and minerals extraction. We had major concerns about Western dependence on unsustainable models of consumption that threatened the very ecosystem from which we derive our living.

Leopold Kohr helped us to visualize this malaise that we called overdevelopment. Workers were now consumers, swimming further and further from the shore of good work in deepening water and clinging to an ever-growing pile of manufactured goods. The image paints a picture of our alienation and dependency on complex bureaucracies for industrial production. Consumerism was threatening to drown out our local economic resilience.

Adopting the ideas of liberation yielded for The Working Centre an integrated philosophy of community tools. We learned from Ivan Illich that the way tools are structured is a reflection on the priorities of that culture. Our starting point was to invert the structure of our tools to ensure that they could be deployed to develop participation in local projects. We learned that people, not the tools, matter to these projects. We structured our tools for meaningful involvement by removing levels of status and by adding hospitality and friendship. The Working Centre evolved into a place of practical projects where people search for their own freedom while using their skills and abilities for the common good.

We had our own experience of brokenness and rejection through Tri-Tech, and this weighed on our understanding. As we developed an alternative philosophy of tools, we did this by addressing the reality of woundedness, of recognizing that people can be crushed equally by their neighbour or by a big system. We tried to become a place of refuge, offering friendly ways to develop skills and knowledge and a place of joy where useful tools inspire imagination and friendship.

PART TWO

Community Engagement

Illustration by Andy Macpherson

The Virtues

A personalist is a go-giver not a go-getter.
He tries to give what he has and does not try to get what the other fellow has.
He tries to be good by doing good to the other fellow.
He is other-centered not self-centered.
He has a social doctrine of the common good.
He speaks through deeds as well as words.
Through words and deeds he brings into existence a common unity,
the common unity of a community.

"Personalist Communitarianism" by Peter Maurin[1]

The virtues live at The Working Centre through hundreds of individuals who have selflessly contributed their skills. A commitment to service inspired Larry Crawford to become a valuable co-worker in the early 1990s after being laid off from the printing trade where he had been employed for twenty years. Larry took a course in numerical machine-tool controls, only to find there were few jobs in that field. Larry did have other work, though. He was a talented jazz musician whose regular gigs around southern Ontario had resulted in a 1970s jazz album.

Larry started working at 58 Queen Street by volunteering on the front desk, a role he modelled to suit his temperament and sociability. He made the front desk like his home office, spending over twenty hours a week assisting people with faxes, photocopies, taking after-hours phone messages, organizing the public message board, assisting users of the public access computers, directing resource centre traffic, sorting newspapers, and keeping the space organized. After hours, Larry connects with friends by phone, does paper work, and discusses contracts with fellow musicians. Larry is often the night watchman, doing his work while listening to shortwave and recently Internet radio.

Larry's parents settled in Guelph after immigrating from the Caribbean in the 1940s. His father was a minister, and the children were raised in a disciplined religious environment. Equality for Larry is deeply ingrained, as is his expectation that people use public space with civility, recognizing the public service being offered. For seventeen years at the annual Mayors' Dinner, Larry has brought together the Centro de Trabajo ensemble to play smooth live jazz, with the intention, as Larry puts it, that "the music stays in the background, helping to make the evening shine."

Countless others have made similar commitments. Nan washed piles of dishes by hand before we bought a dishwasher for St. John's Kitchen. Don spent twenty years doing food pickups for St. John's Kitchen and meticulously displaying hundreds of gift certificates for the Mayors' Dinner auction. Beth, in her work as financial coordinator, developed reporting systems for the centre's many diverse activities that blend responsiveness with the need for efficiency and accountability. All those involved with the centre have found opportunities for personal development and service to others.

We did not have a business plan or management skills when we launched the centre. We learned how to make things work as we went along, finding the expertise we needed for specific tasks. Rather than policies, we found resonance with the concept of virtuous personal action.

In the early 1990s we started thinking in new ways about the virtues. Reading Ivan Illich, Schumacher, Moses Coady, Dorothy Day, Peter Maurin, Martin Luther King, Mahatma Gandhi, G. K. Chesterton, and others, we formulated the concept of the *virtues* as the underpinning of The Working Centre. Virtues are different from values, a neutral word. Love and hate, acceptance and rejection are values. The *Concise Oxford Dictionary* defines virtue as "moral excellence, uprightness, goodness." The virtues now lie at the core of the centre's activities creating the spiritual basis that generates its culture and way of doing things. Culture has many definitions but it is best summarized as "the way we do things around here." Those at the centre practise social cooperation in contrast to the rampant individualism, competition, fragmentation, and isolation so marked in all societies today. The Working Centre seeks to create a different language, a grammar of community, to support the discipline and philosophy of relationships and collaboration.

During the 1990s we slowly started to talk about virtues—ideas in the background that simply flowed from what we were doing. The first four virtues came directly from Peter Maurin, the cofounder of The Catholic Worker, who lived his *personalism*[2] through offering his *work as gift, living simply* to leave more for the other, *serving others,* and *rejecting status.* The next two virtues grew from our work. By the end of the 1990s, when we were frequently renovating buildings, we used to joke that we were literally *building community.* The sixth virtue was our unique approach to mutual aid that we called *creating community tools.* The act of listing and describing them has helped create a habit of virtuous practice. They show how social co-operation is learned and practised in small, incremental ways that enhance personal and community development.

Work as Gift

Work as gift seeks to create places where the work accomplished feeds the human spirit, allowing relationships to flourish and deepening craft and skill. These are tied together by finding the courage of personal responsibility. Work as gift is what people offer in the form of time, skill, and labour to make their community a better place. Work as gift respects the environment, blending social and economic activities in mutually beneficial human interactions.

Work as a transaction in the 9 to 5, Monday to Friday, work world can lead to feelings of stress and dislocation. Work as gift recognizes that everyone has something to offer, from the professor washing dishes during his lunch hour at St. John's Kitchen to someone with a disability helping to arrange the toy shelf at Worth a Second Look. While building the apartments above 66 Queen, some of our best drywalling was accomplished by a fellow whose life was so torn apart that he was living in a tent in a secluded forest. His gift of energy and skill were matched by our support for his situation. It became a lasting exchange of craft and friendship.

Each person contributes to the work of the social good with his or her activity or presence. Opening to the gift of each person—what he or she has to offer—makes communities more inclusive and often more efficient. The Working Centre depends on both paid and unpaid workers, all working together with a common purpose in mind. By sustaining welcoming and practical projects, our work is a gift to each other and to the community.

Work as gift invites us to think outside the traditional employer–employee, boss–worker, staff–volunteer mindset, to challenge ourselves to think creatively and avoid the pitfalls of work as wage labour. It is sometimes easier for volunteers to understand the concept of work as gift than it is for paid staff. For those who earn their income through The Working Centre, our salary policy[3] is the agreement that gives everyone an equal piece of the resources we have to share; our salary is not a measure of our worth. Work as gift gives people a chance to engage the work on an equal level as everyone offers their labour as a gift for each other.

Living Simply

Living simply is the effort necessary to reduce the amount of stuff that we clutter our lives with. Ironically, living simply is complex: it requires the ability to learn new skills, to resist ever-present media and peer messages, to slow down long enough to celebrate the crafts of self-sufficiency, and believe in a world that can be different from the one in which we live. Living simply, as we envision the concept, is not about being poor in an affluent world but about choosing to live with less stuff, depending on self-produced or locally produced goods and services, and stepping as much as possible out of the market economy to meet our basic needs.

Westhues describes this concept as "acquiring skills and seizing opportunities to produce more necessities and luxuries of life on our own or in small groups. Unemployment (or a reduced income) need not mean the loss of the good life, but a chance to redefine the good life in a more genuine, joyful and sustainable way, more in terms of producing power than purchasing power."[4] At The Working Centre this practice means that those of us who receive an income from our work accept a lower wage. This is a fundamental gesture of respect for the many people we work with who live on very limited incomes. The savings from lower salaries get turned back to the organization, enabling us to purchase buildings or create access-to-tools projects. At its core, this is a commitment to sharing our limited resources with a widening circle of people.

We are not prescriptive about the concept of simple living. We work to generate the joy and rootedness that comes from making alternate choices. Fundamentally, living simply is a rejection of the basic premises of the consumer culture that surrounds us. We believe people thrive best in relationships, sharing tools together to make things they need, not as passive consumers serving the growth economy. Living simply can also lead to many of the deep pleasures of life; a meal cooked together made from the food we grow ourselves or purchased from those we know, bicycling or walking as a main form of transportation—these activities help us to see the world at a different pace.

Serving Others

Serving others means engaging in personal action to support the common good. Service can be practical activities such as helping to prepare a meal at

St. John's Kitchen, supporting someone in learning how to use a computer, helping someone fix a bicycle, or signing someone up for a personal telephone voicemail box. Service can also be listening, enjoying a meal together, or walking with someone through difficult times.

Serving others is probably the easiest of the virtues to understand, but it can be difficult to put into action. It is one thing to offer help to someone who is struggling and grateful for the assistance, but what if that person is unpleasant or demanding? What if that person is a co-worker? How can a misunderstanding or conflict become a way to understand the other person more, not a way to strengthen our own point of view? How do we stay committed to listening and responding to the person before us as the day and week moves on? Are we able to respond to a frustrated person with patience?

David Schwartz, in *Who Cares?*, describes the monopolistic successes of large modern institutions. Increasingly, people can only imagine being cared for through formal systems, which have expanded and taken over the space where informal systems previously operated. The problem is that informal supports were unlimited in the context of community while formal supports are by their nature limited and truncated.[5]

Serving others means to continually support "the impulse of people to help one another." Relearning the concept of service to others, rooted in relationships, helps us to recapture the reciprocal nature of responding to one another.

Rejecting Status

Rejecting status recognizes that the work of each person is to be valued equally. The work of a community is only possible when many people contribute. Human nature means that we are sometimes over-sensitive about this issue, especially when work is unpaid or offers smaller pay. Status can often satisfy the need for acknowledgement or recognition.

The Working Centre has a flat, egalitarian structure. People have responsibilities, not titles. No part or project has greater or lesser importance than the other. Communication is immediate, as messages are not held captive by hierarchy. The emphasis is on creating an open atmosphere conducive to skill development and practical action. There are no bosses, only colleagues contributing what they have to offer for the good of the community.

At St. John's Kitchen, volunteers who help to distribute the fresh food market are asked to select their own food last. At Worth a Second Look items are priced and put out on the floor and not vetted first by the volunteers. At Recycle Cycles, volunteers cannot reserve the best bikes for themselves. Paid staff and volunteers work alongside each other in ways where each person's work is valued equally. We work to respect the gift of volunteers above paid work.

We reject status because it is a gift to learn how to address each other as equals. We constantly explore mechanisms for supporting those with wider responsibilities, acknowledging that at The Working Centre the status and role clarification that you find in hierarchies is absent. Issues are discussed at Common Tables,[6] reinforcing the importance of everyone's voice. Rewards come from having greater responsibility for the welfare of the community, not from status or salary. This model of service when practised and reinforced by the virtues helps the human spirit to sing.

Building Community

Isolation, anxiety, and depression are found at all levels of society. What is the best way to bring people together in friendly open spaces? How can these spaces address the dislocation and individualism of our culture?

Jane Jacobs compared community to a forest ecosystem, where "once sunlight is captured in the conduit, it's not only converted but repeatedly reconverted, combined and recombined, cycled and recycled, as energy/matter is passed from organism to organism."[7] In a well-functioning community, innumerable co-operative acts by individuals and organizations create a diverse landscape. A desert, by contrast, is like a desolate community where people don't connect with each other. Deserts are barren because the "the passage of energy is swift," as sunlight filters through the sand and rocks, "vanishing, leaving no evidence of the passage."[8]

Community can be created in specific spaces where people are welcomed and feel some ownership toward it. Hospitality, welcoming the stranger, becomes an essential quality. If we are creating a forest, we need to nurture co-operation so that people see the good in each other. This entails the kind of energy that invites wide participation and responsibility.

In such environments, our spaces face constant challenges: a developmentally challenged man spits out racial slurs, taught to him at an early age, in a space full of New Canadians; a disenfranchised young person displays a swastika tattoo; an angry and frustrated man volunteers twenty hours a week, but his swearing offends another church-inspired volunteer; a young mother breastfeeding her baby offends a shy, socially challenged older man who is volunteering; or someone wants to limit the number of meal servings requested by a fellow patron at St. John's Kitchen. We are invited to get to know one another and build understanding and compassion within a commitment to the common good.

Building community means providing formal and informal support in a complex web. It includes teaching the skills of looking beyond oneself and into the other person, acting with kindness. It means learning how to be thoroughly helpful and inviting others to do the same. Common spaces should not be managed; they are better thought of as forests, places of surprise and complexity where openness to others is practised.

Creating Community Tools

Creating community tools is the social effort to put productive tools into the hands of people. We look at what activity or resource we want to offer and then think about creative ways to strengthen self-sufficiency and social co-operation around it. It is a direct act of community that develops culture around shared tools. How do we make bicycle repair tools more available? What patterns develop around sewing machines? How is a community garden organized? The virtue is ensuring that the common good of each tool is fully actualized.

Some projects do not fare well as a community tool. The administering of a million dollars in flow-through funding to older workers for training costs is best handled through more formal methods because funds must be accounted for. In the same project, a community tool developed in the older worker resource centre where volunteers took ownership and hosted a lively, informal space for job searching, computer access, and supportive gathering.

Community tool projects aim to develop new structures to facilitate sharing. The projects need to be hospitable and neighbourly. Community tools aim to reduce isolation by teaching the benefits of using tools in shared environments. It is a virtue that aims at civic betterment.

The philosophy of community tools helps us avoid the pitfalls of social services or resorting to easier bureaucratic forms. We do not shut down to protect our space; we open up and welcome people to share the resources and make them their own. The act of constantly inviting people into community space, to participate in the work, involves constant conversation. This dialogue creates structures of inclusion and mutual aid.

Integrating the Virtues

In January 1994, we were reminded of the connection between new models of work and the ideals of The Catholic Worker. We were speaking at a social justice retreat in Scarborough, Ontario. Our family was growing—Christina was ten years old, Rebecca was eight, and their newborn brother, Thomas, was six months old. During the workshops we hardly had to look after Thomas—he melted into Sr. Frances Ryan's arms. She gently held him the whole weekend. Christina and Rebecca had the run of the giant retreat house, a perfect place for young imaginations.

We were co-presenting with Len Desroches, a Toronto peace activist who was teaching the link between work and non-violence by telling the story of workers for peace, from Gandhi to Martin Luther King. He included Dorothy Day and Peter Maurin. In between the sessions we learned in detail about Peter Maurin's Green Revolution. Maurin grew up in the communal culture of a small French agricultural village. Later he was taught personalism by a Paris Catholic lay group, La Sillion, who were critical of the bourgeoisie's utter lack of concern for the poor. At the turn of the century, La Sillion sought to end inhuman working conditions by a return to communal guild factories. Twenty-five years later, on the streets of New York City, Maurin's past experience crystalized. He saw workers, the unemployed, and the indigent as cogs in the machine of urban industrial society. Maurin started spending all his time provoking people to relearn the communal aspects of Christianity, teaching the need for hospitality and bringing a spiritual dimension to daily living.

In a providential meeting with Dorothy Day he proposed creating houses of hospitality where meals could be served, housing offered, newspapers produced that debated philosophy, and round-table discussion to clarify thought. Day was ready to receive this message and together with a crew of workers they established The Catholic Worker movement.

Robert Ellsberg joined the New York Catholic Worker in 1975 and was invited to edit their monthly newspaper. Ellsberg's connection to the movement deepened as he spent time with Dorothy Day in her final years. She passed away in November 1980, living in the community she had founded almost fifty years earlier. In 2010, Ellsberg came to speak at St. Jerome's University (at the University of Waterloo) to promote Dorothy Day's diaries.[9]

On the Friday afternoon before his lecture, Ellsberg visited The Working Centre. We wanted to show him our adaptation of Maurin and Day's personalist philosophy. Our approach has blended modern ideas of useful and vibrant public spaces with the old ideals of service and communal hospitality. On that day, the resource centre was packed with people using the phones and the computers, and getting assistance from the front desk. The housing help desk was active, and Maurita's Kitchen was filled with volunteers. Even on that winter afternoon, the bike shop was busy. We talked about the housing we constructed ourselves, our quarterly newspaper, and the daily meal at St. John's Kitchen. All of these initiatives, combined with an inclusive and dialogical culture, represent the practical application of personalist virtues.

When Ellsberg commented that "Dorothy would have loved this place," it was a positive affirmation for the effort our community had devoted toward integrating the virtues into our daily work.

The Pastoral Circle—Discerning Right Action

The pastoral circle was the mechanism we used to integrate the virtues into The Working Centre culture. The forces of bureaucracy, status, and materialism are strong and steady. They put pressure on individuals and organizations to protect themselves to ensure they get more than the other. From our early days the pastoral circle forged a model of reflection that continually challenges how to shape the way forward. Praxis is the synthesis of action and reflection. Our praxis has always included habitual, virtuous action, staying focused on the individual who presents themselves at our door. We learned early that right action must be complemented with thoughtful reflection.

The Pastoral Circle
Discerning Right Action

Social Analysis: Ask: why? Why is this happening? What larger social, economic, and historical forces are at work? Make connections between experiences and structures.

Ethical Reflection: Develop ethical judgements in your social analysis. Discern right and wrong in these larger forces. Look at things through a moral lense. Ask: what is the right thing to do?

Experience: Start with the person, listen to them. Respond to their reality. They don't follow you, you follow them.

Act: Develop an action. Do something. Make a change in the reality.

Credit: Pastoral Circle image and descriptions developed by Isaiah Ritzmann for use in the Laurier Community Engagement Option course. Kyle Murphy stylized the graphic.

Margaret and Patrice, two of our earliest supporters, helped us integrate the pastoral circle into the structure of the original PLURA[10] grant in March 1982. The Study and Action Guidelines from *Unemployment: The Human Cost* were also an example to us. The pastoral circle became fundamental to how we thought and acted. It became natural to engage the daily experience of people, to follow and research the social analysis, to ethically reflect, and to discern right action.

The first step is walking with the *experience* of people who have been left out. When we first opened the doors at 94A Queen Street South, we listened to the experiences of those who were unemployed, often hungry, and seriously destabilized by the loss of their jobs. Understanding this experience was the first step of the pastoral circle, a constant readiness to listen actively, to understand the experience, and let that experience challenge us. This is not a one-time activity. When we absorb the experience, we reflect on how it can change us and help us open up to the experience of the other.

The second step is a thorough *social analysis* of what we are experiencing. Critical questions are asked and answers sought. Why do economic statistics give the illusion of low unemployment rates? Who is committed to ensuring that the unemployed can participate in useful training and apprenticeship programs? Why does society exclude and isolate people who are different? This step entails reading, discussing, and analyzing these kinds of questions.

The third step is *ethical reflection*. This is a place where we reflect on how the six virtues relate to the issue at hand. We start from the philosophy of the go-giver.[11] Whether we are analyzing bureaucracy, the economy, the private or public sector, or the community around us, we are clear that personalism involves being good to the other, being other-centred. This is a very simple statement on common unity.

Practical action is the fourth step. It means the best responsive action. How can we make things better? This step is not revolutionary or about big changes. It is simply a concrete action that leads to new experiences as the cycle is renewed. It is not necessary to get it right as long as we continue to engage in thoughtful action. In the best examples, the cycle becomes a positive spiral, with new learning integrated into new community supports.

The pastoral circle is rooted in the virtues, so each new situation raises new challenges. This core philosophy accepts our imperfections as we learn and invite others into this approach of responsiveness toward creating a positive cycle.

Living the Virtues

For twelve years, Arleen Macpherson coordinated St. John's Kitchen in a steady and compassionate way. She ensured that it was a refuge of support and friendship and a place where surplus food was redistributed through a daily meal.

Arleen knew hardship growing up when her father was injured in a mining accident. The family of nine lived in their grandparents' small hotel in Gowganda in Northern Ontario. Money was scarce, as were jobs. The family made do by pitching in together. Arleen was born in the same year the CBC was established, and she recounts her family's main activity as listening around the radio to CBC.

Coordinating St. John's Kitchen brought Arleen full circle. She could relate to the hundreds of people who came each day for a meal. There were people like her father, unemployed because of a serious injury, young workers who supported families with multiple part-time jobs, and older workers experiencing mental illness and the loss of family.

Arleen symbolized for The Working Centre the good work that comes from reflection and action.[12] Here she describes that process:

> We expect that growing pains will accompany the change. After all, communities require a certain lack of structure, formality, and rigidity to flourish. It may even appear on the surface that they are disordered, messy, and inefficient. But this very disorder allows for the inclusion of a wide variety of people. The need to incorporate both fallibility and capacity must, at times, supersede the need for efficiency. The essence of community is people working together; many different talents and skills are needed. Our ongoing challenge is to create a haven, a space for people that is naturally warm and welcoming.[13]

When Arleen started coordinating St. John's Kitchen in 1988, her goal was to ensure it did not become a place of charity where people have things done for them. Her aim was a community where all could be involved in the daily cooking, the serving, and cleanup. Slowly this ideal took shape as patrons took greater ownership. Arleen guided that process with steadfast hope.

Building Relationships Where People Are Real

In 1998, Ken Westhues's article, *Building Relationships Where People Are Real* helped root virtuous habits into our organizational culture.[14] Westhues was mostly interested in the cultivation of reciprocal relationships. By this he meant not only avoiding relationships of domination and power but replacing them with face-to-face dialogue where differences are admitted, hashed out and new options birthed. His model of reciprocal relationships encouraged us to cultivate the habit of listening to the other: "A reciprocal relationship is more than a contract. I open myself to your demands, you to mine, we surrender ourselves to a common goal beyond words, trusting that our pursuit of it will produce a mutually agreeable surprise. This is our covenant. It is a more human undertaking than a contract, and it promises a more satisfactory result."[15]

It is a step-by-step process to counter the stern messages of power and status that emanate from bureaucratically centralized organizations. People learn to fear the shadows when they are not in control. They learn not to question the illusions of power. It is at the margins and at the edges where new questions can lead to a different path. It starts by recognizing that quality in work comes from acting with initiative and learning the freedom to be responsible for one's actions. Local democracy thrives on the habits of reciprocal relationships.

Dialogue makes us more fully human, whether at home, at leisure, on the job, or giving or receiving a service. By taking turns in a discussion, we learn the art of mutually responsive talking and listening. Pride and humility together, in small or large ways, help individuals remember the experience of caring and being open to the other. Westhues is weary of centralized, institutional society. Rather than be crushed by it, he recommends, "dodging around it, building grass-roots covenants to enrich your own and others' lives."[16]

Rootedness and Loyalty

While Ken was teaching us about reciprocal relationships, The Working Board, of which he was a member, developed its own unique model of relationship-based governance. In the June 2004 issue of *Good Work News* we paid tribute to Maurita McCrystal who had passed away from cancer that spring. Maurita had been our board president for fifteen years. To celebrate her contribution to the centre we featured a picture of Maurita painting in the basement during the renovations of 43 Queen.[17] We could have chosen a more formal picture from the Mayors' Dinner, but it was more authentic to emphasize how Maurita saw her role as working equally with others. For Maurita, the dialogue that occurred while working together was essential. When she became president of the board our meetings featured friendship, food, and discussion. This model, which Stephanie describes below, became the means of enhancing our decision-making capacity through the stability and wide perspective it offered.

Maurita served as our chairperson and president in a way that was both tolerant and impatient. She had a knack for allowing a conversation to roam and develop until we had played out the creative discussion that was possible, but when it was over, it was over. Maurita quickly drew discussion to a close in a decisive way. Through this loose structure we stayed productive in our meetings without crushing the story-telling, the philosophizing, or the random way new ideas flowed together as we reached a common understanding of the ideas at hand.[18]

What kind of public philosophy sustains a commitment to the other, recognizing the importance of embracing all members of society? Simone Weil's definition of rootedness is one aspect of the answer. "A human being has roots by virtue of his real, active, and natural participation in the life of a community which preserves in living shape certain particular treasures of the past and certain particular expectations of the future."[19] We learned that adding loyalty back into exchange relationships encourages rootedness.

Loyalty has almost been extinguished in Western, market-oriented society. Loyalty is a victim of calculation. The world of administration and centralized bureaucracy is happy to see the last of loyalty, content to disregard it as an outdated virtue.[20] While loyalty is expected of those working in a bureaucracy, there is no guarantee that it will be returned when there is a financial crunch or when priorities change. Over time this reality undermines the practice of loyalty. In contrast we have worked on building loyalty in small and big ways; for example, we prize the steadfast long-term loyalty of many of our Working Centre board members, whose sense of duty and attachment to building community is integral to our organization. We had learned that board member terms should be limited to two or four years, but this practice was an organizational challenge as we were constantly educating new members. We found it easier to allow key board members to become committed to our organization through long board terms. In essence, we stumbled into recognizing what long-term experience and knowledge can bring to an organization. It allowed board members to breathe in the culture that they are committing to. Loyalty mixes faithful commitment with an ongoing dialogue and openness to learn from each other.

Loyalty partly vanished as the speed of work quickened and workers were treated as expendable. Our work culture will need to slow down in order to increase loyalty, because "the great benefit of slowing down is reclaiming the time and tranquility to make meaningful connections—with people, with culture, with work, with nature, with our bodies and minds."[21] Slowing down is a conscious act that gives priority to the dignity of human beings over money and economic growth. Instilling loyalty into exchange relationships creates trust and solidarity.

Renovating Using Reciprocal Principals

We learned how to craft open and useful public space when Peter Moberly, from the local Baha'i community, became involved in the early 1990s. Moberly took absolutely nothing at its word. He challenged everything. He got involved in the Tools for Living group and the Public Art Exhibition of Unemployed Workers only because he saw in both efforts the potential for craft, which was his motivating interest.

Peter asked questions, he offered to help, and he kept his doubts silent until he had to verbalize them: they then tended to come out with unusual force. He disliked structures that got in the way of people's creativity, believing beauty and functionality should be the outcome of design. Together we drew up plans for a resource centre with open and inviting spaces and interesting design elements as key concepts. We proposed disrupting the counselling offices in favour of public areas for computers and phones.

In late 1996, we made up a paper model of the plans. A presentation was made to the board, and a plan of action drawn up to start renovations in December. This large undertaking coincided with the Christmas holidays. As a Baha'i, Peter was glad to avoid the non-spiritual fuss of Christmas, so he was enthused to have a project for this time. From the minute we took apart the library shelves and tore down old walls, to the extra effort required to complete the job over the New Year's long weekend, all effort was directed at completing the 1,500-square-foot project. The original red maple hardwood floor was refurbished after four layers of flooring were removed. We had no fewer than ten volunteers every day, ripping out, rebuilding, tiling, drywalling, mudding, and painting. The essential work was completed late on the evening of January 2 when we pulled out the old carpet that would be replaced in the morning.

The whole process could be described as an intense two-and-half-week training camp for learning open-community building. The final result was that the 58 Queen Job Search Resource Centre became a bright and open space with a chrome green tin ceiling and original wooden floors, with counters, work tables, and café tables strategically placed to ensure maximum work and meeting space. With the computers, phones, newspapers, tables, and library it became an interesting, purpose-filled café. It offered a modern look while emphasizing the unique features of our ninety-year-old building.

Peter had shown us the importance of beautiful public space. The community participation in this barn-raising-like effort to refurbish 58 Queen demonstrated how reciprocal relationships can be integrated into the daily work of community building.

A Journey Rooted in the Virtues

Our hope is that the virtues live in the hearts and minds of the people who form The Working Centre community. You won't find a wall poster explaining or listing the virtues in our buildings. Virtues are best learned through action. A spirit of hospitality is the first way the virtues become apparent. They are lived when they nourish our capacity to learn, our ability to teach generosity, and when they deepen our commitment to hear the other. The virtues embody the act of letting go, of dismantling protective barriers in order to share, to help, and to listen. The virtues are not just a technique to engage those who are left out or who have no voice. They teach us and the wider community the benefits of generosity of spirit. The tradition of the virtues is only meaningful when others come to understand them, learn them, and practise them.

The closing of Tri-Tech Recycling led us on a search for deeper answers to the modern malaise of institutionalization and individualism. Modern society wants rootless, selfish non-connected individuals who are prey to institutional power. The institution tells the individual what to do, and for the sake of power, status, and money, the individual follows the demands of that institution even if it degrades his or her spirit.

We found that alternative thinkers were questioning how overdeveloped bureaucracies were causing havoc for the environment, changing the way people worked, and how they related to their communities. David Cayley was already searching for different answers. In his interviews with Ivan Illich, he highlighted the *Declaration on the Soil* which defined virtue through the lenses of shared local culture,

> By virtue, we mean that shape, order and direction of action informed by tradition, bounded by place, and qualified by choices made within the habitual reach of the actor; we mean practice mutually recognized as being good within a shared local culture that enhances the memories of a place. We note that such virtue is traditionally found in labour, craft, dwelling, and suffering supported, not by an abstract earth, environment, or energy system but by the particular soil these very actions have enriched with their traces.[22]

Cayley's writings also referenced Alasdair MacIntyre, who concludes in *After Virtue*, that the only hope for the tradition of the virtues is "the construction of local forms of community within which civility and intellectual and moral life can be sustained."[23] At the same time, Ken Westhues was teaching us about the virtuous habits of reciprocal relationships. These ideas were mixed in with the virtues, already familiar to us from The Catholic Worker. Over time we started to describe these virtues as important to the community of The Working Centre. The virtues started to be reflected in our actions and in the hospitality that each project cultivated.

We learned that our transformative work is about creating communities, places where individuals can express their skills, create access to tools, and build friendships. The bonds of community are strengthened through the humility of seeing the good in the other. Loyalty helps society develop a deep sense of spirit and solidarity. Our projects are about hands-on work with individuals who are listening, hearing, and responding. The virtues are a guide to the complexities of daily right action, a process that is transformative. The virtues offered The Working Centre a way to sustain small community projects by celebrating the human spirit.

St. John's Kitchen:
Redistribution through Co-operation

One of the first patrons to come to St. John's Kitchen was a big, strapping thirty-year-old labourer with a blond flowing mullet, who often did not have work. His workboots signified that he came from a working-class family that had to fend for itself in a harsh world. It doesn't matter the challenges his family faced, whether alcohol abuse, mental health, violence, or abuse. Paul grew up in a world where either his family would rise above these realities or they would be overwhelmed in a downward spiral. Could his father keep his job? Could his mother keep the family together? Families that give way to alcohol abuse, or experience mental health challenges, often must deal with violence, frustration, and shame. Depression, anger, and alcohol-fuelled violence can leave a family's dignity tattered. Their sons and daughters scatter, trying to make sense of it all.

During those early years we knew little about Paul's family. He would tell us about a trauma he experienced at his birth. He was sure the newspapers had covered it, and in later years, he would desperately ask us to help him find the article. Politicians and social service administrators weren't interested in stories—they wanted hard data. St. John's Kitchen had been open only six months, in June 1985, when a review was conducted to find out why people came to the kitchen. The Social Resource Council survey found that Paul was typical of those who came to St. John's Kitchen. He was an unemployed man under thirty-five who lived in the downtown, mostly in rooming houses within ten blocks of the kitchen. The survey of 87 people showed that half were single, 72% had lived in Waterloo Region for two years or more, 17% had no income, while 70% lived on less than $400 a month. These statistics meant little to us. We wanted to know why individuals were no longer connected to their families. Where were the jobs to provide them with employment?

Street life took its toll on Paul, and he was rarely content in his last ten years. He could threaten violence, give a big bear hug, and reminisce in a quick interaction. He would yell, "Why don't you help me, I can't live on the street anymore." He was known to break glass windows and doors when he pounded in frustration. Outreach tried their best to find apartments that could accommodate Paul's larger-than-life personality. At his memorial service, his niece told the story of how sad she would feel when her mother would drive Paul to the House of Friendship hostel. "Why does he not want to live in a house?" she would wonder. Paul would visit his sister once a month but he wanted no help from his family. One friend told how tough he and Paul were. Before churches provided the Out of the Cold shelters, "they used to sleep under the back Working Centre porch covered in blankets and cardboard through rain, snow and ice. We would do anything to live free on the street."

Paul was a member of the St. John's Kitchen community for almost twenty-five years before he passed away. Many like Paul live full lives on the edges of society, where they are never fully accepted, always scouting out a place to spend the night. Many cannot work because of the unresolved trauma or substance use that is circling through their head. They have a ready reason for their choices: "You may have been born into privilege, but I had no such luck." Several, by their actions, swear off work, finding acceptable excuses to refuse to become a cog in the wheel of consumerism. Many know they are on the bottom rung of society, with no chance of climbing up, so they refuse to climb, convinced they have more pride than those that do. Instead, they develop strong friendships on the street and help each other through good and bad.

St. John's Kitchen Takes Root

St. John's Kitchen grew as an idea between 1982 and 1984. During the summer of 1982, The Working Centre listened to, and learned from, unemployed individuals who spent their days scavenging for food and money. Maria and Michael George, two of our early supporters, had recently returned from the New York Catholic Worker, where workers take responsibility for serving a free daily meal. Maria instinctively started making sandwiches to share during lunch at 94A Queen Street. During the summer she addressed the Downtown Ministerial Committee, seeking their support to establish a soup kitchen, but for a number of reasons the churches were wary.

At the same time, the co-chairs of the Industrial Labour Adjustment Program (ILAP) committee helped us secure ILAP funding to establish three Unemployed Worker Centres (UWC). The location at St. John the Evangelist

Anglican Church became a refuge, a place in the downtown away from the rooming houses, offering coffee and friendship.

When the funding ended for the Unemployed Worker Centre in August 1984, the recession continued to leave many people behind. The provincial government established an emergency shelter and food program to help communities cope with the growing unemployment problem. The Ministry of Community and Social Services approached the House of Friendship, a men's shelter, about establishing a food relief project. By this time, the Core Area Ministry Committee (CAMC) was holding regular meetings. Martin Buhr, House of Friendship Executive Director, convened a meeting of the CAMC along with representatives from Waterloo Regional Social Services, the John Howard Society, the YWCA, and The Working Centre. At the meeting, Martin supported the suggestion that The Working Centre extend the St. John's UWC into a community kitchen. The support of the House of Friendship would help our fledgling project take on a large community venture.

The meeting in the late afternoon of October 31, 1984, touched off a flurry of activity. We quickly got Working Centre board support for the project. In early November we went to visit Sr. Christine Leyser, a Loretto sister (IBVM) and founder of the Welcome Inn Drop-in Centre in Guelph, to learn how she was providing a daily meal. We met with Rev. Cy Ladds at St. John the Evangelist Anglican Church to ask the church to host this new project based on the UWC experience. Rev. Ladds had no doubt that his church should open its doors to feed the hungry. With a location secured, a committee meeting was organized to help guide the implementation.[1] Brice Balmer of House of Friendship became a common presence at St. John's. He was committed to ensuring this project developed into a long-term safe haven. He also helped present our case to Regional Council. We had to request a grant worth 20% of the provincial contribution (about $15,000) which was the mandatory local contribution, in order for us to be eligible for the provincial funding.

At Regional Council and in the community there were people who were opposed to establishing a soup kitchen. They reflected the views of rugged individualism: Why do these people not look after themselves? We knew this argument missed the point. We had learned from the Unemployed Worker Centres that a large number of single men lived in rooming houses on meagre pensions or benefits. We saw a community kitchen as an extension of the helping spirit of Waterloo County's farmers. Farming neighbours helped each other to bring in the harvest and build barns. The old settlers had few possessions. They understood that by sharing what little they had, it would be returned a hundredfold.[2]

Organizations in Kitchener had been developing social services since the 1930s. In a 1941 letter to the Mayor of Kitchener, the chair of the House of Friendship reported that in 1940 some 8,727 meals had been served in the dining room and 177 beds given during the winter months. Even during prosperous times, the House of Friendship responded to the needs of isolated and lost individuals. In the 1960s, fifteen thousand meals were served each year to men from Kitchener and Waterloo. The numbers kept growing, with 23,000 meals served in 1978.[3]

When we opened St. John's Kitchen on January 15, 1985, we hoped to redistribute surplus food while co-operatively involving patrons in the daily work. In the first month about 1,200 meals were served, and by the sixth month that had grown to 2,300 meals. Eighteen months later we were serving about 4,200 meals a month. For the next ten years the number of meals served did not change substantially, hovering at 60,000 meals annually. Rose, the St. John's Kitchen manager thought preparing a large meal for 100 people each day was a perfect job for her. "We're part of their daily lives. Most don't eat more than this one meal here. We serve the meal, find clothing, deal with welfare, and make doctor appointments." There were two distinct groups who came to the kitchen. There were those not in the labour market, including older workers, ex-psychiatric patients, people with alcohol and drug issues, and people with disabilities. The smaller group was made up of employable, unskilled labourers between the ages of seventeen and thirty-five.

Edwin Chishol was one of those men. "This is the only meal I get all day," Chishol explains, "I come here every day that it's open. I don't have a job. I am looking though. I'm an epileptic and most people don't want to hire an epileptic." Jean Roche, an injured meat cutter, liked the openness of the kitchen: "This place is good. You walk in here and you can walk out. You don't have to get authorization at the desk. Without the soup kitchen you'd have nothing but a bunch of hungry people."[4] Roche, in his late fifties and living on a $320 monthly welfare cheque, had no chance of finding work again. His last employer had closed its Kitchener plant in October 1984, leaving 630 workers unemployed.

St. John the Evangelist Anglican Church has occupied a prominent corner at Duke and Water in the Kitchener downtown since 1862. It is close to King Street and right beside the block that the City of Kitchener purchased in the 1990s for its new city hall. The entrance to St. John's Kitchen was from the side door off Duke Street. Patrons opened a heavy wooden door and entered a small foyer with wood carved benches on either side, where a retired church member sat, dutifully welcoming each person and directing them to the gymnasium. The gym had once been a popular spot for youth dances, theatre, and basketball. By the 1980s, The Working Centre was its most active user.

As we planned our first meal, it seemed obvious to serve the meal through the three windows that looked from the kitchen onto the gym floor. We quickly recognized our mistake, and learned how bad design can turn into a permanent barrier. In this case, we had allowed a physical divide to form between the patrons and volunteers. Once the habit of serving from inside the kitchen was established, any attempt to change it was brushed aside as not fair to the volunteers, who were more comfortable in the kitchen. After a year of discussion, exasperated, we set a date, then pulled the tables into place and started serving the meal from in front of the windows. Within weeks, everyone agreed that coming out of the kitchen was a more open and friendly way of serving the meal.

Around the same time we were being asked to start charging a fee for the meal at St. John's Kitchen. Waterloo Region's Health and Social Service Committee had required us to co-operate with the Social Resource Council to survey St. John's Kitchen patrons in return for funding from the province's Emergency Shelter and Food Program. The report on the survey included a request that St. John's Kitchen impose a fee and create an ongoing list of patrons. Both requests contradicted the philosophy of our community development effort to turn surplus food into a daily meal shared with those on a minimal income. We argued against both recommendations.

We were facing our own internal problems. The initial work of establishing St. John's Kitchen had been successful, but as we finished our second year, it was clear there were problems with the structure and operation. A document was prepared that outlined the problems and described our hopes that the people who used the kitchen would develop ownership, that patrons and volunteers on the floor and in the kitchen would mix freely, and all would join together in advocacy. In contrast to this lofty vision we were hearing increased complaints about the patronizing atmosphere of the kitchen, that we were overstaffed, that patrons were not trusted, that the new community development worker acted more like a security guard.

The Working Centre perspective was that the operation of St. John's Kitchen was challenging enough but was made harder by a structure that gave the SJK committee power over hiring and moral sway over direction. Alternative ideas are easily overpowered by fear. The committee listened to the kitchen manager's concerns about the patrons and the hard work involved in producing the meal. The worries created a distrustful environment. St. John's

Kitchen was quickly degenerating into a stodgy social service. By August 1988, the SJK committee became a subcommittee of The Working Centre board, formally recognizing our day-to-day responsibility. We were eager for the partnership and the freedom to create the place we envisioned. Over the summer we recruited Arleen Macpherson as a woman of faith and justice to give St. John's Kitchen new direction.

Arleen's first years were spent understanding the issues. In February of 1990, we learned that the province was cutting the emergency food funding we had been receiving. Their rationale was that increases to General Welfare Assistance had reduced the need for the program. The region declined to help us provide the daily meal—we had already rejected their recommendations to create a list of patrons and charge a fee. Other groups with food programs were granted funds if they restricted service by setting a limited number of visits per month. We stuck to our position, which made us poorer in funds but, as it turned out, richer in participation. We knew we did not want to conform to a centralizing system that offered money in return for social control; rather, we chose to use our resources frugally and rely directly on the people who used the service.

A new spirit of hospitality started to catch on. Arleen worked slowly, repairing what was St. John's Kitchen, and quietly injecting new values of honesty, compassion, and volunteerism into the structure. One man noted how he would never forget how Arleen had encouraged him during his drunken grief. When a new tragedy struck, there was Arleen again, willing to sit there each day listening. He was grateful, knowing he could release his anger and despair to a friend rather than with a jug of wine on a park bench.

At a rally held at St. John's Kitchen to criticize the provincial government cutback in June of 1990, Brian Caldwell of *The Kitchener-Waterloo Record,* interviewed Dwayne and Nancy Currie who were both in their forties and who each day walked eight kilometers to the kitchen to get a free hot meal. Dwayne had been laid off six months earlier. Their Unemployment Insurance paid them about $1,000 a month, of which $550 went to rent. They had two children under three, and they had just had their telephone disconnected.[5] Another patron said, "This place kept me alive in the winter months." During these years, Arleen worked with a street kid who over time completed her Masters and now has a family. Arleen documented the barriers this young woman encountered along with her heart-warming success at school.[6]

Grants and other funding had allowed St. John's Kitchen staffing to grow to five positions in the first years. When Arleen arrived and one of the grants ended, we reduced staffing to three positions. This meant there was a cook, a cook's helper, and a floor worker. The loss of the provincial grant in 1991 coincided with the cook's retirement and another staff member taking a leave. We hired a cooking facilitator, who encouraged others to cook, we had a part-time worker for the floor, and Arleen helped people see how they could contribute. The loss of the grant became the means for achieving our original goal of involving the whole community in the work of redistributing food.

In the December 1994 issue of *Good Work News* Arleen Macpherson explained the kind of community we were attempting to create:

> St. John's Kitchen long ago became a place where people gathered for more than food. People come to socialize, meet friends, play cards, support one another, and help with tasks. It is a rare place where people with strongly divergent points of view can spend substantial periods of time in relative harmony. It seems like the ideal place to develop and practise the virtues of gentleness, respect, love, and inclusiveness that sometimes get forgotten in our competitive and often harsh world.[7]

St. John's Kitchen always had a spirit of hospitality, essential to its success. We learned how fragile this spirit can be and how lurking institutional responses threaten to creep into the structure. We were wise to identify the problems early, and Arleen had a calming approach that reinserted the values of co-operation and the ability to listen to people's lived experience.

The Evolution of St. John's Kitchen

When Arleen retired in 1999, Jennifer Mains, the new St. John's Kitchen coordinator, found opportunities to develop outreach services in partnership with doctors and community health advocates who were asking for clinic space in the church. The congregation of St. John the Evangelist Anglican Church continued to be our host until July 2006, when we moved into the newly renovated warehouse space at 97 Victoria Street North. Our relationship with St. John's Church had spanned over twenty-three years, during which over 1.5 million meals were served. They had offered the gift of hospitality and space to ensure the meal was served every day. Now, homelessness was presenting a new reality, and the number of individuals with complex issues was growing. A new approach was evolving, and the church agreed that St. John's Kitchen had outgrown its home. This resulted in a search for a new location.

It had seemed impossible to replicate the large space requirements of St. John's Kitchen. We were discussing furniture recycling with the St. Vincent de Paul Society when we suggested the idea of locating St. John's Kitchen on the top floor of their warehouse building. The building needed significant renovation work, and The Working Centre knew exactly how to revitalize it. Leaders of the St. Vincent de Paul Society helped members to see the greater community good of selling the building to The Working Centre in order to provide a long-term place for St. John's Kitchen to serve its daily meal.

After we purchased 97 Victoria, we engaged our architect, Robert Dyck, who had recently offered services pro bono to help us revitalize 66 Queen. He was pleased and surprised when the patrons of St. John's Kitchen demonstrated their solidarity. At Robert's design workshop, the group met in a circle and a wooden spoon was used as a talking stick. Each person described what they would like to see in the new space. They had clear opinions on how open the kitchen should be, what kind of kitchen equipment was needed, where the dishwasher should be located, what were the best colours, how to design the washrooms, and how much light the windows should let in. The patrons had been thinking for years about the best amenities for a community kitchen.

In May 2005, we started the task of completely stripping down the two-storey, 15,500-square-foot building. The first job was getting the main floor renovated and opening Worth a Second Look (WASL).[8] The second job was renovating the new St. John's Kitchen into a place with an open kitchen, big bright windows to surround the dining area, public access washrooms, a medical clinic, showers, and a laundry area. At every stage new volunteers, job café workers, and unemployed workers on training grants helped us complete the project.

Greg Roberts coordinated the renovations, valiantly holding all the disjointed pieces together, when at last in July 2006 the majority of the work was completed. Don Gingerich assisted with his extensive construction experience, while also developing the job café crew and establishing WASL on the main floor. Together, their combination of skills and commitment allowed the 97 Victoria project to move in rhythm with the planning process and bring the work to completion as quickly as possible.

In July 2006, St. John's Kitchen moved from the church to the new space with brightly painted walls of orange, yellow, and green, shiny kitchen equipment, an accessibility lift, and ceramic tiled floors. The top floor of 97 Victoria had been transformed by a dedicated group of staff and volunteers who worked days, nights, and weekends to go the extra mile to complete the work.

Today when you walk up the stairs at lunch time to St. John's Kitchen you are confronted by a buzz of activity. Some people are scraping and piling dishes, others are entering the medical clinic where the Psychiatric Outreach

Project has open hours, the serving line for the lunch meal stretches past the laundry, and a few people wait to use the shower stall. This can all be observed within ten feet of the stairs. The serving area and the dining hall to the right is filled with about 120 people.

This is St. John's Kitchen. Each weekday, hundreds of people come together to ensure a community meal is served. How do we welcome the stranger? How do we ensure all have access to a full meal? How do we involve people in producing a meal? How do we support those who tenuously cope with problems as they confront personal change? How can this be accomplished with love, without judgment, in a way that respects the dignity of all involved?

The kitchen is an important gathering place that opens at 8:00 a.m. for coffee, jam, peanut butter, and breads. The lunch meal is served between 11:00 and 11:30, when it is ready. If you are still eating at 1:30, people may hover over you to clean the final dishes and get the floor mopped. During these hours there is continuous work to prepare, serve, and clean up for the meal. Many people devote hours of their day to this labour. At 3:00 they leave, knowing they have completed a good day's work. This has been the rhythm of St. John's Kitchen for almost thirty years.

Gretchen Jones has been a rock for St. John's Kitchen, facilitating the shared work of serving the daily meal for twenty-three years. In 2003, when she was recognized with the Queen's Silver Jubilee Medal, she reflected on the 90% of her co-workers who are unwaged or on social assistance but whose work is essential. Every day, the labour of up to forty people who cook the daily meal, assist with the laundry, keep the coffee pot filled, do dishes, or mop the floor is a community-inspired commitment that makes St. John's Kitchen possible.[9]

In 2002, in *Good Work News*, Leslie Morgenson described the different elements that make St. John's Kitchen more than a food redistribution centre. It is partly the "high emotional characteristic of this large community as they mingle with their joys, their woes, supporting each other in the manner of old—freely given." It is a place where the intent is unconditional respect. There are no strings attached; people gradually begin to trust and let their guard down. Gretchen watched the transformation: "It evolved so slowly you can't see it.…The patrons have taken ownership of the place," she says. "It is their community. This is their refuge."[10]

On December 15, 2008, over eighty family members, friends, and members of The Working Centre and St. John's Kitchen community gathered at St. John's Kitchen for a memorial service celebrating the life of Dave Conzani.

In 1986, when Dave was twenty-three, he became part of the St. John's Kitchen community. Dave was taken away from his Aboriginal mother when he was three and spent his childhood in seven foster homes. He struggled with his dislocation throughout his adult life. In the 1990s, Dave shared stories of living, abandoned on the edge of society.[11] Dave asked for compassion and a listening ear, someone, anyone, to hear the voices of those down and out.

In the spring before he died, Dave and his second son, Ben, attended a public meeting to support the Food Not Bombs group at Kitchener City Council. It was standing room only. Dave was with Joe (Mancini) above the public gallery listening to the debate. Dave proudly told Joe that his article in *Good Work News*, "Miracle on Duke Street," gave him standing on the Internet.[12] Coincidentally, within a week, we received an email from Dave's son Chris, inviting his father to his wedding. Chris had made the connection by searching his father's name online.

Two months later, Dave described the wedding as the best day of his life, so pleased to share it with both his sons. Both Dave and Ben were well attired, having found two tuxedos at a thrift store. Dave died six months after Chris's wedding, satisfied that his two sons now knew each other. Ben has remained an active friend of The Working Centre community, enlivening us with his adventures as he finds his own place in the world.

Liminality and Integrated, Inclusive Downtowns

Liminal spaces (thresholds or transitional spaces) create opportunities for people, ideas, and ventures to find acceptance. We started learning about liminality and anti-structure during a wintery weekend in Pembroke in 1998, at a retreat on community economics. We were part of a dialogue with Jim Lotz, who had just published *The Lichen Factor*. Lotz gave us words to understand that community is a form of "anti-structure," a "counterforce to the secularized, rational, ordered society in which we live and move and have most of our being."[13] Liminality is about initiating personal and collective development by creating places and spaces where people can re-engage in community, and thereby remember to trust the other, reflecting back the openness they experienced. As large-scale organizations leave people behind, one role for community groups is to develop liminal spaces where people can reconnect with meaningful community.

Lotz talked about the Antigonish Movement, where Fathers Coady and Tompkins combined adult education with economic action to help farmers and fishers to organize ventures to market their goods. Tompkins started by helping his poverty-ridden parishioners to organize themselves so they would not be easy prey for the fish merchants. They used adult education to inspire people to believe in new structures like co-operatives, producer groups, stores, credit unions, and housing that could lift them out of their poverty.

Tompkins liked to advocate for "co-operation in spirit, not just passing pork and bologna over the counter to your neighbour."[14] His goal was to teach people to do things for themselves, not to be reliant on larger economic entities that exploited their advantage over the poor. Today in downtown urban areas, we confront a new kind of dislocation. A hundred years ago, it was still possible for workers to regain control over their tools. Today, the institutional control of society by large public and private bureaucracies means that increasing numbers of individuals are not attached to work, family, or community. Ironically, many of these top-heavy, rule-oriented, depersonalized bureaucracies perpetuate dislocation and addictions. Bruce Alexander calls this *The Globalization of Addictions*, where individuals with less and less psychosocial integration combat the universalization of addictions, depression, and rejection. Increasingly people see this reality in their families, in their workplaces.[15]

Can we create communities that invite people in who have lost their spirit? Downtown Outreach has walked with many individuals abandoned by family and society, who have been deprived or have deprived themselves of nourishing social relationships. They end up having few places to turn. Is the answer a doctor offering mental health support, a friend walking through the pain, an outreach worker helping to make connections, a judge in the Mental Health Court offering compassion, or a local retailer taking an individual under her wing? Every attempt is another undertaking to create community, a way for a wounded person to bounce their character off another in the search for healing. The task is to develop open, inclusive, integrated communities that encourage participation, opportunities for good work, support through the maze of bureaucracies, and public gathering places.

Inclusive downtowns need public squares and embedded structures of solidarity. The Working Centre models co-operative and productive ways of contributing. Since 2005, Job Café crews have been sweeping downtown streets along main routes on three-hour shifts. The project supports those living downtown who are excluded from the regular labour market. The street sweepers have a stake in the downtown. There are countless groups that need access to places where they can organize craft and cultural societies, spiritual discovery, and productive co-operatives. These all create room for the practice of reciprocal relationships, creating opportunities for co-operation, the life-blood of the city.

An important part of integrated communities are the interconnections between people that help build community. The liminal space of informal and formal supports is a refuge that people use to bump into each other and form reciprocal relationships. New cultural supports develop when people engage each other in community that supports the direction they are trying to move toward.

Downtown Outreach at St. John's Kitchen

When Jennifer Mains started to coordinate at St John's Kitchen she wondered what kind of place has 150 people for lunch and only two staff: "The place could easily be chaos. Mutual respect was the only option. I am not someone who ever wants to use force or rules to control. I would rather have mutual respect as a means to establish community conversation and non-violent intervention as a means to responding to issues."[16] Building trust and friendship cannot be done from behind a desk. It has to be earned by listening and supporting people who face many barriers. Jennifer found new resources for the kitchen, such as offering a daily market program organized by the people who could take the food home to cook it. Most importantly, a culture grew among the patrons and workers at St. John's Kitchen as they learned to listen and search for solutions together.

The idea for Downtown Outreach grew from conversations with business owners and people on the streets and a commitment to work on building relationships on all levels. It was agreed that outreach workers should support the issues people faced on the street and that this would improve relationships all around. Jennifer described the process as "not something where you can just parachute someone into the role. It takes time to develop relationships and build trust. Only then can you work on solutions."[17] We describe this approach as walking with others, enjoying the beauty of each person, looking past appearances, and working on problems together.

St. John's Kitchen became the base for a growing outreach initiative. How can we help an individual deal with stomach cancer who has not had stable housing for years? What of an older gentleman, who seems to be without family while his dementia erases his memory? Who will get him to his rooming house? What are the chances he will stay there on a cold night? What happens when a severely depressed volunteer is admitted to the psychiatric ward? Who will be a friend, who will visit?

In a recent gathering of Working Centre staff, the importance of careful listening was emphasized over and over again. How do we help without taking control of the situation, stand beside the person without determining the outcome? This requires thoughtfulness and care for others.

Early one morning, Joe picked up his phone messages to hear a desperate 3:00 a.m. phone call: "I can't go on living, this is the end, there is too much to figure out, no matter how hard I try. I just wanted to let you know." Joe was pretty sure he knew the voice, but it was slurred. As Joe walked to St. John's Kitchen, Paul jumped off his bike and angrily complained to Joe about being harassed by a bus driver: "It is not fair, this guy has been on my case since we worked together at Hoffman Meats. Everywhere I go, he calls me names. One Christmas I even bought him a bottle of whisky to stop the taunts, but he didn't care, he kept harassing me. Now I have been banned from using the buses." "Wait, Paul," Joe asked, "why have you been banned from the buses?" "Don't you understand, these people are against me! This guy is now a bus driver. When I boarded the bus, I put in my adult ticket and this guy tells me I need a juvenile ticket. I couldn't take it anymore, could you? Why is he still harassing me after all these years? Then I started yelling at him, pretty soon the police were there, I get arrested and now I can't ride the buses. You have to do something about this guy. He is harassing me, he won't let it go."

Joe listened as Paul got increasingly angrier. Then Matthew walked by and distracted the conversation. "Are you still working?" Joe asked him. Matthew had been on the streets after he and his girlfriend got into drugs. Eventually, he broke away and found housing in one of our transitional units and soon started working part-time, baking in Maurita's Kitchen. He wanted full-time work, but then moved in with a friend who had just given birth to twins to help look after her three children. This was a second chance. We helped connect Matthew to a local bakery. He told Joe that his job was good, the twins were doing well, and that he and his girlfriend were happy together.

In front of St. John's Kitchen, Bill tells Joe he can't do flyer delivery this year as "his body is too beaten." But he needs a loan. He used what money he had to buy his sister a wheelchair. The problem is that he is battling his landlord over essential apartment repairs. Bill knows he will lose the fight if he can't pay his rent and so he asks if we can help him out. "Don't worry about getting paid back, you know I would never stiff you." Just them a chirpy fellow comes bounding down the St. John's Kitchen stairs. "That phone call, last night, are you all right?" Joe asked. "Yeah, I usually don't do that, I think I got things figured out. You have to stay positive, I just lost it last night. I am glad I made it to the morning."

In line for a meal at St. John's, Joe talks with a hard-working volunteer. He lives for his dog, which he cared for even when he was homeless. Because of his disability he is not able to work full time. He is a calm and warm presence. He

Continued

Box, continued

spent many years helping a woman who could not settle down for her addictions, but he was always there for her, offering his place when she needed it. Now she has passed away, adding to his dislocation. Recently he was whisked to hospital because of an overdose of over-the-counter pills. He is a bit embarrassed but determined to get stronger. He is back volunteering full-time at WASL.

The welfare state, which imposes order from above and requires specific outcomes, fails on many levels. Access to basic necessities of life is often denied because someone does not fit into bureaucratic categories, or because they cannot navigate complex rule-based systems.

Resources to support such people are often difficult to secure and to maintain. St. John's Kitchen has leveraged a range of government supports for this outreach work, but it also depends heavily on voluntary contributions. Dr. George Berrigan offers a clear example of the effort necessary. Upon retirement as a general practitioner, he searched for an alternate place to offer his services. He quickly found a home in the Psychiatric Outreach Project (POP) at St. John's Kitchen. He billed what he could through OHIP and built a new practice, taking courses on psychiatry and addictions and noting the minimal connections often made between the two. He spent hours reading on the Internet, learning new approaches to caring.

Dr. Berrigan summarized the POP approach in this way:

As a family practitioner, I am used to being my own boss. At POP, I work in a different way, here we work in a circle. We are reaching out to individuals who have major illnesses, addictions, and mental health issues. These are truly the walking wounded and who is there to listen to their pleas? This is why the model of care is that of a circle. We who do this work are outliers as the model of professional service in usually based on top-down approaches.

The model we are using helps us avoid the tunnel vision we all have. Rather than only hearing the story of an individual from one perspective, our team usually hears the perspective of the doctor, the nurse, the social worker, and the outreach worker. Each hears in a different way and we put together a more accurate story.[18]

POP is embedded in the village of supports that have evolved at the place of St. John's Kitchen, where the daily meal is prepared in an open kitchen while patrons gather at tables, and services like showers, laundry, and fresh- and canned-food distribution takes place. Funeral services help the community grieve, while opportunities for work and volunteering make the kitchen a place where primary health services seem natural.

The psychiatric outreach nurses are an important part of the clinic. They all take less money to participate in this creative endeavour. The clinic nurse is a friendly face you see when you walk up the stairs to St. John's. You can often see a nurse with a backpack talking to someone on a street corner, accompanied by an outreach worker. Over two thousand patient records have been opened, mainly for those who are homeless or at risk of homelessness. This project has been supported with resources contributed by the Lyle S. Hallman Foundation and the Region of Waterloo,[19] and now through CMHA from the Waterloo-Wellington LHIN.[20] Doctors, nurses, and outreach workers work together and use their skills and compassion to meet the needs of marginalized people.

Jennifer Mains, an impassioned and ethically strong person, sees moral truth quickly, mentoring others in the complex yet simple work of walking with others in a spirit of unconditional love. Her clarity of purpose grew as she worked with a sixty-year-old man with a drinking problem. He had liver cancer and was in tremendous pain and had no place to live. He had once held a well-paying job but was laid off and saw his family life disintegrate. This dying man was unable to access proper health care because of his irrational behaviour and his drinking problem. He had no money and no housing, and his mental stability and grip on reality were tenuous, symptoms often related to liver disease.

The Working Centre purchased the two rooming houses next to our 97 Victoria Street property, hoping to turn them into a hospitality house to support people without stable housing who are dealing with debilitating illness. Jennifer brought the reality of the people we serve to the attention of hospital administrators and doctors. How can we support acutely ill individuals who do not fit into the hospital system and have no place to live? A plan for Hospitality House was drawn up and support secured from the Waterloo Wellington LHIN.

Right action and community development must be interconnected. Jennifer has overseen the growth of the outreach work that includes the Hospitality House, the Psychiatric Outreach Project, the Kitchener and Waterloo Outreach Workers, the Bridgeport Café in Waterloo, the Streets to Housing

Workers, the At-Home Outreach Worker, and The Working Centre's transitional supportive housing. Stephanie Mancini talks about the mindset needed to cope with the details of these non-traditional projects. It is a serious game, with so many balls in the air, so much fluid movement between the projects, to find and sustain the resources needed to accomplish the work. We deal with government bodies that want to create static structures, but our intent is to develop a flowing architecture that encourages good work by creating the freedom for individual initiatives in an integrated, co-operative structure. Our pragmatism ensures that all this juggling makes good work possible. But it also increasingly involves busywork that takes valuable time and energy away from the task of building community.

Our work often replaces the family and community, which formerly looked after their own. Outreach workers support individuals where they are, on the street, through traumas, housing searches, medical appointments, dementia, mental health issues, bill paying, or securing social income.

Outreach involves a nurse and her willing husband going out at 10:00 p.m. on a cold, rainy, late-October night to search for Martin in the alleys of uptown Waterloo. She was committed to ensuring Martin would get his psychiatric and pain drugs every ten hours to help him deal with his growing cancer. That night, Martin was found under a storefront overhang sheltering from the rain. A relationship, built over many months, grew into a friendship that Martin shared with others as the fog in his head slowly cleared. In the Freeport Health Centre, nurses and outreach workers surrounded him and became his family. When Martin died of cancer at age forty-one, over two hundred people gathered at his memorial at St. John's Kitchen. Martin walked ten years of his life on the streets. He was known for his long dreadlocks, beard, and heavy unkempt coat. He said very little but watched everything.

Community ownership of small projects in a decentralized environment demands loyalty and devotion to one's work. The ability to throw oneself into work is reflective of craft, which thrives when individuality is matched with co-operation with others doing similar work. Unlike work imposed by hierarchical structures, those who control their own work develop a sense of ownership of what they produce.

Centralization has difficulty dealing with the ethics of mutual aid, personal decisions that leave more for the other, and the call to develop co-operative structures. Integrity threatens the status and power of large systems. Centralizing forces lose power when faced with commitment engendered by co-operation. Here is the place where co-operation, reform, and the status quo meet head on, what Lotz calls the cross of community. Top-down efforts to change come in conflict with bottom-up initiatives, insiders with outsiders. They each press in to add their piece to the unfolding story. Possibilities for rebirth and renewal work themselves out at the point of maximum tension, the centre. Operating at the centre demands a spirit of grace, grounded in loyalty to a particular place, a craft or calling, and to family and friends. This spirit builds discipline, avoids resentment, and finds hope in possibilities of change in individuals and structures of society. This is change that takes shape before our own eyes, change that happens because hearts have been moved.

Community Engagement

Jennifer describes community engagement through outreach in this way:

> We walk with people only. That is what we do. We are not setting goals. We are not case managers. I am not trying to improve that person's life. I am not out there to see if I can get that person to change. That is not the issue. The point is to ask, "Where are you? What do you need help with?" And when the person says, "You know, I think I want to go to detox," to respond so that there is no pressure. "Good, so do you want me to make the phone call with you? How do you want to do that?" It is the person leading the way—we are supporting.[21]

St. John's Kitchen has walked a long road for thirty years, creating liminal space for co-operative action. It is impossible to quantify the daily work that thousands of people have contributed to serve the daily meal. They have contributed to decentralized models of community development that grow from the bottom up and are dependent on the creativity of individuals. It takes discipline to develop the habit of joyfully preparing, serving, and cleaning up the daily meal. To address the globalization of addictions means to build the kind of community that helps each person become more human. It takes the efforts of many to weave community. It is a craft, expressed as walking with the other, allowing each person to change us as we engage together, one moment as the helper, another as the one who is helped. Together it becomes a co-operative exchange for the common good.

Searching for Work at the Help Centre

Evolution of the Job Search Resource Centre

The Working Centre's location at 58 Queen Street South became a place that job searchers could rely on. In our first four years we had struggled to consistently maintain a self-help resource centre. Funding from the Ontario Help Centre program injected new possibilities. That first morning in January 1986, men from the House of Friendship shelter came to check out job leads, and others applied for our office re-entry training project and inquired about options for job searching. We were able to build on our model of supporting individuals through listening, active involvement, and support as people navigated the challenge of job searching.

One Friday afternoon, Ramsay and Stephanie were hosting the resource centre space. Ramsay, a Newfoundlander, had worked in labouring jobs until his back gave out, subsequently spending many years in pain. He found a place at The Working Centre and eventually settled into a long-term relationship with another Working Centre volunteer. In the door came a rather intense, weathered, and aggressive fellow. He was just out of jail and wanted to know where he could go to get help, primarily a place to stay. Ramsay leaned over, immediately cutting to the quick. "Here's where you want to go," he said and directed the visitor to where he should go and why. The visitor was not interested in socializing, he just wanted a place to settle before the weekend and Ramsey had the answer he needed.

In late 1987, we learned that the Region of Waterloo Social Services wanted to submit a $250,000 proposal to the Ministry of Community and Social Services for a Municipal Employment Program grant. We were disappointed they had not talked with us. Over the weekend we connected with Paul Born at the Cambridge Unemployed Help Centre and together we submitted a proposal to do the same job at two sites for under $70,000. Just before the regional committee meeting, the *Kitchener-Waterloo Record* published an article with the blaring headline "Waste of Money," supporting the community solution over the government plan.[1] The regional officials were furious and a lively debate ensued at the Health and Social Service Committee. The proposals were sent off for study by the Social Resource Council.

At the next council meeting Lynne Woolstencroft, a Waterloo councillor with whom we had previously met, passionately explained the importance of supporting community employment projects, contrasting them to government-organized programs. She emphasized that vulnerable job searchers needed additional community resources to help them compete in the labour market. Regional council was in favour of our grassroots employment work and voted 8–1 to support the community-based option.

Bruce was the kind of job searcher Woolstencroft had in mind. He was at our door any morning he didn't have a labouring job. By 1988, he had stopped renting apartments; he laboured during the day and took his chances on finding shelter at night, often ending up at the House of Friendship. Bruce had grown up in a broken home and had his own reasons for liking the street life. Val, one of our dedicated employment counsellors, was Bruce's eyes and ears on the labour market. She signed him up for training programs and attempted to get him into the Labourers' International Union, as well as addiction counselling. Bruce trudged on for ten years, taking any construction or landscaping job he could get.

Chris joined us in 1984 and immediately learned employment counselling. Along with Val, he became a key strategist in our early years. Soon after the new space opened, Chris met John, who lived in an abandoned house on Victoria Street. John was a foster child who was a bright and articulate young man. He already had two children of his own that he did not see. He wanted desperately to break the cycle of drinking. Chris walked with John through the steps of moving past alcohol and developing a resumé that highlighted his many skills. Although we have helped thousands of workers over the years, those with difficulties competing in the labour market received the most attention.

For over thirty years we have been supporting workers left out of the labour market while keeping our eye on provincial and federal government policy. Our community-based work has been shaped by government policy that has accelerated the growth of the contingent labour force, while we have integrated a philosophy of work and localism into the resource centre.

Shaping a Community-Based Job Search Resource Centre

Our outspoken friend Jon Buttrum, founder of the Citizen Action Group in Hamilton, taught us that government must be challenged because poverty and unemployment cannot be solved by half-hearted bureaucratic responses. He dramatically made his point at the 1989 Ontario Help Centres conference we helped organize. The government speaker was Dalton McGuinty Sr., Minister of Skills Development, who was in the middle of his speech when Buttrum vigorously challenged him to develop programs that would help unemployed adults. McGuinty walked out, refusing to engage with Buttrum. In the early 1990s, the provincial Jobs Ontario program applied top-down planning to manage training and jobs subsidies. The result was short-sightedness and community favouritism. Buttrum was frustrated that his workers had to navigate layers of bureaucracy in order to establish job placements. He wrote an article in the *Hamilton Spectator* renaming the program "Jokes Ontario." The provincial government sued him.

At the resource centre, daily we listened to the stories of dislocation and frustration. The Working Centre did not treat workers as cogs in the wheel of the economy. We wanted a welcoming, informal kind of place where mutual support could lessen the sting of unemployment. We celebrated with each person as they found a new job. Others came back to adjust their resumés and keep in touch. There was also a core group we supported who were unlikely to ever transition back into the formal labour market.

We defined the front receptionist role as a main volunteer position in the 1990s. We feared that our front reception was turning into a gatekeeping role that turned people away from the services they were trying to access. We eliminated the standard-issue front desk and replaced it with a long counter against the wall to visually create a more open-ended helping place.

On a snowy Saturday evening in November 1992, Joe was busy constructing the new counter for our volunteer reception area. To the door came a big burly man with a red overcoat and a bushy white beard covered in snow, knocking to get our attention. Our daughters, who were 9 and 7 at the time, were scared and excited. This was clearly Santa Claus coming to The Working Centre. Bernie had once been a family man and a Volkswagen mechanic who owned his own garage. He now lived in an abandoned factory, where he had a small room. He had few possessions besides his bulky clothes and bike. He earned his income from delivering papers. He had finished his route and needed to make a phone call—warmth and conversation were a bonus. Bernie did not ask for much, just a welcoming place.

The experiment to change the front desk was an overwhelming success. Volunteers took on vital roles, personally ensuring the reception area was a place of hospitality. Jim had worked as a millwright for twenty years but had a tendency to drink whisky over extended periods and eventually faced family breakdown. He offered his natural ability to fix things and took on the challenge of providing our resource centre with refurbished computers. He also sat patiently in the resource centre, teaching computer skills, coaxing old computers back to usefulness, and helping us see the possibility of well-used technology. He initiated competitions for keyboarding skills by installing games to see who could be the fastest typist. A downstairs closet was heaped to the top with computer parts that he hoped to bring into public use. He orchestrated computer thinkers and tinkerers to expand their reach. Jim helped us understand that computers could be a useful community tool.

People marginalized from the work world taught us how change can grow from below. Those with the least power look at the world with different eyes. They wonder what is missing, how things can be organized differently, how people can contribute co-operatively. It was important for us to understand how this process created new ways of sharing tools for the common good.

We became known as the place to go when there were few other options. "My brother died in Hamilton and I am trying to find bus fare and clothing so I can go to the funeral." "My daughter is in a hospital just outside of London and I would like to visit her. Is there someone I could pay to drive me there two times a week?" "I am new to Canada and I am trying to find work as an engineer." "I am living in my car but I have a dog, so I have to find a job quickly so I can find a place to live." "This person is very hostile and angry; do you think you can help them?" Hospitality, listening, and openness to the person requires that no question is too big or small.

As government rules have multiplied, we have combined volunteer and staff roles in an ever-changing balance of service and hospitality. Case notes, we learned early on, were like putting someone's hopes and dreams in a brief case. Intuitively, we knew that maintaining files and statistical tracking forms was intrusive, but we did not know just how intensive and invasive outcomes-based projects would become. Always justifying our work for funding purposes, and the data management that entails, takes increasing amounts of time in the name of accountability. This approach teaches bureaucratized help over creative support of individuals.

In *The Canadian Condition*, Henry Mintzberg describes how Canadian provinces demand the federal government provide money without conditions and then turn around and impose conditions on municipal activities.

Provincial decentralization hardly ever creates autonomy. Provinces recreate hierarchy with intermediate levels that look down and "control the people who actually deliver the service."[2] The neutral bureaucracy of the provinces takes away power from those who deliver the service. Local bodies have little independence to chart a creative path. The lack of real and perceived freedom results in a dulling of process, and the focus on the ends stifles imagination.

Mintzberg's critique must be addressed in order to free the present structure of work from the octopus tentacles of public sector bureaucracies. The forces of centralization tie up billions of dollars in unproductive activities.[3] The political goal of freeing this money for the common good through interdependent activities, especially in the community sector, is the challenge ahead for all concerned with human scale development.

The model we envisioned is the open and welcoming approach of our resource centre. Our focus has been on assisting large numbers of unemployed workers with a practical, responsive, and scrappy approach. We have questioned funding models that continuously reduce the capacity of organizations through financial micro-management and increased statistical and outcome demands. We have opted to create a common-sense approach. There are 3,500 people a year who use the job search resource centre. Most need to get back into the labour market right away, and our goal is to help them find the shortest route. For others, it is a longer process of developing relationships and new skills as they go through the process of discovering their career path. Community job search centres can develop multiple paths that job searchers use to find work that best suits their situation. They can focus on being responsive to the people who come in the door, making a commitment to follow the individual and use creative and useful strategies to help people through their unemployment.

Plant Closings and the Growth of the Contingent Labour Force

In March 1988, we walked up Queen Street to the Canada Employment Centre (CEC) to count the number of jobs listed on the ten bulletin boards. There were a total of 560 available jobs with 45 per cent paying under $5.00 an hour and 72 per cent paying less than $8.00 an hour; 21 per cent were part-time. The bulk of the jobs paid low wages for unskilled labour. When we published these details in our newsletter, we received a letter from the CEC manager demanding that we never count the job boards again.[4]

We were writing multiple stories about the insecure, low-wage labour market. One woman, whose husband worked for $6.50 an hour, was looking for permanent work. "I had some work with a temp agency, but it isn't steady and I can't rely on it…. How am I supposed to make ends meet if I can't get a job that pays enough to live on?" Another described her situation this way: "There aren't any opportunities without having more education. There are lots of jobs that don't pay much."[5]

Thousands of workers lost their jobs in a new wave of plant closings. The first large layoffs started in the late 1970s with the Budd Canada layoffs, but by the 1990 recession, Waterloo Region's manufacturing base was dramatically shrinking.[6]

The closing of Domtar Packaging taught us the impact of employees being laid off with hundreds of co-workers when jobs were scarce. These workers had laboured together for years and now competed with each other to get new jobs. The Action Centre, started in the Domtar plant, was designed to offer solidarity, a place of gathering, and a place for job-search support. Calls were made to local employers, promoting the skills of the workers, cover letters were written, and courses were offered by the local college. The Action Centre moved to a back room at The Working Centre when the plant doors were shuttered. Some workers quickly found jobs while others became part of our community, travelling in and out of jobs.

As plant after plant closed, we worked with these displaced workers to design customized group discussions and workbooks. We developed, with the local college, specialized training packages to make use of government supports. It was important to support the emotional roller coaster of job loss while at the same time offer assistance to navigate employment insurance, severance, and other income support. We helped the workers who built on their people skills by helping and coaching their co-workers. They staffed the action centres and learned about employment insurance and community-supported job searching.

When one thousand Uniroyal workers were laid off, we set up job search and resumé groups for eight hundred workers over ten weeks. With such large numbers it was a struggle to help each person feel that they had something unique to offer, to help them to make decisions about their next steps forward, and deal with the anger they faced.

Recently, government intervention has stifled the creativity that was common in Action Centres. Supporting laid-off workers through plant closing work has become systematized while the labour market is less forgiving. Three years after the shutdown at Kitchener Frame, 30 per cent of workers were still unemployed. "The majority of workers have lost $10 per hour off their income. Only 46 per cent have permanent jobs with thirty or more hours a week."[7]

Many of these workers joined the temporary workforce, taking short-term jobs, in what is called the contingent labour market. The development of practical projects for this group has helped us understand the challenges of dislocation and a growing globalized economy.

The process of job deskilling intensified as full-time, well-paying factory jobs were eliminated. The few remaining large manufacturers in the region mainly hire through temporary agencies, and many positions are part-time. Private and public organizations are deploying technology to displace workers while Canada's support for the global wage arbitrage by signing free trade agreements has accelerated the process of factory jobs moving offshore. The contingent labour force is the result of increased service-sector jobs and a hollowing out of middle-paying jobs.[8]

We have learned first-hand about the contingent labour force. It includes those who primarily work at temporary, contract, or part-time work, along with the unemployed who are ready and willing to work. This group can be made up of older workers, those who have worked in a skilled occupation, people who are in and out of the labour market, self-employed individuals, young people seeking alternative approaches to work, and longer-term unemployed people. Many find only part-time or lower-skilled work, and many become dependent on income support/living allowance options.

In the early 1990s, the business lobby attempted to "discipline" the labour force by reducing the availability of Employment Insurance (EI) and social assistance. Across Canada, governments from all political parties changed the rules for social assistance to increase the barriers for qualification. Seventy per cent of unemployed people in Ontario are no longer eligible for EI benefits. Ontario Works, the new name for welfare benefits, instituted "workfare" legislation that came with a 24 per cent reduction in benefits and sophisticated software that could automatically close a file of a recipient who did not respond to a letter within a week. These measures left people scrambling for the "safety" of the labour market.

One way of quantifying the contingent labour force is to count the number of workers not in the full-time labour market. Andrea M. Noack and Leah F. Vosko, labour studies researchers at York University, report that this new kind of temporary work now represents 20 per cent of the labour market in Canada. Additionally, 15 per cent of all workers are self-employed, but about half this number would choose full-time employment if available.[9]

If we consider the unemployment rate in Waterloo Region, which hovered between 7 and 9 per cent in the three years up to 2012, then add the number of full-time temporary, part-time permanent, and part-time temporary workers, the contingent labour force is shown to comprise 34 per cent of the labour force in the region, including 7 per cent unemployed, 20 per cent temporary/part-time workers, and 7 per cent of the self-employed who do not earn a living wage. These workers have no benefits, are constantly job searching, are often laid off, start small businesses, and are struggling to maintain a livelihood for themselves and their household.

There is another group that should also be considered. In 1997, the Ottawa Economic Development Corporation released a detailed study called *The Hidden Workforce*,[10] which estimated that the unemployment rate would grow by 20 per cent if all the discouraged workers and employable social assistance recipients were added to the employment rate. This explains why The Working Centre's Job Search Resource Centre is filled each day with people looking for work. Last year we helped 3,500 different people, including new Canadians, people who face long-term unemployment, workers with physical disabilities and injuries, former factory workers, recently laid-off workers, entry-level workers, and skilled workers. They are all members of the contingent labour force and the reality is that only a per centage of them will find regular full-time work. More likely, they will travel through an array of part-time and contract work to piece together an income. Plant closings, globalization, technology, and changes to the income safety net have left the labour market a harsh and unfriendly environment for workers.

Toward a Philosophy of Work

Billy is a contingent worker with more resilience than most. He is slight of stature, with long hair that can look menacing as he walks down the street. His happy attitude can easily turn when he becomes frustrated. We first met Billy when we helped him enrol in an adult education upgrading course while he was stuck on welfare, a victim of the factory layoffs in the early 1990s. Whether he was making good on a promise to pay back a loan or to follow through on his schooling, there was no denying his honesty and determination. Once Billy knew something was "the right thing" to do, you could always count on an upfront effort to get the job completed.

For six years, Billy lived in the back parking lot of a machine shop where he was employed as a forklift driver. This arrangement worked because he longed for a place that was his and where people would leave him alone. He landed a forklift driver job and then picked out a place that he could turn into a home. It became a permanent residence that he was proud of. He talked about how he could roll out of bed and start work and in return, he offered twenty-four-hour security. He wanted to work where his efforts mattered. By living at his work and being available on weekends, he became a valuable part of the crew.

Not every employer would take a chance on a Billy, or tolerate him setting up his home on the premises. In that way, Billy's story is unusual. But what isn't unusual is what Billy was looking for. It is what we see over and over. People long for "integrated" models of work that serve their needs and that of the community. It takes people like Billy and his boss to create integrated work. Mainstream work culture hardly ever offers such opportunities to contingent labourers.

Integrated work requires "new eyes and a new heart, capable of rising above a materialistic vision of human events,"[11] capable of grasping how the dignity of each man and woman is tied to their ability to use their skills to contribute to the development of community. What builds commitment is adapting the work to the circumstances of the individual. People should not be slaves to work, but rather work should fulfill the intrinsic goals of an individual. The essence of equality is when people are given equal opportunity to use their varied and often unconventional gifts to contribute in unique ways.

The frustrations of the labour market ensure that people are mostly blinded to their equality with others. In our resource centre, a frustrated older worker approached Joe, "I am not like these other thirty people in the centre. They would work for $11 an hour, but not me. I have skills. I have knowledge and forty years of marketing and retailing experience." A conversation developed as he went on: "Companies are all tight organizations; they are reluctant to let someone new in, and especially someone who knows more than they do." Here was someone who had clearly been left out—he wanted to join in, to find a way to contribute, to be part of something, but his anger reinforced how different he felt from everyone else. The competitive labour market intensifies people's insecurities, reducing trust and creating divisions.

The opposite process can be seen at Maurita's Kitchen, where, each morning, there can be ten people chopping vegetables, baking bread, creating a roasted vegetable salad, baking muffins, making hummus, frying falafels, or washing dishes, all in the service of making affordable and delicious vegetarian café-style entrees and desserts for the Queen Street Commons Café and catering orders. To work at Maurita's Kitchen is to experience equality, something that rarely happens in everyday work exchanges.[12] Peter Maurin used to say, "We need a philosophy of work."[13] He meant that we need a wider vision of work that engages people as equals, where tasks are co-operatively completed even as the work provides useful services and products.

Tom Moore understood what it was like to lose his livelihood but learn a new spirit. His setbacks included losing his twenty-year driving job after his eyesight failed, his divorce, more job losses, and a bicycle accident:

> Bad luck you think? Well I don't think so. There are certainly some things I miss from the lifestyle before—the fine dining, the theatre, and the security that was once there. However, all of the things that have happened in the last few years have changed my outlook on life…. I have been shown a part of the community that I never knew and I have met many fine, fine people. I have experienced a community spirit that would lift a person from the depths of hopelessness and depression and give that person a new look on life. It has for me![14]

Tom found community by becoming one of the volunteers who make the resource centre an important and useful public place. Common sharing provides new ways for people to deal with hardships by working together to solve problems, breaking down individualism.

Increasingly it is only on the periphery of the labour market where you learn about a philosophy of work. This means experiencing work that is not about money but about self-discovery, where the cultivation of intrinsic values is recognized as the primary reason for work. Would the labour market be substantially different if workers were less inclined to out-earn one another? How can society create the conditions where wages are less important than the common work accomplished together? How can the cultivation of intrinsic values be mirrored, expanded, and spread widely through all work experiences? A philosophy of work is the way that society can reach a higher plane of equality.

The choice to control one's role in the labour market starts with understanding that the labour market, for the most part, has been an instrument for creating winners and losers, raising some people's status over that of others. Ironically, labour market statistics prove how relatively equal the majority of workers are when comparing income, a fact that is shocking to many. Most people are unaware that the majority of workers earn close to the average wage of $35,000. They don't realize how counterproductive it is to compete for ever-increasing wages when the reality is that for 75 per cent of the labour market participants, they are already on a relatively flat path.[15]

Livelihood: Economics Based in Relationships

The Job Search Resource Centre offers a place of calm in response to the alienation and dislocation of unemployment. The centre demonstrates an alternative culture that emphasizes support for each other. We invite unemployed workers to become engaged in informal work, offer their skills in new ways, and participate in a creative community setting.

We help people to find a niche within the labour market to obtain the most suitable work. The ASSETS program helps people establish micro home-based business.[16] We support the BarterWorks network where people exchange and trade goods and services. We encourage conversation about taking more control of one's work by reducing living expenses, working part-time, and doing a home business on the side. Alternative income sources can be patched together with part-time jobs or with income generated from a hobby. These ideas appeal to older workers trying to support themselves into their retirement, those left out of the labour market, and those not interested in regular work. Some people seek well-paying jobs, but many others seek to pragmatically support their livelihood.[17]

Livelihood is defined as the means of securing the necessities of life, and thus encourages us to think beyond the acquisitive culture that surrounds us. In his book *Deep Economy*, Bill McKibben shows how a shift to local economies builds community through meaningful economic exchanges that use fewer resources.[18] The environmental limits of the earth and the challenges of peak oil will by necessity challenge how we live and work.

By building the habit of thinking locally we take a major step toward creating a new kind of local economy. Wendell Berry reminds us that we do not need anyone's permission to start buying locally and create a local food economy, an "economy in which local consumers buy as much of their food as possible from local producers, and in which local producers produce as much as they can for the local market."[19]

We have seen the ingenuity of people doing exactly as Berry hopes. One woman became a local farmer, a couple turned their home into a bed and breakfast, some used their computer skills to make technology accessible, others started artistic home-based businesses, a retired counsellor supports people who cannot afford counselling, some supplement their social income with sewing, cleaning, or baking, and more. Our three-acre market garden located near the downtown is another example. This work builds vital and active community.

Purchasing at a local level is often inconvenient. We must first learn who the local producers or service providers are. To support the growth of these ideas, The Working Centre has the developed a new community tool called the Commons Exchange, which consists of a help desk, a website, and a marketplace to connect people, resources, and opportunities related to the production of local, relationship-based goods and services. Its goals are to support creative livelihoods as they make, do, grow, and connect; provide opportunities for people to consume in a socially responsible manner; and to foster community and interdependence through expanding networks and deepening relationships.

Livelihood may mean living with less money, but it is not about living with less. The practice of local sustainable livelihoods stands in sharp contrast to the dislocation and isolation encouraged by the growth economy. By reclaiming local connectedness, by embedding exchange relationships in local networks, we can reclaim the meaning of neighbourhoods.

The Job Search Resource Centre Today

Presently, with over 250 people using the job search resource centre every day, the core concept of openness to each person remains our steadfast goal. New Canadians are increasingly finding their way to Kitchener-Waterloo.[20] Few were prepared for the regulations around professions in Ontario that required more schooling to start the licensing process. Many had risked their savings and their security to come to Canada to build a better life for their children, or they were refugees fleeing intolerable conditions in their home country. Their skills were in demand in Canada, but they faced roadblocks with respect to language and licensing not to mention convincing employers that they had skills to offer as they built their cultural understanding.

It was around 2000 when we started focusing on researching licensing issues and potential employers for new Canadians. We developed bridging projects for universities and colleges to integrate the skills and challenges of newcomers. We have seen the cost, however, of the new global economy on families as they struggled with cultural shifts, the lack of social inclusion, and the reduction in their status.

The rate of change was daunting for a couple from India and their two children as both searched for work and held multiple survival jobs. A Brazilian woman with an information technology (IT) background took work as an administrative assistant, where her language skills were challenged despite her determined efforts. Five years later, in a new job, she was praised for the quality of her work. A Pakistani woman adapted quickly with her family, only to be challenged when her father became ill and she had to support him through the daunting Canadian health system.

We forged many friendships over these years, bonding with people who were making a new life for themselves and their families. Settlement issues mingled with licensing problems, language skills were coached and studied, and participants became friends as we strategized through life changes. We focused on specific areas like health care, accounting, IT, the financial sector, teaching, and social work, by connecting with educational bodies, meeting employers, and mentoring and advocating with each person. We helped new Canadians use their transferable skills to become employment counsellors, offering their broad cultural, faith, and language experiences to help others in the same situation.[21]

In 2011, The Working Centre implemented the Targeted Initiative for Older Workers (TIOW). We had two months to create the materials, recruit participants, and develop a program. We opted for our traditional self-help approach ensuring unemployed workers have a voice in determining their direction. We were the transfer agent for one million federal dollars per year distributed toward participants' living allowances, training, and transportation costs. The reporting and administration was heavy, but the focus remained retraining and job searching.

One-on-one assistance and groups have been important for helping older workers share experiences, to break down the discouragement of unemployment. It takes three to six months longer than average for an older worker to find their next job. The jobs available are often part-time, contract, temporary, unstable, and low-paying. The TIOW participants went from jobs like technical writer to retail sales, from manufacturing to security guard work. A sequence of jobs like these is emotionally draining and it gets harder to rebuild both financially and emotionally. For some, a significant part of TIOW was the stability of a very basic living allowance that reduced the stress of unpaid bills. Despite a 68 per cent success rate for older workers finding work or training, the program was scheduled to end in March 2014. We were relieved when the February 2014 budget gave TIOW a three-year extension.[22]

Community-based centres are constantly under pressure from different levels of government. In January 2014, the federal government advertised the Canada Job Grant, even though it had not been implemented. Ottawa planned to pay for it by cutting transfers to the provinces for existing training programs that support vulnerable workers, including immigrants, persons with disabilities, Aboriginal people, youth, and older workers.[23] This is another case of a top-down bureaucratic funding model. In this environment, our goal is to continue supporting contingent workers who eke out a living in a labour market where they have few friends.

The Job Search Resource Centre supports over 3,500 unemployed workers per year, providing assistance with the following:

- preparing a basic resumé and writing a cover letter;
- faxing and making photocopies;
- access to an employment counsellor, job leads, and employment opportunities;
- workshops on job searching, interview preparation, portfolio development, and researching occupations; and
- access to affordable computer training in basic and complex office computer programs.

Job searchers become frustrated and discouraged by the process of rejection and lay-offs. We try to walk alongside as people make significant choices and changes.

We have honed our understanding of the specialized labour market by investigating different sectors along with employment culture and by teaching researched job search. We produced a detailed web-based job search tool that shares knowledge built up over the years. We assist people to stay organized, to seek training, and to follow through on job-searching tasks.

Entrepreneurial supports have been integrated into the resource centre, including BarterWorks the local bartering exchange, WRAP's home-based self-employment training,[24] and the Local Exchange website and a help desk to assist small entrepreneurs to develop wider access to local markets. These projects especially help women, refugees, new Canadians, low-income workers, and those on a limited income.

The Money Matters Help Desk assisted 3,750 people to access tax credits, learn about tax benefits, establish and keep bank accounts. Many have benefited from non-judgmental budgeting and problem-solving. Volunteers helped two thousand individuals file their income tax returns. The resource centre also hosts the housing help desk, the reduced-fair bus pass program, and is the home for a new project, Community Access Bikeshare.

During these thirty years we have witnessed a major shift in the labour market. Previous to 1980, many sectors of the economy provided lifelong jobs with a retirement pension plan. After 1980, a growing contingent labour market was established with temporary contract work as the primary mode of employment. The Working Centre has been a buffer, supporting workers as they tested options to find work that reflected their interests and abilities. This search for meaning has resulted in the creation of a unique community space that explores alternatives and provides practical support. The Job Search Resource Centre continues to be a vital place of connections in downtown Kitchener.

The Nuts and Bolts of an Alternative Organization

Making Decisions for Right Livelihood

We are in an old farmhouse near Millbank, on the outskirts of Waterloo Region, on a frigid December evening. The kitchen is big enough to hold all ten couples around a large oak table. We are visiting a collective of farmers who provide vegetables to our Commons Market CSA (Community Shared Agriculture) project. Rebecca and Joe, having arrived late, join the discussion with the farmers about the ups and downs of the past season and talk about extending the market with winter root vegetables. This old farmhouse kitchen has held its share of community meetings. The farmers gathered by horse and buggy, their chosen way to get around. Our hosts are gracious, and homemade cookies and hot chocolate are served. The large table and much of the furniture is handcrafted, probably with wood they have harvested.

These past few years, our daughter Rebecca has been coordinating the CSA. If she put a clock on her hours coordinating this project, it would be hard to justify. The farmers, too, work for free, but these farmers are less governed by an hourly wage—they work toward household livelihood. Together we focus on growing food, building relationships, and creating a viable market. The farmers are in weekly contact. Is it possible to sell bushels of potatoes, how about extra gladiolas? The CSA boxes start in June with early greens and salads, adding vegetables like peppers, turnips, and potatoes as we move through the summer, and in no time the season ends in October with lots of carrots, squash, onions, and beets.

The CSA Commons Market generates city sales for Amish farmers through our commitment to sell food box shares in advance. The program provides education to the city dwellers as they learn to have patience with the farmers, who have little control over drought conditions and other complications that affect what produce comes in the box.

A Short History of the Evolution of Urban Agriculture Projects

How does The Working Centre decide which project it is going to support? How did we get involved with this group of Amish farmers? The pattern of our decision-making can be seen in the way each project develops through accumulated knowledge, which comes from responding to ideas, skills, and energy that individuals and groups bring to projects. How do these factors fit together? To an outsider it may seem random, but in fact it is thoughtful relationship building, trying to fit pieces together and finding project support that results in growth. The following describes the journey of urban agriculture projects at The Working Centre over fifteen years.

Queens Green Community Garden

The Queens Green Community Garden was our first urban agriculture project.[1] In 1997 we helped two recent university graduates to apply for a City of Kitchener grant to establish a community garden on a vacant flood plain lot near our office on Queen Street South. For more than fifteen years, the Queen's Green Community Garden has demonstrated how neighbours can keep a garden looking beautiful while growing vegetables and herbs in a co-operative environment. The Working Centre community has often gathered for fellowship around the garden and bake oven that we built on the site.[2]

In the same year we started tending a large garden plot at Meadow Acres Garden Centre in Petersburg. This project started when Gretchen Jones, cooking facilitator at St. John's Kitchen told her cab driver about the kitchen. The cab driver mentioned that his family had a large acreage beside their nursery that was not being used. A meeting was set up with the owners, and they were excited to put aside land for the purpose of growing produce for St. John's Kitchen. The project was the recipient of hundreds of volunteer hours and was an excellent learning opportunity, with key volunteers almost living out at the garden the first summer. One thousand pounds of potatoes, thirty-four bushels of tomatoes and more were grown that year. We learned that the first-year bumper crop had been helped along by a spraying of Roundup that had kept the weeds at bay. In the second year, without any spraying, the weeds started winning. By the third year, driving twenty kilometres to combat weeds lessened the enthusiasm and it was clear that we could not sustain the operating costs. Volunteer effort had made this market garden possible.

GROW Herbal

In 2003, we were asked to support a garden project called GROW Herbal in Bloomingdale, only six kilometres from downtown.[3] Along with the herbal gardens, we were offered another acre to produce vegetables for St. John's Kitchen. In our first year at Bloomingdale we came up with a temporary solution that made it easy to get volunteers out to the garden. A BarterWorks member, an organic market gardener, was earning side income during the winter driving a mini school bus. In late April he got permission to drive the van from St. John's Kitchen to the GROW garden and then do a return trip later, giving St. John's Kitchen patrons an easier way to get involved.

The Bloomingdale St. John's Kitchen garden was productive, producing in one year twenty-five bushels each of beans, tomatoes, zucchini, and greens along with a long list of other vegetables and herbs. Over one hundred volunteers offered 1,200 hours of labour to produce vegetables for St. John's Kitchen.[4] In our newsletter, *Good Work News*, Sue Gallagher describes the satisfaction after a morning of harvest, "with garden workers admiring the bounty in the van of fresh, organic vegetables and herbs to be shared at St. John's Kitchen."[5] The half-acre GROW Herbal Gardens were designed as beautiful, meditative space that offered therapy, training, and enterprise opportunities. They produced quality culinary and medicinal herbs and taught herbal crafting and seed starting. Soap, herbal products, and paper-making became part of GROW.

By 2005, the urban agricultural projects consisted of the two Bloomingdale gardens, three community gardens, and support for the community gardening network along with the community bake oven and the ongoing Patch Match project that pairs landless gardeners with households with unused garden space. We also offered an ongoing series of organic gardening workshops with a focus on increasing thinking and acting on growing food in urban areas. It was at this time that we were approached to support the Fair Share Harvest CSA, a collective of Amish farmers who were practising low-tech, subsistence organic farming.

The GROW operation in Bloomingdale reinforced our commitment to developing sustainable infrastructure for urban agriculture, but without Charley's bus, volunteer participation at GROW had declined. We continued to search for a combination of projects that would be easier to sustain.

Lancaster House and Greenhouse

In 2006, The Working Centre was rapidly evolving as we completed renovations at 66 Queen Street South. The changes included adding computer-recycling space, eight units of transitional housing, and new consolidated employment-counselling space. All this enabled our larger plan of establishing Maurita's Kitchen and the Queen Street Commons Café, which would link our urban agriculture initiatives with cooking and serving local food. We saw the revenue potential of developing a social enterprise around a commercial kitchen and café, in contrast to the Bloomingdale gardens which had generated minimal income. We loved the work at Bloomingdale but we questioned our ability to support the project with so many priorities on Queen Street.

We thought of building a rooftop greenhouse on 66 Queen South during the construction project, but decided it would be more accessible and require less maintenance to build the structure in the backyard of a property we owned on Lancaster Street and move GROW Herbal to that location. Over the next three years we wound down the St. John's Kitchen Community Garden in Bloomingdale and started moving GROW Herbal to Lancaster House. We added activities on Queen Street by expanding soap making and paper craft. We made bread dough at Maurita's Kitchen and baked weekly in the Queens Green bread oven. At Lancaster House we thought of ways to combine gardening, herb processing, and soap making.

Lancaster House is an early-1900s four-bedroom house that The Working Centre has renovated and used for community housing since 1995, accommodating interns, visitors, and refugees, a place of shared living and respite. We wanted to continue the spiritual ecology that Sr. Margaret Maika, the first resident of the house, had established at the house. Margaret's gardens were recreated into herbal and flower gardens for GROW. In 2009, Job Café workers tore down the old garage and laid the foundations for a greenhouse and a workshop space.

The project coordinator's building knowledge was complemented by his ability to trust the enthusiastic Job Café workers to build according to the plans he patiently laid out on scrap pieces of paper. The greenhouse structure used the new double wall polycarbonate sheets that offer a higher insulation value than glass. The greenhouse was designed to operate for ten months of the year to grow microgreens and seedlings with minimal additional energy. After we installed the first hydroponic unit in the greenhouse, an environmental resource student from a local university earned a fourth-year credit for testing the growth rates of the seeds and establishing cleaning routines. Adam Kramer, now coordinating our urban agriculture project, took this information and started producing microgreens, which proved popular, and two more units were ordered.[6]

We upgraded the Lancaster House basement washrooms for greenhouse volunteers and fixed up the porches. The gardens connect with our house on neighbouring Mansion Street, the lack of fences allowing an easy flow between the properties. In the late 1990s we had many volunteer and staff gatherings in this shared space, including the wedding reception for a couple who met at The Working Centre. Our large backyard became an oasis of four-season raised-bed gardening with plenty of sitting areas. Our six compost bins have been feeding our gardens for more than twenty years. The two properties are now tied together by pathways that wind through the gardens.

Hacienda Sarria Market Garden

In June 2011, Joe was told that a man by the name of Ron Doyle was waiting for him at 58 Queen. Ron was committed to establishing gardens and orchards on his property as a social outreach project and was convinced that The Working Centre could join him to create a large garden to teach market gardening skills. A few days later Ron showed Joe the 1905 factory that he had meticulously converted into a Spanish villa. Ron had sketched out each design feature and then worked with artists and craftspeople to ensure rich colours, natural materials, and beautiful columns.

Ron's three-month journey with his son on the El Camino trail in Spain had inspired him to create this unique place that emphasized the shape and beauty of craft. He placed four shipping containers in a row to define the space, with green roofs installed by his daughter. Two of the containers already had washrooms installed and Ron offered the other two for garden storage and processing. It did not take us long to start planning a garden that would teach urban food production and develop sustainability through selling market produce.

Over the next year a great deal of work was accomplished.[7] Ron started the job by bringing in two hundred loads of top soil and landscaped the garden areas. Old concrete slabs lying around the property were used for terraces and art pieces. In April, we started planting and purchasing tools and equipment, including a rototiller, which was essential to loosen the soil. With the help of Fr. Toby Collins CR, who had offered to lead a landscaping project, a plan was put together to lay six thousand square feet of interlocking brick pathways. Over just ten days the paths quickly defined the garden. Fr. Toby's clarity and landscaping knowledge combined with volunteers and Job Café workers added functional pathways to the beautiful gardens.

We still had a lot of work to do. Ron sourced a big water tank, and we installed an irrigation system. We built a cooler in one of the containers. Ron commissioned a local metal worker/artist, Sandra Dunn who in the 1990s had participated in our Tools for Living groups, to craft a metal statue of Don Quixote. It now stands proudly in the middle of the garden pointing at the water tower, which now has a windmill on it. That fall we planted perennial flowers for beauty and eventually for selling. While we were planning the garden we learned about SPIN (Small Plot INtensive) market gardening and purchased the manuals, which gave us a map for growing fresh organic vegetables and selling them at regular market rates.[8] SPIN continues to be our source book whenever we have questions about planting, pricing, and succession planting.

The Hacienda Sarria Market Garden has given us a sustainable base for the development of urban agriculture. We are now training four interns each summer in urban agriculture and greenhouse management along with a group of thirty volunteers that are part of both projects. The greenhouse has produced more than fifteen thousand seedlings for selling and planting at the Hacienda. We developed humidity beds to increase seedling production, a goal we had been working on since 2000. During the winter of 2013, we added an aquaponics demonstration unit on the last bit of greenhouse floor space, which is now producing heritage grape tomatoes and kale. This year we are filling sixty CSA orders through the Hacienda garden and an equal number of ongoing orders from small stores and restaurants, and we sell microgreens and herbs at various locations. Each step of this long journey has taught us new aspects toward building a sustainable urban agriculture project.

Building Local Democracy

The ups and downs, and twists and turns, of our urban agriculture projects reflect how producing food, doing it in community, and bringing together divergent ideas and people are building blocks of The Working Centre. The story of the development of these projects is a metaphor for how concepts take root. Community development organizations are most effective when they listen to the ideas in the air, pay attention to the signs of the times, and direct positive energy into common-good projects. The process starts by being open to the possibilities that can be heard in people's stories. Where do ideas come from? They come from discussion, debate, and connections to others. Each individual has contributions that can form a foundation for new links and associations. Other individuals have plans, skills, materials, and even land that they are willing to use toward fulfilling a project they have formulated. An organization with a master plan may miss the nuances and diversions that result from multiple ideas coming from different directions.

In our early years, Ken Westhues wrote about how the increasing scale of organizations, the level of professionalization, the concentration of capital, and the growing bureaucratization of work were conspiring to reduce meaningful relationships between democratic citizens. The main problem is simply that the kind of meeting of which humans are uniquely capable—generative, constructive, productive meetings that enrich and enliven all who partake of them—are becoming less common in the workplaces of Canada.[9]

Urban agriculture was an experiment that grew from the bottom up. We created productive work projects that developed co-operative, reciprocal relationships that engendered new structures that influenced our direction. This deflected us from a bureaucratic path.

The Working Centre is a model for social change, guided by a vision of integrating community into practical work. If we follow institutionalization then we turn our backs on the people who want to engage community projects at the grassroots. We envisioned new ways of working to ensure people have control over the tools they use. Anything less would reinforce the cultural norm in Western societies that leaves community building to experts. We have interpreted access to tools in urban agriculture as community gardens, public herb gardens, teaching the skills of herbal crafting, taking vacant land and turning it into public space, teaching market gardening and greenhouse techniques, and teaching vegetarian cooking and baking knowledge in a commercial kitchen and café environment. These are examples of how community organizations can channel grassroots energy into community betterment.

Structures that focus on the professionalization of skills reinforce the exclusion of people from practical neighbourhood building. Local democracy comes alive in the interplay between projects for civic improvement, the structure of the tools that are used, and the inclusive, dialogical relationships developed in these projects.

Tocqueville's journey through America in the 1830s identified the inherent contradiction of democracy. He observed that after citizens vote they can easily become unambitious toward making their communities better. Utilitarian self-interest can lead to "democratic apathy."[10] Even today, the act of voting can relieve one's conscience, as if this civic duty was enough. Barriers to political engagement are high; people lack confidence and then rely on public opinion to guide their thinking. The system conspires to tempt people to surrender to the powers of the working government.

The Working Centre has evolved a new model for community work, designed especially to combat the inertia of individualism. We have developed structures that are effective at generating efforts to bring people together to address social issues. Community tool projects integrate the philosophy of access to tools by ensuring open structures that invite a wide spectrum of people to add their skills and ideas. Wide and interconnected organizational pathways give people options to become involved in issues they care about. When groups form within projects, this invigorates interest and participation. In a community organization, it is the combination of structure and anti-structure that creates space for people to involve themselves. People find meaning when the work they envision is matched with opportunities that grassroots groups make available.

Creating a Distributed Network

Local participatory democracy has the means to gently break down hierarchy. First, it is important to recognize that hierarchy is an instrument to ensure that bills are paid, grants are attended to, financial goals are met and daily work is accomplished. In other words hierarchy, on the surface, can be effective. At the same time, a strategy is necessary to avoid the demands of organization that result in top-down structures dominating. The goal of injecting local democracy into organizational structure is to ensure that equal relationships create a free flow of information and discussion. The Working Centre reduces middle management by starting with a flat organizational structure that interconnects the coordinators who lead the projects. The coordinators engage in dialogue that identifies roadblocks and problems while seeking good direction. Some coordinators have a larger role because of the nature of their project. When coordinators provide updates on project development to other coordinators this is done collegially. Goals are achieved through reasonable consultation. An important aspect of co-operative work is building in extra resources, whether through staffing or for unexpected costs, to allow for mistakes or experimentation. Hierarchy can be broken down when the structure supports engagement and discussion, and participants in the discussion are enlivened by the shared horizon of the accomplishment they seek together. Distributed, decentralized, networks and local democracy come alive through shared responsibility that shifts the emphasis from demands toward the co-operative end goal.

To accomplish this goal we have tried to avoid certain types of managerial descriptions. Managers and bosses were terms that we discouraged. We liked calling the project leaders "coordinators," because of the collegial tone. We

Project Groups of The Working Centre

A Distributive Web

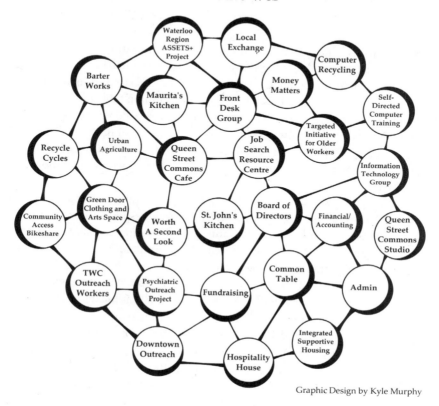

Graphic Design by Kyle Murphy

chose the phrase "common table" to describe the concept of wider coordination meetings that take place either in the projects or in the broad organization. Rather than portray a tightly woven organization, we like to recognize the creativity of each project, demonstrating a decentralized model or one that is more like a distributed network. Changing the language is one aspect of developing different ways of acting.

We have learned that this model works best when coordinators are linked in order to evolve a distributed network of interconnected projects. The common table provides a forum for debating and discussing direction, staffing, philosophy, and financial issues. The common table members then share information both into and from the network. Individual projects also meet as common tables, such as when Worth a Second Look thrift store has a common table meeting of volunteers and staff every two weeks. Outreach workers meet every two weeks, employment counsellors on Wednesday mornings, and different cluster groups meet on specific issues. All of the projects have regular meetings of some form.

The common table has a main role in the organization, but it does not exert ultimate control, leaving room for dialogue and debate. It started as a small group in the 1990s and grew to include the financial coordinator and the kitchen coordinator at St. John's Kitchen. The common table now comprises ten to twelve people from different projects. The accompanying diagram shows our distributed network represented by projects or nodes that all share responsibility. The interconnections are dense and diverse, making it possible for the function of the common table and board of directors to be shown as off-centre.

This is not to say that The Working Centre has no traditional structure at all. What we do have is determined by our legal responsibilities as a non-profit corporation with charitable status. Payroll, insurance, building ownership, and government contracts all demand accountability structures. Fundraising, administrative, and financial nodes are interconnected but with separate meetings. The common table deals with administrative issues with the goal of resolving issues with wide participation. This means ensuring that administrative requirements are tempered by relational priorities.

A soft network is the idea that the administrative core of the organization does not overwhelm or dominate the nodes or projects. At the project level a higher level of responsibility is taken up doing the daily work. In urban agriculture it is teaching skills, growing seedlings, planting rows of seeds, weeding etc. At Worth a Second Look it is the sorting and pricing of housewares, organizing the truck for pickups and deliveries, repairing furniture, organizing Job Café crews, managing the work around the cash register, and so on. These tasks are about building relationship with workers, volunteers, and customers. The common table should support this work as a servant, finding ways to usefully assist the projects.

It is important to treat projects as integrated into a network. The primary function of a project is to operate as best as it can and to have the tools to pass on information in a distributive way. This means learning to give information and power away. Networks function best when people are informed. A network is not about exerting power but finding a light-footed way of accomplishing work by being open to involving others. The further the network spreads out, the greater the potential for groups and individuals to offer ideas and suggestions. This is the place of "dense, diverse, decentralized exchange."[11] The project will experience growth as it listens and responds to the issues and ideas being generated. The project grows through the connections that are nurtured to sustain it.

The Working Centre core started humbly and saw its role as helping support the best ends for the growing network. The common table is now the place for new ideas to get a hearing and to find organizational support. It is the place for modeling the virtues, debating the community-tools approach, and demonstrating non-hierarchical ways of working. These are tangible ways that local democracy has developed within the organization.

Sustainability

Our model for developing local democracy has benefited from a carefully developed frugality toward all things related to money. Our goal of developing sustainability is more than jargon, and we seek to raise more than 50 per cent of our revenues from sources other than government. The pressure to raise this revenue has made us reluctant to seek out grants that cannot be sustained over the long term. Urban gardening was an initiative that needed a revenue base, but this was impossible in the early years as we were experimenting. As the story unfolded, we abandoned projects like the Petersburg and Bloomingdale gardens because their lack of revenue meant they could not sustain active involvement.

When revenue generation is essential, is it possible to ensure that co-operation is a deciding value? While it is crucial to have one's eye on the balance sheet, just as important to our model is inspiring a learning culture to benefit from the knowledge accumulated during the twist and turns of the venture. Failed new work can be viewed as an experiment with potentially profitable lessons. The learned knowledge comes from combined sources and experiences that should be shared openly. Projects conclude for many reasons—it could be that opportunities for growth are blocked or that there is an inability to raise enough ongoing revenue. Sometimes, the best idea is to close down with the hope of using the learning in a new successor project. These decisions are made in consultation with those involved in the work, with the recognition that financial pressures are finally resolved within the central nodes. The goal is to do this in a way where there is respect for each person involved.

At The Working Centre we have had our share of outright failures, but we have tended toward restating the learning into new projects. Addressing grassroots social issues is complex and it is hard to avoid these pressing realities. If we did not get it right the first time, we recalibrated for another approach. New challenges have helped us listen better, to involve a wider group in an alternative direction. The effort to build co-operation looks the same as the effort to build sustainable revenue. The two must walk side by side with neither dominating the other.

Failure can be disheartening, but we can only learn if the experience builds relationships. When projects flourish, they demonstrate the possibilities of co-operation; failure means understanding how the connections were broken. The gift of working together is the basis of sustainability.

Good Work News and Fundraising

At an early stage of The Working Centre's development we undertook to build a relationship-based fundraising model, recognizing that our grassroots work would need widespread support outside of government. We mailed out our first *Economic Justice Newsletter* in September 1984 to a group of 150 potential supporters.

We committed to mailing our newsletter four times a year. The first ten issues focused on community development, plant closings, worker co-operatives, and employee ownership. The next ten focused on St. John's Kitchen, the Help Centre, and Tri-Tech Recycling. After Issue 20 new ideas were introduced on reciprocal relationships, producerism, local food, and access to tools. By Issue 37, with our mailing list growing to four thousand names, we converted to a newspaper called *Good Work News*. We learned we could tell community stories about our projects, the philosophy they grew from, and push the boundaries about work, unemployment, and consumerism. We found authors who were thinking critically about these issues while we described creative alternatives, often the projects we were developing. In 2014 *Good Work News* reached Issue 119 with a mailing list of eleven thousand. Another thousand copies are distributed locally; thirty-seven issues can be accessed online.[12] We have been thinking and sharing widely in print, developing a conversation, exploring with our readers practical grassroots thinking that the mainstream media cannot possibly cover.

Our main approach to fundraising has been to send out a letter once a year, in November, to our mailing list, letting people know that their contributions our important. We cannot even begin to express our gratitude for donations that come in year after year. In *Good Work News* we have highlighted extraordinary contributions, but we can hardly keep up with all the ways the people of Kitchener-Waterloo have supported our work. Fundraising contributes between 25 and 50 per cent of our revenues in a year.

The Mayors' Dinner

The Mayors' Dinner started in 1988 as a fundraising idea from Will Ferguson, a labour-oriented Kitchener municipal politician, who helped us organize a public dinner to celebrate Kitchener's colourful and populist mayor, Dominic Cardillo, who had been a local politician for twenty-five years.[13] The evening was topped off with a monologue from Canadian comedian David Broadfoot. Working Centre staff and volunteers were amazed to have pulled off a successful event, selling out the Kitchener Market. We asked Mayor Cardillo to expand the idea and call it the Mayor's Dinner.[14] Jonas Bingeman was chosen as the next guest of honour and another sold-out event told us that people in Kitchener-Waterloo liked this way of publicly recognizing individuals who had made substantial community contributions.

A committee was organized to select each year's guest of honour and guide the event. The Bingemans, a prominent family with a thriving hospitality business, helped with planning and keeping ticket prices reasonable. Neil Aitchison, a local broadcaster and speaker, joined as the master of ceremonies for Betty Thompson's Mayor's Dinner in 1990. Twenty-four years later, his comedic skills offer great entertainment with humorous local storytelling that helps make the dinner a long-running project.

Guests of honour have wholeheartedly embraced our fundraising efforts. Ken Murray, the tenth guest of honour, was determined to raise enough money to pay off the mortgage on our 58 Queen building. When local businessman Peter Hallman died in a motorcycle accident, his wife Brenda and brother Jim created a wonderful community celebration of Peter's life. In 2002, Waterloo mayor Lynne Woolstencroft joined the organizing committee, turning it into the Mayors' Dinner, plural, uniting the efforts of the cities of Kitchener and Waterloo.

The Mayors' Dinner has created memories and has honoured an outstanding group of citizens from Kitchener-Waterloo. The evenings usually attract over seven hundred guests. For the dinner's twenty-fifth anniversary, our friends Margaret and Bob Nally were chosen as guests of honour in civic recognition for their community contributions and for their role in helping to found The Working Centre, which was marking its thirtieth anniversary. The evening was a grand success with over nine hundred people in attendance.

On the twenty-fifth anniversary of the Mayors' Dinner, we invited and gathered together almost all the families of the first twenty-five guests of honour. At the special reception we thanked each family and gathered for a group picture, symbolizing not only the cultivation of friendships but how the good spirit of this group has intertwined with the development of The Working Centre, linking us in immeasurable ways with the wider K-W community.

Golf Tournament

The golf tournament is another example of relationship-based fundraising. We had minimal golf knowledge, but board member Sue Oberle saw the value of developing a tournament.[15] In our first years we barely managed seventy golfers. Slowly, Sue knitted together enough labour union locals that would each sponsor a foursome. Our golf tournament evolved as a province-wide union gathering, attracting the president of the Ontario Federation of Labour and the leadership of the Canadian Auto Workers. The Working Centre in turn developed wider union connections and established a big prize table. Other groups, such as businesses, churches, and service clubs, have also participated. We have found in the labour movement a commitment to raising funds to support our work with the unemployed.

Around the tenth year of the event, two CAW organizers who were both effective and boisterous got behind the tournament and soon we were signing up 240 golfers. They worked on negotiating with the CAW Social Justice Fund for a $70,000 contribution toward the renovation of 97 Victoria and the new home for St. John's Kitchen. In the early years the tournament was a great deal of work, but the friendships and the connections to labour have turned out to be a wonderful gift to The Working Centre.[16]

The Third Sector

We fell into non-profit development by accident. As we learned the stories of those who had neither work nor money, the experience instilled in us the desire to organize a framework for building community. We learned about non-profit corporations and charitable status. We entered into a lease, we secured a telephone, a typewriter, volunteers, and furniture. Stephanie learned bookkeeping; we struck up relationships with groups like the labour council, church committees, community organizations, activists, government bureaucrats, politicians, and the social service network. Soon enough we had legal status, a formal board of directors, a grant to work with unemployed auto workers, charitable status, another lease agreement at St. John's Church, and employees. To us it seemed like we were a growing concern. To outsiders we looked like an unsteady, minimally funded venture on the verge of collapse.

The Working Centre was straddling two different eras. We read up on the self-help movement, but we were fortunate that there were no manuals for the kind of non-profit development that we had in mind. The business manuals held little sway over us, and thus we consciously avoided status quo advice about organizational development. We were left with intuition and our reliance on friends who were our original board members. This began a tradition for The Working Centre of conducting board meetings with a loose structure. The purpose of a meeting was to air ideas, to strategize, to let everyone have a say in the next project. Jim Lotz describes this informality as partners getting together to determine innovative ways to meet human needs and aspirations.[17]

Gord Crosby, long time Working Centre board member and president with a diverse background as an orphan, Olympic athlete, police officer, and successful Volkswagen/Audi car dealer, describes our tradition of effective informality.

> I have trouble with this word—governance. When I look that word up I get a definition like, "rule or control with authority, conduct policy and affairs of (an organization)." Governance is not what we do on The Working Centre board. We are not trying to control or rule with authority. We are doing the opposite. We are there to engage in discussion and dialogue to really understand how the organization is doing.[18]

What became important over time, in an era of ever-new layers of imposed bureaucracy, was for us to come up with our own definition of transparency, one that meets the demands and tests of the people we serve and our volunteers. These are the groups most affected and involved in our work. We focus especially on three tests or proofs of our commitment to serving the common good. The first is that our buildings are open, free-flowing public spaces that are hospitable and welcoming to all who enter. Second, these public spaces are used for practical projects that serve the public good and are not dominated by offices or bureaucratic paper shuffling. Third, there is a test that analyzes the whole organization from top to bottom, from left to right, including small jobs and big jobs equally, ensuring an ethic of equality and respect for the work that is accomplished each day. This test takes the form of an ongoing discussion that takes place in the projects and at the common tables. It is only possible through constant involvement in the day-to-day work. Side by side, working and walking together is the true way of understanding what is going on. When issues arise then structures, people, and philosophy have to be evaluated and reconsidered.

We have refused the franchise model of community development. Since the 1980s, the adoption of a franchise mentality has allowed an insidious concentration of power. Previously, small enterprises operated independently, defining their own scope. In *Age of Access*, Jeremy Rifkin describes how small businesses are increasingly being "tied together in a rigidly defined network of mutually agreed-upon contractual arrangements."[19] This is not ownership, nor even small-business entrepreneurship, but strictly defined access that can be pulled away at a moment's notice. The franchise process has hijacked the formerly broad distribution of independent businesses into a regime of dependent lessees.

Community-based organizations can be subjected to this same process. Government bureaucracies, larger-scale non-profits, and powerful foundations aim their power at small, independent non-profits. They use their instrumental power to impose rules from above to enforce their own agenda. Talk of empowering the local, is usually top-down monitoring and controlling of the process. This franchising-in-disguise model diminishes creativity and hinders collaborative development.[20]

The ideas presented in this chapter describe how we have avoided bureaucracy. Useful community engagement starts from and remains rooted in the locality from where the idea grew. When groups distance themselves from the people they serve, they move further away from their original objective and invite bureaucracy.

Informal Work

Perhaps the strongest reason why The Working Centre has not fallen into the traps of bureaucracy is because it has been intent on creating what Bob Nally described as, "a beehive of social innovation."[21] It is a place that works at building relationships at the grassroots.

We have celebrated the culture on the streets of downtown Kitchener. We are proud of all the services and projects that have rooted on Queen Street, Victoria Street, and Market Lane, the downtown streets we constantly walk. A streetscape transforms into a place of meaningful attachment through frequent walking and biking to work, school, or leisure. A Saturday-morning trip to the Kitchener Market is filled with people connecting to others through formal and informal ways, purposefully building their place in a community.

As Joe locked up his bike by the market wall, a Working Centre volunteer was sitting on a bench enjoying a plate of pancakes and sausage. They talked about Al's struggle to gain compensation after an injury ended his twenty years as a welder. A retired president of the K-W Labour Council who volunteers his time at The Working Centre had been helping Al with his claim. Having lost his family and work, Al is learning the computer trade at Computer Recycling, where later that afternoon Joe saw him helping a new Canadian woman purchase a computer.

Walking down the ramp, Joe saw Claude walking unevenly toward the market. Claude is eighty and quite ill. For twenty years he supplemented his pension by busking on King Street and at the Kitchener Market. A regular at St. John's Kitchen, he had been laid off in his late fifties. He spoke to Louisa D'Amato, a *Kitchener-Waterloo Record* reporter on what it is like to be unemployed and hungry:

> What do you think people do when the cheques run out? You learn that because you have to go without … your stomach adjusts and you drink lots of water or whatever is free. I can go without food but I have a bad time if I can't buy any tobacco. Even for those who know how to budget—and most don't—it's impossible to eat and stay warm after you pay rent. If a guy's lucky, he's left with less than $90 a month. That means you often go hungry.[22]

Among the market stalls, Chris was assisting a vendor selling fruits and vegetables. When the market closes, she will hustle as much food as she can from vendors willing to unload their surplus. By Sunday, twenty people will be involved in sorting, distributing, and moving this food. Chris's energy makes possible a grassroots food program that uses minimal resources, and serves those who most need it.

Leaving the market, Joe locked his bike at the back of The Working Centre, where he could see the Food Not Bombs volunteers using Maurita's Kitchen to prepare the meal they serve Saturdays at Kitchener City Hall. A local grocery store usually stocks them with fruits and vegetables, but this week they borrowed from Maurita's Kitchen to top up the two pots of soup. The Food Not Bombs volunteers pick up produce, prepare it, serve it at city hall, and then come back for cleanup, all with a spirit of justice.

At the back of the Queen Street Commons Café, a steady stream of volunteers and bicyclists were either smoking or making their way up the stairs to Recycle Cycles. At the market newspaper stand, Normie, a retired cop who used to volunteer at St. John's Kitchen, had told Joe, "They are a great bunch at that bike operation and they know how to fix bikes. They helped me out yesterday and now my bike works great."

On the street, Shiraz called out, "Joe, how are you doing?" Shiraz is a volunteer working at Computer Recycling, where his role is to disassemble the computer parts for recycling. Most of the volunteers there tend to be on the quiet side, but Shiraz is all fun and games. That day he asked Joe about the picture he had taken with Stéphane Dion when the Liberal leader toured through The Working Centre. As a new Canadian without permanent work, he would value this picture representing his contributions to Canadian society.

Conclusion

The Working Centre has stayed rooted in the Kitchener core. A trip downtown on a Saturday reveals how much work and effort is facilitated by informal connections. This is crucial for underfunded grassroots work. Resources are best developed through the co-operation and integration of networks of support.

Urban agriculture is a case in point. With minimal government funding, there exists a two-acre garden that supports a CSA and other markets along with a greenhouse that produces microgreens and seedlings, a commercial kitchen for teaching vegetarian cooking, and a café that specializes in affordable homestyle vegetarian entrees and delicious home baking. Community gardens, a bake oven, soap making, herbal products, and ongoing skills training in organic gardening are important off-shoots. This economically viable food-to-table model has grown through relationships, dialogue, hard work, and organizational commitment. This slow developmental work is the practical application of local, participatory democracy.

An organization does not exist in a vacuum; its creation and survival is dependent on diverse support. Networks develop through connecting people together, harnessing added energy, new ideas, friendships, and storytelling. Diversity is strengthened when everyone in the network is recognized as important as the other. The Working Centre builds on the powerful need for humans to be connected to one another. Dialogue and reciprocal relations ensure people are listening to what is being said. These are the nuts and bolts ideas that have helped The Working Centre to prosper.

PART THREE

Toward a Philosophy of Work

Illustration by Andy Macpherson

Ethical Imagination: The Working Centre's Approach to Salaries

It has been our experience that people thrive in a working environment that prioritizes co-operation, community-building and strengthening relationships. The following story describes the evolution of The Working Centre's salary policy, demonstrating that it is possible for workplaces to develop practices that embrace less-materialistic values. The ethical imagination that formed this policy emerged from a consistent ethic of sharing and simple living, and it has invited people into a culture of equality.

The Evolution of a Salary Policy

By 1987, The Working Centre had two operating projects: the Job Search Resource Centre at 58 Queen Street South and St. John's Kitchen in the rented church gymnasium of St. John the Evangelist Anglican Church. During our first five years, all the full-time roles were paid equally, but this approach was questioned as unrealistic for the long term.

A professor of organizational psychology, who had recently joined The Working Centre board of directors, suggested a standard workplace model that scored each job description for its functional role. This process was initially adopted despite the fact that we did not have written job descriptions and we were resistant to creating job checklists. For five years we had avoided narrow job descriptions with lists of responsibilities, believing this counter to our co-operative culture, which focused on completing the tasks at hand.

Right away, it was recognized that the process of ranking job descriptions numerically was biased. The executive director position scored 50 per cent more than the others. Everyone else felt their jobs were under-scored and less valued. The questionnaire was skewed to recognize formal responsibility over informal co-operation. Adopting this organizational system would have put us on a contradictory path—trying to develop alternative community projects with a hierarchical salary structure.[1]

A meeting was set in the basement of 58 Queen to discuss the results of ranking the job descriptions. Ken Westhues offered, as his first assignment on The Working Centre board, to observe this meeting. Westhues was an accomplished author and professor of sociology at the University of Waterloo. He was able to think critically using a non-hierarchical perspective. At the meeting, he asked some questions, looked closely at the questionnaires and delivered his verdict. He decided to leave, pointing out that he did not want to be part of The Working Centre if this was the direction it was heading.

Within days, Westhues phoned and suggested a different kind of salary policy. First, he apologized for leaving the meeting, admitting that he felt bad about doing so. The incongruity between the stated goals of The Working Centre and our willingness to subject ourselves to organizational management had upset him. He went home discouraged that social projects could be derailed so easily, but thought about alternatives to the hierarchical traps into which we were drifting.

The simplicity of his plan immediately won our confidence. He started by asking if we (Joe and Stephanie) would limit our salaries to the average industrial wage, as this reflected the level of wages paid to our employees at The Working Centre. By capping salaries at this rate, Working Centre wages would remain on par with 60 to 70 per cent of the workforce, who earn this wage or less. It would demonstrate the centre's commitment to the unemployed. The rest of the policy followed naturally. In keeping with the centre's value of reducing hierarchy, the salary pyramid was designed to be relatively flat, its five levels starting at 86, 80, 74, 68, 66 per cent of the director's salary.[2] Over seven years, staff would earn between 98 and 74 per cent of the director's salary. This was achieved by granting a 2 per cent increase each year over seven years.

Advancing through the steps was independent of ongoing mutual evaluations. This delinked performance from salary, another important aspect of Westhues's thinking, which inserted trust, relationship, and dialogue in place of arbitrary decision making. Wages would increase when the board raised the director's salary. Over the years, few positions were hired in levels four and five. Westhues's salary grid created a workforce where the lowest-paid full-time worker can earn 88 per cent of the director's salary in seven years.

The decision to cap our wage was an easy one. We had already made such a commitment and in the early years of the centre, we often worked without a wage. Staff immediately saw this new structure as exceedingly fair compared to the job description process they had started with. The Working Centre salary policy was officially adopted in February 1989 and twenty-five years later is as vibrant and relevant as ever. Its virtue is felt in the development of a culture of equality. Community grows when people can relate to each other without the burdens of concern for who is making more money or who will get a raise before someone else gets it. The salary policy can be understood as a foundational concept that generates a wellspring of reciprocal relationships. It reinforces the ideals of The Working Centre by practising what it preaches in the core function of wages.

Going Beyond Competitive Wages

The new salary policy gave The Working Centre a practical document that addresses the problem of competitive wages, and it was exactly what our emergent organization needed. We had recognized the conundrum of wages, wondering how we could be an organization of justice if we took wages that were substantially different than the people we were supporting or developing community with. Even in the beginning, we chose to use surplus dollars to build community infrastructure rather than increase wages.

Our founding ideals critiqued consumer culture. It seemed to us that high school, college, and university were merely preparation for a suburban life whose rhythm was controlled by a job, a house, a car, and seasonal shopping in the malls. The Working Centre aspired to create a different reason for working. A job could be about substantially giving back to one's community. It could encompass meaningful work, serving others, frugal spending, and rich relationships.

Over time, the main benefit to The Working Centre was that the salary policy became ingrained into our culture reinforcing how equally paid each of the jobs were. The more workers understood this organizational commitment to equality, the more they trusted the honesty of the enterprise. The burst of energy that created our wide footprint of community development infrastructure can directly be traced to developing a salary policy that respected each individual's efforts equally.

Richard Layard's *Happiness, Lessons from a New Science* affirms what we have learned in practice at The Working Centre. His book challenges economists to move away from behaviourist economics, the belief that purchasing power explains everything. Layard states, "if we cannot know what people feel, we cannot organize things so that they are happy."[3] His work is an attempt to integrate new understandings of human decision making within the framework of economics. Why, he asks, do our political and economic leaders sacrifice economic security to the dictates of competition? Individualism and consumerism are both fuelled by competition. Both encourage the growing social distortions rooted in the decline of trust among people.[4]

The core of Layard's argument is that we in the West are richer than we acknowledge, don't work nearly as long as our great-grandparents did, have universal access to health care, can travel anywhere we want, and live longer—yet we are no happier. Society is more anxious, distressed, and disconnected, constantly fighting addictions. What economic policies would discourage the pollution that people cause by seeking to gain more relative income for themselves?

> Every time they raise their relative income (which they like), they lower the relative income of other people (which those people dislike). This is an "external disbenefit" imposed on others, a form of physical pollution. If people do not take this pollution into account when they decide how much to work, they are behaving just like someone standing up at a football match. The result will be too much work and a distorted work–life imbalance.[5]

Layard is in favour of people enjoying their work and the camaraderie that develops through meaningful endeavours and believes work should not be about a quest for more money. Economic policy that removed the "pollution" that results from pursuing greater status through large income increases would contribute to a more content workforce.

Robert Frank, author of several books on economics, reports that for several decades, wages have been stagnant for the middle class. In order to spend more on houses, cars, and all kinds of consumer items, families have had to work longer hours, reduce savings, go deeper into debt, buy cheaper houses further away from their workplace, resulting in longer commutes, and sleep less.[6] All these options are stressful, they increase the pressures of work, and they feed consumer buying behaviour that reinforces the problem, offering little additional satisfaction. Frank does not blame this on a character defect of the middle class. He thinks that they have been falsely led into a "positional arms race" that defends goods and status, in the long run leading to welfare losses like reduced leisure, increased stress on families, dislocation, and fewer dollars to support the environment we live in—money that could be used to develop the infrastructure for community living—bike lanes, interconnected transit, naturalized parks, water conservation, and so on.[7]

The research of Layard and Frank is less commonly known to the general public. Many do not make the connections between the social inequality and welfare losses and the practice of seeking higher incomes at the expense of family and community. The Working Centre was able to avoid this pitfalls thanks to Westhues, whose policy helped to develop beneficial income structures that demonstrated a different approach to wages.

Rooted Principles

The Working Centre salary policy integrates solidarity, reduces income comparisons, creates harmonious environments, and teaches co-operation, embracing a philosophy of generosity among the employees. When West-hues found himself at our board meeting, where another "positional arms race" was about to be played out, he wasn't interested in waiting around to see who would be the first to blink. "Sociology is more than knowledge," he says. "It is the interplay between disciplined empirical social thought and social action." The goal of activist sociology is to respectfully "design and implement social practices that improve on existing ones."[8]

The result was a salary policy that integrated philosophical and ethical principles into the core of the organization, combining theory and action to create the conditions for sustainable social change. The continuous growth of our community development projects rooted in wide participation demonstrates the synergy possible when people work together as equals.

Solidarity with the Unemployed

The primary social goal of the salary policy was the alliance and identification with those who are unemployed and/or living in poverty. It gives the Working Centre a mechanism to root our founding ethos into the fabric of the organization and share it widely, reflecting the broader goal of moving the values of society toward equality. In the short term, it demonstrates the right thing to do, in contrast to organizational management methods that reinforce status and power by rewarding executives with significantly higher levels of pay.

There are several ways in which this policy aligns itself with those who earn low incomes. The first is that the search for more income is self-defeating when you have already reached a level of relative income or have met basic needs. We believe society's resources are best used to augment the incomes of families and their children who struggle to meet basic needs. Secondly, society's resources are best directed at community-based projects and services that make community living more dependable and secure. Local investment can make community living inexpensive for all, if it is aimed at co-operative structures designed to reduce basic costs of housing, food, and energy.

The Working Centre has made these kinds of investments. In total we have taken $350,000 in direct government housing grants and created forty units of transitional housing that supports hundreds of people through low rental rates and high social supports. We found sufficient internal resources to create this housing without going into debt. It has been a conscious decision to direct resources toward assisting those who face multiple barriers to gain access to proper housing. This process added supportive housing structures to our community.

Layard's research shows that "extra dollars make less difference if you are rich than if you are poor."[9] Savings from our salary policy are redistributed to community-based projects that assist people to live richer lives. This happens in our bike shop, café, community kitchen, thrift stores, and gardens. Solidarity for The Working Centre has been interpreted widely to mean developing access-to-tools projects that directly assist individuals living on a low income to need less money.

Reducing Invidious Comparisons

Externally, the primary goal of our salary policy is solidarity with those we serve. Internally, the primary benefit is the development of a culture that reduces invidious comparisons between workers. Salary inequality in a workplace has a specific way of undermining performance and organizational pride. Free-flowing communication inevitably breaks down when there is widespread knowledge in the workplace of wage inequality. This situation creates distrust and results in an unsatisfactory and unproductive work environment.

The Working Centre has endeavoured to create a level playing field so that each worker can reach their potential. Our work culture has been enhanced by not linking salary to a performance evaluation. Many jobs, especially in the human service sector, cannot be objectively measured for performance, and developing elaborate systems for punishment or reward only invites unjust comparisons, ignites old social wounds, and undermines trust. We have seen that happiness and satisfaction do not come from getting ahead or triumphing over colleagues, but from making one's community a better place and from the personal recognition of a job well done. Reducing job and pay comparisons helps people enjoy their contribution to the social product.

Becoming accustomed to the benefits of a pay raise, such as a company car, can mean that two years later the family cannot manage without it. Having to earn enough income to support a second car is like being on a treadmill that keeps moving while you get no further ahead. You have to work harder to continue paying for this new expense. The Working Centre salary policy helps people to get off the treadmill by offering a different way of working. The policy promotes long-term stability by helping people identify their income expectations. A co-operative work environment is found through doing what is necessary to support a community of workers attempting to use their skills in the most productive way.

Over four years ending in 2007, The Working Centre added greatly to its community wealth. We renovated two old warehouse buildings, established a thrift store, relocated St. John's Kitchen, adding a medical clinic, showers, and laundry, established the Queen Street Commons Café, created five units of crisis housing for women, combined employment services under one roof, expanded Public Access Computers, relocated the computer recycling lab, and built five new units of transitional housing on the second floor of 66 Queen. This was made possible by a dedicated group of staff and volunteers who were willing to fill in holes, pitch in, and do whatever was necessary to complete this vision of community. The shared sense of ownership and the celebration that ensued with the completion of each project were a visible sign of the harmony and social co-operation that made the work possible.

By reducing competition, workers recognize that there is not a ladder of status, where people climb over other people in an effort to get to the top wage rate. Organizations whose philosophy emphasizes co-operation over economic social climbing can benefit from constant positive communication between workers, enabling daily business to be completed efficiently. This is an important part of developing a prosperous organizational culture.

Greater Income Is Not a Guarantee for Harmonious Social Relationships

The goal of commercial advertising is to convince consumers to purchase goods or services, often exploiting feelings of emptiness they hope will be filled by a shopping spree. Advertisers make extravagant claims to lure the viewer to spend more. This constant barrage can lead consumers to seek higher-paying jobs to afford all these opportunities. This vicious cycle draws a false picture of the meaning of work. We think we have to work for money when in fact most people would rather work to learn and create new things. People strive to find meaning in work that has lasting benefit. It is this divide in society that needs to be understood. Why is it so common to trade away meaningful work in order to take a higher paying job? New research is showing that greater income can lead to social distress. When money is the sole goal of a job, then the chances of that job turning out to be unsatisfactory, bureaucratic and stale are high.[10]

Canada in the 1970s had a base of stable industrial jobs and homelessness was not widespread. Forty years later, Canadian society is richer,[11] but according to a Canadian survey in 2000, emotional distress now affects 20 per cent of the population.[12] During our years of operation we have witnessed a substantial increase in emotional and mental illness. Even as we are richer, our communities are less secure. Homelessness in every major city in Canada continues to grow. Our Psychiatric Outreach Project at St. John's Kitchen registers over two thousand people with over 1,600 contacts each month.

Under the patina of our consumer society is an ever-growing array of depression, anxiety, substance abuse, and impulse disorders. Many of these psychological responses are the result of unpleasant, harsh environments. Canadian society, like much of the Western world has placed a high value on money, possessions, and appearances at the same time that long-term secure jobs have been replaced by a growing trend of temporary positions and insecure working conditions, making these goals more difficult to attain. Layard discovered that many countries with annual per capita income of $5,000 had almost the same level of happiness as rich countries, defined as those with incomes per person of between $15,000 and $25,000. In rich countries happiness from larger increases in wealth were increasingly cancelled out by "greater misery coming from less harmonious social relationships."[13]

What happens to individuals when they work in order to be a functional consumer? What is lost in the process? An individual's intrinsic motivation is vital to personal definitions of success and that is what gets buried under the social compromises necessary to win a higher paying job. It may be counterintuitive, but social researchers are now documenting the kinds of motivation that lead to unsatisfactory results. Daniel H. Pink documents how financial reward for work performed, also known as the carrots-and-sticks approach, reduces motivation, diminishes performance, decreases creativity, and encourages shortcuts and short-term thinking.[14]

The Working Centre may be a micro example of Pink's research. The original ideas for our first projects, the Job Search Resource Centre and St. John's Kitchen, started with unpaid work. The same is true for Computer Recycling, Public Access Computers, Recycle Cycles, Community Access Bikeshare, our first Community Gardens, and our first renovation projects at 58 Queen Street South. The whole infrastructure of The Working Centre had its beginnings not with paid staff but with volunteers who were creative and intrinsically motivated. They were responding to gaps in services, human needs, and concerns for environmental and heritage conservation. There were organizations with money to address these issues, but it was people with limited resources and higher motivation that took decisive action to address these social concerns.

The Working Centre salary policy is not designed to help our workers become better consumers but to respond creatively to the community around them. We opted to pay each other relatively equally at modest levels, but this egalitarian model comes with its own problems. Even before the concept of a consumer society, Alexis de Tocqueville was warning about egalitarian social solutions. He loved democracy for the equality that it created, but he wondered what would happen if democratic citizens were too equal. Tocqueville might have projected that treating our workers equally might mean they would settle for mediocre desires.[15] He would have taken for granted that a society of equally paid people lacked intrinsic motivation. Tocqueville would wonder who would do the dishes, who would clear public spaces of clutter, who would work the extra hours to accomplish burdensome tasks, and who would plan the sustainability of economic ventures. Peter Maurin of The Catholic Worker summarized such concerns this way, "Everyone's newspaper is no one's newspaper."[16] These have always been real concerns in our projects.

The Working Centre demonstrates that a co-operative work environment can be both equal and productive. It starts by creating an ethic of service, at every level, each striving to do well for the other while achieving the organization's goals. The salary policy embedded this ethic into the leadership of The Working Centre. This gift has been returned a hundredfold by a co-operative group of workers who have seen the opportunity for creating new structures that serve people in new ways.

We have learned that community organizations are at their best when they create co-operative projects that promote lively dialogue and opportunities to directly contribute. This work involves teaching people to use tools "that allows the user to express meaning in action."[17] Community problems are solved most effectively by processes that generate meaningful work and the ability to overcome obstacles, and that develop pride in the work accomplished.

Hierarchical organizations tend to pay one group of workers substantially more than other workers. At The Working Centre we take a different perspective. In a highly functioning organization it is essential that those who have broad skills to analyze and act on complex situations are free to use those skills to their maximum potential. Traditionally these skills have been valued more highly and receive the highest pay. We question whether it is fair that some skills are reimbursed at many times the rate of other skills. What about practical skills that entail physical endurance, like cooking, cleaning, gardening, moving, repairing, and all construction skills? How about more cerebral jobs like listening, counselling, bookkeeping, computer programming, report writing? When you reflect on the continuum of jobs in an organization, then fairness demands that each job is as important and as necessary as the other. Our organizational structure is strongest when there is an easy flow of communication between workers and projects. Structures of equality make these daily transfers of information convivial, and this reduces stress and makes possible an ongoing harmonious place for workers and volunteers.

A winners and losers environment replaces social relationships with money. In contrast, The Working Centre has created a harmonious social milieu by promoting equality and simple living, an environment that has resulted in bursts of social innovation. In decentralized projects, where hospitality and inclusion bring people together to solve problems, an ethic develops to look after the hundreds of small details. If Tocqueville toured The Working Centre we think he would be intrigued by the easy way each project serves community.

Teaching Co-operation

Our research and experience shows that dislocation in our society is the result of misplaced attachment to material goods. It leaves people alone, isolated, and lacking human connections that are necessary to help us through good and bad times. People often choose consumer products over cultivating relationships. Disconnection is made worse by advertising that fills the air with messages aimed at feelings of self-doubt and boredom. But what are the alternatives? What can communities do to teach and model relationship building?

From its beginnings, The Working Centre has supported grassroots, co-operative, self-directed, skills-based learning as integral to its service. Every day at our centres people gain competencies in cooking, sewing, computer repair, bike repair, and so on, but the primary skills are not the only things taught. The approach used reinforces distinct and invaluable social skills such as how to teach, learn, and live in a respectful, reciprocal, democratic way. Hierarchical, top-down models of teaching are avoided; instead, teachers and learners take turns talking and listening, showing one another how to do new things.

The Working Centre creates many teaching opportunities through projects that have little or no government support, such as the community bike shop, Speak English Café, BarterWorks, the vegetarian cooking taught at Maurita's Kitchen, the housing help desk, Waterloo Region ASSETS Project (A Service for Self-Employment and Support) Project, public access computers, self-directed computer training, free public computer repairs by volunteers in our computer lab, a bustling furniture and housewares thrift store, and the work skills learned serving the meal at St. John's Kitchen. Community is enhanced when scarce resources are freed up to build access to projects that build relationships.

The Diploma in Local Democracy is a fourteen-week course that helps people explore a philosophy of citizenship. The project is about teaching how reciprocal relations in everyday life form the roots of a democratic society. Local democracy is an expression of building community, of ensuring people are not left behind, of practising the skills of equality and peaceful coexistence, and challenging hierarchy by affirming equal relationships. All these skills can be practised in workplaces, public agencies, community groups, schools, and at home.

Participants define local democracy in their own terms: "These two hours a week have been meditative. Therapeutic in the sense of growth. The notion that a small community can have a voice, can dream out loud, being able to share ideas that I would not have had the opportunity to share otherwise. It makes me want to take this model elsewhere."[18]

The local democracy project started in the late 1990s and it continues to evolve. It cultivates an environment where individuals learn how to responsibly put the community above themselves. This is the essence of teaching co-operation, reinforcing a core virtue that is essential for community development.

Happiness arises from seeking the well-being of others by paying attention to their feelings, realities, and economic circumstances. You limit your own ability to be happy when you are an obstacle to others, when you are jealous of their success. The Working Centre has developed learning initiatives to help individuals co-operate toward sharing the abundance of our society.

Ethical Imagination

When Ken Westhues typed out the salary policy he was thinking along the same lines as Peter Maurin in "Better or Better Off": "Everyone would be rich if nobody tried to become richer, and nobody would be poor if everybody tried to become poorest. And everybody would be what they ought to be if everybody tried to be what they want the other fellow to be."[19]

Layard came to the same conclusion seventy-five years later. "So we have in the First World a deep paradox—a society that seeks and delivers greater income but is little if any happier than before." He adds that in the First World there is now more depression and addiction than reported fifty years ago.[20]

For twenty-five years The Working Centre has implemented a salary policy that pays a fair average wage with equal benefits and holidays, which reduces comparisons and supports a workplace that is productive and useful. This is economics as if people mattered, E. F. Schumacher would say; it means putting money in its place facilitating beneficial exchanges.[21]

The Working Centre salary policy works for future planning by giving workers time to collaborate to develop frugal skills, to learn sharing and partnering, and to strengthen their surroundings with rich social bonds. A salary policy is only a piece of paper. What is most important is a workplace where supportive relationships thrive. This means giving workers time to be with family and friends when they are grieving or supporting the sick, recognizing the importance of building personal relations as we work together. It is vital to offer volunteers and staff, the people who form The Working Centre community, the same kinds of mutual support that individuals get through our services. This creates an unbroken chain of solidarity.

We believe that human beings are made for giving, and relationships and community develop together as people give of themselves, striving for the best they can achieve. Society is in every way richer when a co-operative environment is encouraged. Gifts of the spirit, offered in friendship, offered for the building of community, in a spirit of peace and joy, are gifts of the heart that emphasize our commonness. Our experience at The Working Centre has shown us that a community dedicated to seeking the happiness of others will find that joy returned a hundredfold.

Community Tools

Building Community in the Parking Lot

Bev shakes her head; it is Friday before the Canada Day weekend and around the Victoria Street buildings there are people everywhere, "It is like a zoo, there are so many people shopping, volunteering, and coming to and from St. John's Kitchen. I don't know what to do!" Don Gingerich, coordinator at Worth a Second Look (WASL) holds the project together with moral courage. Don is constantly teaching. All day long volunteers, Job Café workers, and shoppers encounter a place where the main goal is co-operation and sharing.

In the WASL garage Scott and Fig assemble the single speed bikes for our Community Access BikeShare project that we are piloting with help from the City of Kitchener. As Scott describes the mechanism for locking the adjustable seat, volunteers bring goods into the warehouse and arrange sold items for delivery.

Sammy shuffles by the garage and is in a reflective mood. For the last twenty years he had lived by his wits, delivering flyers for income. Last summer, we called an ambulance when we found Sammy slumped over his motorized cart in the parking lot, sweltering in the hot sun and losing consciousness. Pat, a WASL volunteer, sensed something was wrong with Sammy's living conditions, and after discovering he was living in a flea-infested apartment, he contacted the landlord to get the problem addressed. Then Pat personally cleaned up Sammy's apartment.

Sammy's medical problems were acute, however, and he was able to get a bed at the Hospitality House, beside 97 Victoria on the WASL side. He has major liver failure but looks remarkably healthy. "How can I complain?" he asks. "In the middle of the night I can ask for a peanut butter and jelly sandwich and they will get it for me." Life at the Hospitality House is different from a rooming-house existence. The staff act as family, ensuring everyone eats properly and gets to their medical appointments, creating a warm and welcoming place of support.

While Sammy is talking there is more drama in the parking lot. An old Lincoln Continental suddenly accelerates uncontrollably, narrowly finding its way between two parked cars and over the concrete parking barrier, flying in the air, thudding to the ground while turning rapidly into the laneway and crashing to a halt over a wooden barrier. Slowly an old man emerges, wobbling as he describes his knee locking his foot to the gas pedal.

As a crowd tries to lift the car off the wooden barriers, Jenny shakes her head. "That is dangerous—doesn't he know people like to sit on those wooden barriers?" Jenny has a tenacious will to volunteer even while battling her addictions. Don has recently asked her to stay away when she is drinking. "I just wanted to say hi," she says. "Would that be all right?"

This anecdote represents a regular afternoon at 97 Victoria, where friendships flourish among recyclers and those involved in food redistribution and health care. Here the idea of *community tools* flourishes.

Developing the Philosophy of Community Tools

Community-tool projects received a boost of energy when University of Waterloo environmental studies students started showing interest in practical projects aimed at environmental issues. BarterWorks emerged as a community venture through the efforts of two students who re-energized the K-W Local Employment Trading System (LETS).[1] They used their fourth-year university course work to revitalize the system by using word-of-mouth marketing, holding barter fairs, involving university students, and visiting businesses. They organized a community of people dedicated to sustaining a local currency.

Community-tools projects evolved at The Working Centre by combining community service with social enterprise. Each tool is structured to create an environment that allows maximum involvement, creating ways for people who have been excluded to contribute. The resulting projects invite people away from isolation to become involved in serving others, to use tools productively, and to become part of a group that serves a public need. In this way, community tools offer opportunities to combine work experience, skill building, civic involvement, and a new freedom to contribute in a positive way.

Community tools are a response to the competitive labour market, which leaves many people without a way to contribute to society. They are models of sharing that focus first on community building and secondly on revenue generation. These projects start as new creations that become ventures by learning to earn their own revenue. Projects maintain the affordability of their services and goods while developing and identifying potential income sources. Donations are used to subsidize service activities such as free children's bikes, kitchen and café employment training, and market gardening intern training, as the projects strive to generate their own revenue.

Over 160 people gathered at our November 2010 volunteer dinner, which, in our tradition, is cooked and served by our own hands. This annual gathering to celebrate our work has taken many forms over thirty years. Falcon, a volunteer at Worth a Second Look thrift store, wondered why he was called a volunteer. In his opinion it demeaned his role in a vital recycling venture. We need new language, he said, to describe this liberating work not tied to money, one that relates unpaid work to community building. Community tools can create that language.

From *Tools for Conviviality* to Community Tools

The Working Centre learned from the writings of Ivan Illich how to think about access to tools. Illich believed strongly that we should write an epilogue for the consumer age. His bold assertion was rooted in his analysis of the destructive bias of centralized organizations and their complicity in undermining virtuous action. People who are slaves to institutions lose their ability to see autonomous work as essential to civil society. When Illich was writing during the late 1960s, large-scale production dominated the landscape as small shops and small farms declined. Centralized techniques solved some problems but created many more. Illich perceived the future as holding an escalation of institutionalized management that treated people and things like slaves rather than humans working together.

In *Tools for Conviviality* he visualized an intentional society in which people used tools in ways that enhanced the common good. "People need not only to obtain things, they need above all the freedom to make things among which they can live, to give shape to them according to their own tastes and to put them to use in caring for and about others."[2] For Illich, the first step was to recognize that for a century, the concept of progress had been based on a false premise that machines can replace slaves. Long after Illich wrote *Energy and Equity*, Andrew Nikiforuk contends that we are not much closer to ethically understanding how our dependency on oil is another form of slavery.[3] Illich's goal was to not only think ethically but to change the structure of how we use tools: "The crisis can only be solved if we invert the present deep structure of tools; if we give people tools that guarantee their right to work with high, independent efficiency, thus simultaneously eliminating the need for either slaves or masters and enhancing each person's range of freedom."[4]

Illich advocated the local production of goods and services that created connections between people, not for money and prestige but for mutuality and reciprocity. Work should lead to the development of meaningful relationships. Goods crafted with the skill of an artisan are not assembly-line products. Growth can be directed toward ensuring that basic things that people need, such as water, electricity, urban agriculture, household goods, and child care, are made available through face to face micro-enterprises that involve networks of people committed to human betterment.

How Community Tools Operate

Illich describes alternative ways of structuring tools, while Jane Jacobs's minutely describes the interweaving between entrepreneurial efforts and co-developments. New work is work that is not being done but that could be accomplished if organized in an efficient way. New work arises by continually listening to what people say, scanning the landscape, analyzing the social factors, and understanding why the work is either being discouraged or why no one is interested in pursuing it. It involves finding those who know something of this new work and co-operating to accomplish it.[5] This search for new work and its co-developments has led us in surprising directions.

Over the last fifteen years we have called this new work *community tools* and established projects like Recycle Cycles, BarterWorks, St. John's Kitchen, Maurita's Kitchen, Queen Street Commons Café, Integrated Supportive Housing, Computer Recycling, Worth a Second Look, Hacienda Sarria Market Garden, Green Door Clothing and Arts Space, and the Queen Street Commons Studio.[6] Each of these projects have endured in one form or another as interdependent work within the community of The Working Centre. We have learned the importance of adding energy, infrastructure, and a method to incubate new projects. Community Tools projects share the following characteristics:

- Projects incubate new ideas in an informal atmosphere.
- Projects use materials that are often free because they are being recycled or procured very cheaply.
- Project administration is minimal, consisting of general coordination and the maintenance of a co-operative, friendly, and inviting atmosphere.
- Projects provide low-cost useful services otherwise not available.
- Projects inspire people to use tools in creative ways and consistent with Working Centre philosophy.

- Projects have benefited from Working Centre support during the project's initial development and ongoing activities. They are not expected to earn income in the initial stages because it takes time to develop infrastructure, and to build public engagement with the services being offered.
- Projects are inclusive and provide concrete ways for individuals to contribute to the common good.
- Projects create cultures of livelihood as workers support each other and the people who use the tools in the building of community.
- Projects are a unique form of social enterprise. They are not rigorously tied to the market, allowing for that liminal range where creativity and the common good come together for many different reasons.
- Projects with a higher degree of administration frequently record a corresponding decrease in participation.
- Projects have evolved from or have been sponsored by The Working Centre and rarely received support from long-term government grants. Some projects have benefited from summer students or youth training projects.
- Projects with a coordinator aim to generate income for that position from products or services in the range of $30,000 per year. Some projects may only raise a fraction of that amount.
- Projects at The Working Centre are not charged rent unless the income generated can sustain this. These projects benefit from our philosophy of public space.

Community tools projects are designed to develop skills and provide self-help opportunities for creative livelihood. In *The Lichen Factor*, Lotz shows how community is created through "mutual aid and interdependence between humans that mirrors the symbiosis found in lichen."[7] By sharing energy, creative activities thrive in diverse, decentralized environments. Community tools have inspired recycling initiatives, opportunities to control one's work, and supportive places that help people find meaningful work. Each owes its origin to the process of listening, analyzing, reflection, and creative action. Each has a story.

Work as Freedom

Community tools question why our culture excludes thousands of people from working in the labour market. Excluded people constantly seek opportunities to use their skills and talents.

Up to twenty-five people a day contribute to Worth a Second Look Housewares and Furniture (WASL), Kitchener's largest furniture and housewares recycling centre. Thrift-store work is labour intensive. Material acquired is sorted into the categories of furniture, small wares, electrical items, books, sporting goods, and so on. Items are priced, shelves stocked and restocked. Cashiers and helpers respond to questions and problems. Generating work is only one purpose of the WASL experience.

Turning a thrift store into a community tools project has been a surprising experience. Don Gingerich, the store's coordinator, has taken pure delight in creating a respectful and welcoming place. In any half hour he could be, in his own words, "paying workers out for Job Café , helping someone to put a hold on a TV and to hold their money so they don't drink it away, while filling out two delivery receipts and tagging furniture items for a customer, and running to the bank for change."[8] Don started with the remnants of a former thrift store that had lost its energy. The first step involved energizing a group of people to take ownership of the work through servant leadership. This has meant modelling every job and teaching people how they could become involved.

The first year focused on establishing a positive environment in which all can contribute. Within a few weeks of re-opening, fifty people became involved. We were still finding our way as volunteers took responsibility for the work. The first crew was made up of people living in our housing, people on social assistance, men living at Out of the Cold, retired individuals who offered skills and leadership, people recovering from addictions, and a young, talented, home-schooled kid, who would only do things her way. This diverse crew knew they were creating a thriving thrift store dedicated to low prices and service to the community.

John Maier did his MSW placement at WASL under the banner "social work is moving furniture." When he walked into WASL, he "noticed the hustle and bustle of people working tirelessly every day.... The number of tasks that needed to be accomplished seemed endless." But there were always volunteers ready to do the work. He wondered why so many gifted and wonderful people gave so much time and why they had been rejected by the labour market. People told him, "it was something about the place, an atmosphere that made it welcoming and exciting to work at." He concluded that at "WASL, co-operation grows along with mutual aid and trust, as volunteers work together to make the community a friendlier and more helpful place."[9]

The most important variable for satisfying work is a workplace that embodies good spirit and opportunities to positively contribute. Confidence and usefulness grow in an environment of trust. An accepting place is important for acquiring skills. WASL has an atmosphere where people are invited and trusted to engage and accomplish the daily work, on terms that respect what they are able to do. Friendships develop from co-operative work. Solidarity emerges from the effort to make the enterprise sustainable and from providing a useful and meaningful service.

Rooted in Community

We accidently learned how to produce housing as a community tool through our renovations on Queen Street South. The tangible benefits of building apartments demonstrated how housing can bring people together. Our first endeavour was to convert two empty apartments into functioning units. We knew little about building codes, but we knew that construction costs can escalate quickly. The building project evolved using the electrical, plumbing, drywalling, and painting skills of The Working Centre community, skills easily found among ordinary people who are unemployed.

We had more challenges on the next project, which involved renovating the third floor of 43 Queen. A city of Kitchener building inspector told us frankly that because of the number of windows required and their prescribed placement, he doubted apartments could be built. Despite his superior knowledge of the building code he would not help us find a solution, saying he was not a consultant and it was our problem to figure out.

We needed a fair bit of ingenuity to take out the top back quarter section of the roof and a portion of the back wall. The two new inside walls that form part of the large balcony added four windows and a door to the apartment. This solved our window problem and it made an interesting outdoor space for the tenants. We created two apartments of 1,500 square feet, each with three bedrooms. These units have been continuously used as transitional housing for twelve years by individuals without housing options. We soon were providing affordable, clean housing that included phone, heat, hydro, cable, and laundry for $360 a month. This integrated housing offers people the chance to escape the world of drugs and drinking found in downtown rooming houses.[10] We did this without government subsidy, showing how it is possible to create small-scale, low-cost housing through co-operative work.

Another project involved creating two Hospitality Houses to provide seven rooms of supportive housing for those who are homeless and at risk and experiencing debilitating health problems. Street life, complicated by addictions and mental health challenges, leads to chronic health problems such as liver failure, hepatitis C, and diabetes. The Hospitality House provides stable housing and access to health care.

The workforce that upgraded these houses consisted of excluded workers. The crew of about twenty workers each contributed one day per week. The renovations to create the space required the full range of construction skills, and decisions were made co-operatively as the project evolved. On a cold day in March, Joe asked one of the crew how he felt about only working one day a week. He replied, "Sure I would like to work more, but by sharing the work we all gain a bit." As the project neared completion, the crew was pushed to finish the final touches as residents waited to move in. This pressure was not resented because the workers knew what kind of housing we were creating. Renovations rooted in community means learning how to be flexible and inclusive. The Hospitality House renovations were a gift proudly offered to the community.

The production of housing is an example of community building from the bottom up, the kind of autonomous action that Illich described in *Tools for Conviviality*, the kind of action he believed was crucial for human development.

Making Public Space Common

The Queen Street Commons Café (QSCC) is a community tool that is creating a new definition of public space. The café was pieced together with donated equipment, trial-and-error vegetarian cooking, and affordable fair-trade coffee. The renovations at 43 Queen had created a three-thousand-square-foot main floor that initially housed The Front Window craft store, public computers, and employment counselling. Next door to us was the popular café and Kitchener landmark, Café Mozart. When the owners retired, they closed the business and sold us their coolers, chairs, and tables, which we used to convert the main floor into café space. Over these eight years, the café has evolved. The serving area grew, and there is now a stage and sound system with video projection. The chairs and tables are constantly rearranged to fashion a homey, vibrant space. We designed a separate coffee bar that brought presence to the back area and features a micro fluid-bed coffee roaster. Customers can now get freshly roasted organic, fair-trade coffee and choose from fifteen single-origin coffee beans. The Commons has the freshest coffee and is a unique gathering place in the downtown.

We knew exactly the kind of place we wanted to create. In the mid-1990s we had learned from Christopher Lasch the idea of "third places": "Civic life requires settings where people meet as equals, without regard to race, class, or national origin. Thanks to the decay of civic institutions ranging from political parties to public parks and informal meeting places, conversation has become almost as specialized as the production of knowledge."

Lasch describes third places as informal, lively, and inclusive. The pub or coffee shop contributes to the civic arts by encouraging freewheeling conversations, thereby giving substance to the idea of democratic debate. Lasch laments their decline, because "neighbourhood hangouts give way to shopping malls, fast-food chains, and take-outs."[11] Third places resist lifestyle marketing claims—Lasch thinks of them as grittier, quoting Mary Parker Follett, who notes that "we may like some selected group better than the company of our neighbours, but the satisfaction and contentment that comes with sameness indicate a meagre personality."[12]

Third places are like decentralized village squares, different from home and work, where people can hang out for good company and lively conversation. Discussion and banter are the heart of grassroots democracy that is facilitated by places that are accessible, inexpensive, and easy to navigate.[13] Third places anchor community life by their welcoming nature. It is pedestrian-level democracy; people live in walking distance and drop by to meet their friends, knowing they can make a connection. With the arrival of franchise restaurants and highly organized food-service organizations, communities need real spaces where interactions are not determined by marketing studies. At the QSCC there are constant informal gatherings. On a recent Saturday, a band was practising their new songs publicly for the first time. People were enjoying their coffee while the band was honing their skills.

The QSCC is anchored by volunteers and training projects in food preparation and service. We have developed a wide selection of affordable, homestyle vegetarian foods and baked goods that add to the atmosphere of a welcoming place.[14] QSCC sells books through Books for Sustainable Living, homemade products made by people associated with The Working Centre, BarterWorks products and services, and GROW Herbal. There is a continuous stream of gatherings such as the BarterWorks fairs, the Speak English Café, lectures and movies, the Wednesday Commons Market, inclusive Open Space gatherings for people with disabilities and their friends, informal concerts, Friday Night

Jazz with The New Vibes Jazz Quartet, and CD and book launches. The café is a meeting place for housing, employment, and outreach workers and other projects and services. It is open from 8:30 a.m. to 9:00 p.m. each weekday and 10:00 a.m. to 4:00 p.m. on Saturday.

QSCC has brightened up the Kitchener downtown by developing an alternative to franchise coffee shops and bland suburban enclaves. It is a third place that facilitates skill building and volunteerism, like a lively village square.

The Three Sisters of Community Tools — Serving Others, Work as Gift, and Building Community

Community tools encourage solidarity through integrating the virtues into projects where individuals can use their skills, access tools, and form friendships. Projects build organizational capacity to operate without stringent rules through on-the-ground practice. This is a transformative process that many organizations have trouble navigating.

Recycle Cycles is a community bike shop where volunteers contribute their time and skills to promote bicycles as an inexpensive, non-polluting way of getting around. A bike shop is successful when it creates a friendly environment that welcomes all contributions. Community spaces can be challenging when they are inclusive and accept the full range of human gifts and follies. Acceptance involves listening to the stories of each individual with the goal of solving problems through dialogue and a focus on the practical work of the project.

Jesse Robertson, the Recycle Cycles coordinator, is not only a friendly face; he is familiar with every kind of bike problem and repair. He saw the potential of the bike shop and worked with volunteers to more than double the number of bikes recycled, to seven hundred per year, and the number of bikes fixed yearly on the public bike stands to 4,500. The shop is singularly designed for the purpose of recycling and repairing bicycles. If you already know how to fix your bike you may only need help in locating the right tool or part. If you have less experience a volunteer will work with you to find the best course of action. A new brake cable, a gear shift adjusted, a general clean-up, and your bike is tuned up for another couple of months.

The virtues of *serving others, work as gift,* and *building community* have benefited the Recycles Cycles bike shop. Serving others means helping people keep their bikes on the road and making refurbished bikes available. On a low income, paying for a bike repair can be unaffordable. A shop that teaches and assists people to maintain their bikes is a gift of service. A community shop also needs to hear the anger of frustrated individuals who may be experiencing challenges. This demonstrates a willingness to dialogue and solve problems together. Episodes that create tension are learning experiences toward helping the shop develop a supportive framework.

Recycle Cycles encourages work as gift. At the shop, a bike-mechanics culture has taken root, where there is pleasure in refurbishing abandoned bikes. Those who have learned the skills of bicycle repair teach others. A bike with worn brake pads and a misaligned gear shifter is repaired. Skill and knowledge are shared as the bike owner learns from the volunteer how to make the proper adjustments. Little money changes hands. The work is a skill and a craft, learned and enhanced over time. The workers add service and gift, deploying bike tools for the common good.

The Recycle Cycles community attracts a wide range of people, from mechanics who no longer ply their trade to retired factory and office workers, teachers, and university professors. There are volunteers who are not in the workforce, computer science students, and stay-at-home mothers. All enjoy the opportunity to repair and give away children's bikes. A bike rider comes in frustrated and angry because of a flat tire and they find a shop designed to repair the tire quickly. They leave with a smile. Volunteers know they are building community when someone buys a refurbished bike for riding to their new factory job. At Recycle Cycles, you can see what is possible when mechanical skills and community skills are combined in a shop space with tools designed to help people keep their bikes on the road.

Decentralist and Integrated

Community tools operate within The Working Centre as decentralized nodes. This model of subsidiarity ensures decisions are made as close to the source of the work as possible. Projects are decentralized to allow each group to express their independence through distinctive cultures that take their shape around the shared use of tools.

The Working Centre provides an indispensible framework of philosophy, infrastructure, labour, and financing to help new projects mature. Projects have grown out of ideas about expanding access to tools and community service in the areas of gardening, computers, bikes, bartering, and sewing. Integration with a larger entity gives small, decentralized projects meaning and direction while still retaining the freedom to create their own culture with different volunteers, different ways of service, and different use of tools. We strive to make the integration and decentralization feel seamless. When people take responsibility for their work and help build a wider community of services, they are accomplishing community work, not in isolation but through engendering co-operative development.

Subsidiarity gives volunteers who are the main workforce a voice in the labour they are contributing. This ensures that those who benefit from the services are "directly involved in their planning and implementation."[15] It avoids the pitfalls of paternalistic social services. The advantage of subsidiarity is that social concern becomes tangible and new ideas emerge as people involved in the work make project decisions. Pope Benedict XVI said, "The principle of subsidiarity must remain closely linked to the principle of solidarity and vice versa, since the former without the latter gives way to social privatism, while the latter without the former gives way to paternalist social assistance that is demeaning to those in need."[16]

The Working Centre uses an incubator model to assist new projects to attain sustainability. The supports we offer include centralized bookkeeping and accounting, staff and project development, fundraising, proposal writing, funder relationships, and wide community contacts. Our salary policy reinforces the spirit that everyone at The Working Centre is in it together. Our newly renovated buildings offer great locations. Our established projects, despite fragile funding, demonstrate stability and concrete services. The Job Search Resource Centre adds expertise in job search, job training, and placement knowledge. The scale of volunteer commitment at St. John's Kitchen underscores the community tools model. All these practical instruments of our social infrastructure strengthen solidarity by demonstrating a larger vision.[17]

There is tendency among community groups to immediately start planning their independence as an organization. For-profit organizations have financial mechanisms and incentives to hold successful entities in their corporate sphere. Community groups must do this by moral persuasion. The Working Centre philosophy of community tools helped hold together these projects. We developed a mutually supporting system where participation in this cluster of projects added value and knowledge, representing a shared approach to community building.

The Green Door Clothing Store can be seen as a start-up that benefited from The Working Centre's integrated supports. When 37 Market Lane was purchased, it meant that the store and renovations could be organized with long-term thinking. Volunteers at WASL had ideas and energy toward planning and opening the store, and the renovations were accomplished with Job Café workers. The IT group installed phones, a computer network, and the Internet while the accounting office set up the financial system. These supports helped a decentralized project get established.

The integrated supports offer a base for start-up and long term support. An effective decentralized project must still operate on its own merits. Its efforts are focused on recruiting volunteers who become immersed in the work of preparing meals, fixing bikes, or recycling clothing and furniture. Each group must then use their own initiative to connect to the broader philosophy.

To be authentic, a commitment to decentralization must be expressed at every level of the organization. On December 17, 2009, St. John's Kitchen held its twenty-fourth Christmas dinner. The Working Centre board of directors have always come together to enjoy the Christmas meal, and no special fuss is made. We meet at 12:30 when the majority of the five hundred people who come for the Christmas dinner have already eaten. This makes it a bit easier to find a table for seven or eight people. The scene is similar each year. Hundreds of people enjoy the meal with friends while the regular St. John's Kitchen crew, made up of patrons and community volunteers, work as fast as possible to keep up the supply of plates and utensils. With steel band Christmas music, gifts, cards, and greetings being exchanged, it is a festive atmosphere unique to St. John's Kitchen. The board of directors take pride on this day in their faithful support of a direction that allows community to grow in ways that could not have been described twenty-five years earlier. They line up for their Christmas dinner and their plates are filled to overflowing just like all the plates that day. A fair bit of jostling is usually necessary, but soon enough, tables are pulled together and we enjoy being part of a wonderful community.

Access to Tools

At first glance, there is nothing unusual about a thrift store, a community meals service, a bicycle shop, a café, a commercial kitchen, a community-share agriculture project, a bartering system, public access computers, or computer recycling. Underneath each of these projects, however, is a renewal of theory and practice, an effort to reduce social service paternalism, to enliven democratic thinking, apply environmental values, and cultivate the virtues within the rhythm of each project.

These ideas grew from our efforts to develop access-to-tools projects that help in small ways to create meaningful work. Margaret Maika, a volunteer in our sewing space, picked up the idea:

> A belief was steadily growing [...] that a meaningful and alternative way of working with and being with others was possible. My work included craft afternoons, providing access to heavy duty sewing machines, and informally teaching the basics of using a sewing machine. I was learning a new kind of positive

energy that combined access to tools, an inclusive accepting environment, a priority on the value of human relationships and a focus on people's active participation as opposed to established bureaucratic and hierarchical structures people often experience.[18]

Few people who use The Working Centre and St. John's Kitchen own a car. They recycle clothing and furniture and tread lightly on the earth. Bikes are always parked outside of our projects as an affordable and easy way of getting around. The same frugality can be observed when public access computers are cannibalized from old computers and when people contribute work to make meals available. Community tools projects have enhanced what we saw people struggling to create and have supported people to live more easily with less money.

New work arises, Jacobs proposes, out of work already being done. There must be "an insight and, combining an idea or observation with the suggestion from the work itself."[19] Jacob's idea of new work can be understood by considering the example of bike repair. There are many privately owned shops that do this work. A community shop is both imitative and a variance on work already being done. Our departure was to equip the shop with a co-operative spirit and to address the lack of places that teach bike repair skills. New work is about adding new goods and services, for a new market, by combining the creative use of labour while refashioning the scope of the tools to make that service and product more accessible. New products and services take root if they evolve efficiently and economically.[20]

The community tools projects are highly productive. Worth a Second Look sells three thousand items a week. Queen Street Commons Café has up to four hundred customers per day. Maurita's Kitchen produces two thousand entrees and desserts each week. St. John's Kitchen serves 250 to 350 meals at lunch each weekday. Forty units of housing have been created with minimal government investment. Public access computers are used one thousand times per month, and five thousand bikes go through Recycle Cycles in a year. There are five hundred volunteers working in this model. These projects generate the majority of their revenue from their own activities.

These decentralized projects have a unity. Volunteers are invited from those who use the services (and from the wider community) and are involved in developing and reforming the work process. Projects integrated through a co-operative network have far more supports than would an independent entity. The development of this network of community services teaches the philosophy of redistribution, good work, recycling, and access to tools.

Community tools are places for new work, new ideas, and new servant leadership. These gains have been hard won through constant attention to sustainability, co-operation, and subsidiarity. This is a step-by-step process of breaking out of the constraints and conformity imposed on charities and social service organizations from government agencies or corporate structures. We have offered a new direction by inverting the structure of tools to enable workers to use their skills to serve the community and to do this in co-operation with others.

Small Is Beautiful: Re-embedding Reciprocal Relationships in Daily Work

Development from the Bottom Up

The Working Centre community has always started projects from the bottom up, finding energy and co-operation for integral development. Margaret Nally, Patrice Reitzel, and Stephanie and Joe Mancini combined theory with practice to get The Working Centre up and running. Planning started in early March 1982 and by the end of May we had a small grant, an office with a phone and message service and we were typing people's resumes as we reached out to the unemployed.

The Core Area Ministry Committee agreed to support a soup kitchen project on October 31, 1984. We would have begun operations in December at St. John's Church, but the fire department insisted we install a vented hood and fire-suppression system over the stove. We served a hearty meal on the second week of January from a small kitchen and then washed all the dishes by hand.

Tri-Tech Recycling started in November 1988 after a year of planning. We leased a warehouse space and worked long hours to sort, bale, and ship the material that kept arriving. Every Saturday long line-ups of people dropped off materials for recycling at our depot. We had no choice but to process the ever-growing volume of material.

When we took ownership of 97 Victoria Street North in May 2005, we inherited an old thrift store on the main floor. While doing the renovations, we opened with remnants of the old store in a small sectioned off area, learning the thrift store business. Plans accelerated to create a different kind of store. By December with renovations completed we officially opened Worth a Second Look with a focus on furniture and housewares. We had almost fifty volunteers, our signs, shelves, and store displays had all been hand built, and there was excitement for this new initiative.

Our method of grassroots development has been responsive, practical action. The goal of each project has been to create meaningful relationships, help individuals produce things for themselves, and create new work by addressing critical social issues. Our aim has been to cultivate the art of co-operation.

These examples of community development in action illustrate how individuals and groups can blend their creative abilities and evolve a common will to take responsibility for issues that concern them. Mary Parker Follet understood what happens when even three people combine their energy, personality, and will. Surprising results emerge when people bring a sense of determination to a project. "We must grip life and control its processes. Conscious achieving is leaping into view as the possibility of all. We are capable of creating a collective will, and at the same time developing an individual spontaneity and freedom hardly conceived of yet, lost as we have been in the herd dream, the imitation lie, and that most fatal of fallacies – the fallacy of ends."[1]

Follett understood the creative process that happens when people allow their ideas to enrich each other. This happens when authority has been delegated and people are engaged at the level where problems are best solved. When people work at their capacity, with knowledge and skill, they can arrange their priorities and address the work that needs to be done. Hierarchy gets in the way if people worry about who is above and who is below. Follet describes how the merging of minds combines independent thinking with interdependent action.[2]

Economics in the Lifeworld

The study of economics is increasingly recognized as divorced from real-world transactions that take place on the street. Economists spend their time analyzing the transactions of states and corporations. Their world is valueless. They accept inequalities along with externalities of overconsumption, pollution, and resource depletion. Economics is mainly concerned with efficient transactions. In contrast, The Working Centre and business thinkers like Follet are more concerned about what happens in the lifeworld, the place on the street where daily transactions take place that affect people's lives.[3]

The lifeworld is the place of civic engagement in neighbourhoods, ethnic communities, associations, and churches. It includes the spoken and written word, deliberations, discussions, and agreements on how we act, how we use common pool resources. The lifeworld is community, the place where we interact with each other, pursuing common efforts to make the world better.[4]

The Working Centre has managed to stay rooted in the lifeworld of grass-roots economics by embracing thinkers who resisted the fatalism of market economics. Polanyi, Lasch, Illich, and Schumacher had no patience for markets designed to leave humans as cogs in a machine. Instead they sought the virtue of honest transactions mediated by the distribution of tools that enhance community sufficiency.

Teaching Local Democracy and Social Inclusion

Lifeworld transactions are the heart and soul of The Working Centre. Ideas grow from the bottom up when there is a democratic and inclusive culture that listens, respects and acts on the voices of volunteers, staff, and participants. Local democracy is incorporated into the working of the centre through combining self-directed, skill-based learning with opportunities to participate in grassroots, co-operative projects.

The Working Centre has been a school where people learn computer repair, sewing, cooking, gardening, retailing, construction, soap making and bicycle repair. People learn while serving others and practising the social skills of shared enterprise. The process of teaching is never hierarchical, nor is the way the community tools projects organize themselves to value participation. It is about respectfully inviting others to share the joy of gaining new skills while helping others gain access to tools and things they need in a reciprocal environment.

The Working Centre introduced the Diploma in Local Democracy to teach the skills of participatory and co-operative engagement. We call these skills the habits of democratic culture: "In a democracy, citizenship means more than voting. Democracy happens as we engage each other day by day in producing our own goods, our own culture as we share experience, skills, knowledge. We teach and learn co-operatively, respecting each other individually and thereby bring democracy to life."[5] Local democracy is recognizing that we inhabit community space together. There is always tension between developing an appreciation of the other while having personal voice and agency. These ideas intermingle in democratic public settings where people are drawn out of themselves, common concerns are identified, differences debated, conflict negotiated, and mutual aid becomes possible.[6]

How can social inclusion be woven into the fabric of our culture? After centuries of exclusion, increasingly there is a common understanding that we must include and not leave people behind. In *The Joy of the Gospel*, Pope Francis makes an ethical and moral call for inclusion:

To sustain a lifestyle which excludes others, or to sustain enthusiasm for that selfish ideal, a globalization of indifference has developed. Almost without being aware of it, we end up being incapable of feeling compassion at the outcry of the poor, weeping for other people's pain, and feeling a need to help them, as though all this were someone else's responsibility and not our own. The culture of prosperity deadens us; we are thrilled if the market offers us something new to purchase. In the meantime all those lives stunted for lack of opportunity seem a mere spectacle; they fail to move us.[7]

Exclusion results from a culture dulled by bureaucracy and centralization, that fails to recognize how rigid structures construct an impermeable veneer that leaves wide segments of the population on the outside. In contrast, celebrating small, local work and building community has been The Working Centre's model to develop creative and inclusive democratic structures. Our aim is to develop a society of skilled and small-scale producers who ply their trade in creative reciprocal relationships.[8]

E. F. Schumacher believed that individuals and groups could generate productive small human communities and described this in *Small Is Beautiful*, where he took aim at bureaucratic, centralized society. This literate and humanistic book argues for the decentralization of organizations and questions the limitless use of resources.[9]

Writing in *Good Work News*, Geeta Vaidyanathan observed that: "Schumacher…believed that an entirely new system of thought is needed, based on attention to people, an economics 'as if people mattered.' But people, he notes, can be themselves, only in small comprehensible groups, and he concludes that we must learn to think in terms of small-scale manageable units."[10] When work is organized to be monotonous, nerve wracking, and unsatisfying, Schumacher believed, it is soul destroying and just short of criminal, indicating that goods are more important than people.[11]

Schumacher looked to Gandhi's moderate development approach, which saw value in labour-intensive work, appropriate technology, and local village planning. Moderate development would help villages find practical ways of producing what they needed. The logic of production should be based on what makes a community better, both materially and spiritually.

The philosophical journey of The Working Centre has included the juggling of many complimentary concepts and ideals that are integral to local democracy. We have found that social inclusion is the result of implementing local development through participation. This has meant understanding the roots of development, ensuring that our work was based on a solid foundation. Producerism taught us the importance of creating the means for people to control their tools. Distributism is a philosophy that similarly teaches how ownership of tools creates dignity. Substantive economics reminds us that honest trading of skills and goods plays an important role in binding communities together. In the next sections, each of these ideas are further explored providing lenses on how social inclusion and local democracy help establish genuine social relationships in daily work.

Roots of Development

In 1980, Joe remembers searching through dictionaries and books to find a definition for the word "development," only to find statistical references to alleviating poverty in developing countries. Even E. F. Schumacher defined the concept in relation to the foreign aid policies of Western governments.

The definition Joe was searching for was in Jim Lotz's *Understanding Canada, Regional and Community Development in a New Nation* which was published in 1977.[12] Joe had noticed this book among Lotz's writing credits but had never seen a copy of it. While visiting in 2009, Jim promised to find a copy of the first edition. It arrived within weeks and the first chapter had a sparkling definition of development as "signifying an unfolding, a growing from within, an organic process that involves a fuller and richer working out of what has already been started, the achievement of a higher level of sophistication or of completeness ... the idea that there will not only be more of what currently exists, but that things will be better."[13]

Community development for Lotz "focuses on the process of enabling people collectively to achieve goals and to influence actions together, rather than as individuals." By its very definition there is no guarantee that such a process will not dissolve into tension and dissention. Community development is a human process of finding common values that rely on co-operation with internal and external resources. There is a balance to be found between how an organization supports individuals to become the best they can and how individuals in the organization foster a learning culture to ensure the right people have the right technical knowledge like money management or customer service. The skills of community development are rarely taught—it is expected they be learned by osmosis—yet these tools are essential if communities are to improve the conditions that surround them.

Growing up in Liverpool during the Second World War helped to foster Jim Lotz's philosophy of equality. In line for lunch at St. John's Kitchen, Jim turned to Joe and said, "It is a good thing that you went to the back of the line. If you had taken me to the front, I would have left you there and gone to the back." Later that night at St. John's Kitchen, as part of his lecture for the Local Democracy project, Jim made clear that involving human beings in the process of achieving their true potential demands subtlety and complexity. He told the story of how Moses Coady of the Antigonish Movement would help people believe they could do ten times more than they thought they could do. Jim has a way of summarizing common sense actions into pithy phrases; for example, "If you want to change the music, you talk to the organ grinder, not the monkey." Practical action takes common sense, good timing, and an ability to distinguish who are the right people to talk to at the right time. It is easy to be sidetracked by someone who has no interest in your issue. Community work demands a sense of humour and a great deal of patience, he declared, adding that if you can't work like that you should get out of the way. Government is not your enemy, it is your servant, he continued. Many grassroots initiatives confuse their relationship to government by losing their critical sense and mimicking government with bureaucratic-inspired solutions. Lotz offered a final piece of advice: "Be a bridge and remember that people walk over bridges."

Jim emphasized that community development is usually rooted in small groups but cautioned that this does not diminish levels of complexity. Community development requires new methods of including people in creative, affordable, local production of housing, food, energy, and other staples. Such initiatives require ongoing learning about the complexity of the self, the community, and the world.

When The Working Centre was established in 1982 we naively set in motion a commitment to learn as much as we could about some of the fundamental truths of community development. We did not understand what it would mean to cultivate knowledge and actions that build a social infrastructure dedicated to what Gregory Baum calls, "the vision of a peaceful, co-operative society where all can eat and where all can be friends."[14] We learned over time that such a vision is best accomplished by creating co-operation and solidarity in specific projects, workplaces, and neighbourhoods. We emphasized hospitality, looking after one's neighbour, using local resources in co-operative and participatory ways to create new structures to enhance human betterment.

We learned to understand the subtle intricacies of creating community. The most fundamental action that holds community development together is the commitment to hospitality and relationships: how to be welcoming, how to be trusting, how to let the other in, how to refrain from dominating the other. These are the hospitable acts that build trust and relationships. These are the acts that take us away from bureaucratic organization building into the wonder and diversity of human relationships.

Developing an organization that opens itself to strangers goes against the grain of traditional organizational methods. Organizations have a habit of protecting themselves from all kinds of people they perceive as rivals. When we opened our doors we met people who told us we had no business being in this field. Others told us that we should be wary of this organization or that organization and warned us against others who didn't share a similar philosophy. Introspection plays an important role in developing clarity. We needed to understand why people were seeding doubts and fears as we learned the difference between building trust and creating walls of anxiety.

We chose to focus on the stories and experiences of the people we met in our homey second floor office at 94A Queen Street South. Its comfortable unofficial feel was enhanced by the previous occupant who had a flair for matching purple and blue tones. Here we learned stories from those who became our friends. They told us about getting kicked out of shelters, of surviving with no money in their pocket, of stealing food in order to eat, of families in distress because of unemployment. Concepts of organizational development meant little when compared to finding ways to support and assist this growing group of friends who told stories of a system stacked against them. We learned early that it would take a long-term commitment to enhance community through relationships. We needed a formula for organizational growth and to nurture the growth of human potential.

Community development that grows from the bottom up has a point of view and a methodology. We slowly learned how to integrate productive work that builds relationships into projects that respond to identified needs. It seemed to us that institutionalized growth was about chasing after problems by injecting money into unsustainable structures. Development from below patiently fits together puzzles of skills, revenue, location, needs, and culture. It helps communities do more than they thought possible, by learning to work co-operatively together.

Producerism: Combining Craft and Labour with a Sense of Limits

The word "producerism" was once used to describe the development of villages throughout North America during the nineteenth century, when blacksmiths, carriage makers, farmers, mill operators, and householders formed the lifeblood of the economy. This was a time when craft was infused in everyday activities. When people give up control of their work, they lose meaning and their ability to contribute to the common good. Virtue comes naturally to those working their land to produce food for the many. Producerists celebrated the skill and knowledge of the baker, planter, tiller, cloth maker, miller, tanner, and blacksmith—the trades that incorporated art into work.

By the middle of the nineteenth century, the small producers, farmers, artisans, master craftsmen, and journeymen formed the majority of business people. They created capital and became the communal strength from which villages grew into towns and cities. These were the people in North America who, on mastering a trade, purchased a small plot of land and offered their useful trade to residents of the town and villages. Robert MacFarlane, a mid-century labour leader would say that the "true foundation of a stable and firm republic was small but universal ownership."[15]

Producerism in North American history has been the attempt to develop rooted communities in which economics and social relationships were intertwined through labour, craft, church, and civic improvement. In contrast to consumerist culture, producerism is a means of producing virtue through the cultivation of friendship, craft, and adherence to a calling, not for status but for service to others.[16]

Christopher Lasch saw producerism as an idea that recaptures a moral vision now largely misunderstood. Producerism critiques the "pretensions of progress" while emphasizing "a sense of limits, a respect for accomplishments and aspirations of ordinary people, a realistic appraisal of life's possibilities, and genuine hope without utopianism which trusts life without denying its tragic character."[17] The tradition of producerism seeks civic virtue through the habit of useful daily work that contributes to community growth.

If you look around you can still find producerists. In early 2010 Joe joined the Kaufman family for lunch at the Queen Street Commons Café. Brothers Edmond and Carl were then both in their nineties and respectfully referred to Jacob Kaufman as grandfather. Grandfather Kaufman, who died in 1920, was an archetype producerist. He learned carpentry as a farm boy while working at a lumber mill near Stratford, Ontario. Jacob married the mill owner's daughter, Mary Ratz and, in 1888, set up a planing mill in the village of Berlin (now Kitchener). Jacob started numerous enterprises, best known of which was the Kaufman Rubber and Boot factory. A hands-on owner, he ran the boiler, supervised construction, and made deals to bring the rubber industry to Berlin/Kitchener. Jacob served on town council, contributed substantially to rebuilding the Zion Evangelical Church, and converted the old church into apartments that became the first home to the YWCA. Edmond tells of Jacob's woodworking shop, which crafted the wooden dashboard for the first car produced in Berlin in 1902.

Carl and Edmond, who both recently passed away, carried on the tradition of hard working producerists. Carl is known for pioneering vegetable oil bio-diesel for cars. Every day was a work day for Carl. He came from a tradition that was critical of public or private sector bureaucrats. Carl would challenge any bureaucrat that protected what he saw as a corrupt in-house culture that prevented good work from being done. Carl asked hard questions with the purpose of generating useful work, in the tradition of his family. Up to his last week, before he died at the age of 94, Edmond managed the large warehouse building on Queen Street South built by his grandfather in the 1910s. Edmond had his own business, Schlichter's Motors, and rented to two ethnic grocery stores, a billiard hall, and the Kaufman Arts Studio, a project of his grand-daughter. Carl and Edmond both appreciated The Working Centre's building revitalization projects and our commitment to involving people in good work.

After studying the ideas of Christopher Lasch, The Working Centre was ready to put producerism into action. In 1994, three factors came together to allow us to purchase 58 Queen Street South. The first was a desire to own our own space to control our destiny. We had learned that Tri-Tech Recycling's fragility was partly dependent on our status as renters. As recycling piled up on the loading dock at Dotzert Court it was only our moral position advocating for increased recycling that prevented our eviction. The next factor was the closing of Uniroyal on Strange Street. We had secured the plant-closing contract to assist the eight hundred workers who were losing their jobs. This contract allowed us to save enough money to make a substantial down payment to purchase 58 Queen. The third factor was that our landlord, overextended because of the recession, offered us the opportunity to purchase the building. We were buyers with a vision, excited that 58 Queen could become our base of operations, an open space that fostered diverse activities.

The empty apartments on the third floor presented the possibility of adding housing to our list of projects. We modified the concept of squatting, engaging two Working Centre volunteers who were living at the House of Friendship shelter to live in one of the apartments. Instead of paying rent in their first months, they agreed to renovate the apartments and make them fit for occupancy. We rented the other apartment to a couple who met while volunteering at the centre.

This was a direct way of making available low-cost housing without government subsidies, a housing social enterprise making its own decisions without relying on a distant authority. The people in the apartments became part of our community, taking responsibility for computer maintenance, cleaning, and volunteering in other areas. Many had keys to the main floor. One tenant allowed a litigious fellow named "Tiller" to work through the night. Working in the basement on his many legal cases, he did not need to rent a room.

The burst of activity in our first housing initiative resembled that of new homeowners who purchase a duplex that needs lots of work. The sooner the apartments were occupied, the quicker they generated revenue to pay the mortgage. This is the discipline of home ownership. Significant efforts went to both pay off the mortgage and to make the place look bright and welcoming. In *The Democratic Malaise* Christopher Lasch describes how democracy is best served when it rests on a broad distribution of property. "Democratic habits, [they thought]—self-reliance, responsibility, initiative—were best acquired in the exercise of a trade or the management of a small holding of property."[18] Our creativity blossomed as we demonstrated how a community group could instill its building with pride of ownership, a diversity of projects, a growing core of volunteers, and our own base for growth and development.

Property and the Distributists

In the early 1900s, a group of English thinkers, called the distributists, held that the ownership of the means of production should be spread as widely as possible among the populace rather than centralized under the control of the state, large businesses, or the wealthy.[19] Distributism proposed that workers become the owners of their tools. They supported artisans who were losing work to assembly-line thinking.

G. K. Chesterton, a vigorous proponent of distributism, recognized the important role of property in deciding the economic and spiritual welfare of communities: "Property is merely the art of democracy."[20] The Catholic Worker picked up the essential ideas of the distributists; on one hand, Dorothy Day emphasized the communal tradition with the maxim, "property, the more common the more holy it is." On the other hand, she saw ownership of property as necessary for the good life: "I believe that we should work to restore the communal aspect of Christianity as well as some measure of private property for all."[21] In one sentence Day combined the tradition of property holding with that of communal responsibility.

The Catholic Worker struggled to maintain ownership of the properties used for their houses of hospitality and the serving of daily meals.[22] The Working Centre had to address these same issues. Tri-Tech Recycling taught us how financial pressures can crush emergent projects. As we purchased other buildings, we worked to quickly pay down the mortgage with donations, allowing the operating projects more range. We became frugal and astute with money from donors and public funds.

As we completed the renovations at 43 Queen Street South, we worried about translating The Working Centre culture into the new space. We learned soon enough that the spirit of volunteerism, the public nature of the open space, and the access-to-tools projects meant that our producerist culture could be dynamic.

It was a surprising turn of events that allowed us to revitalize 97 Victoria Street North. We were pleased that our good fortune meant that we had an adequate space for the new St. John's Kitchen. The discipline of ownership permeated the renovations of 97 Victoria as it evolved quickly into a campus for St. John's Kitchen, Psychiatric Outreach, and Worth a Second Look thrift store. Two houses next door were soon purchased and converted into the Hospitality House.

The conversion of an old warehouse into a multi-use facility was a long-term project. By the sixth month we were already operating the thrift store and St. John's Kitchen moved in seven months after that. A few years later, when a local Rotary Club presented The Working Centre with a cheque for $200,000 from the proceeds of their Dream Home Lottery, it went directly to the Canadian Alternative Investment Co-operative. This social investment arm of Canadian religious organizations had granted us a mortgage with open terms. Our goal was to pay off the mortgage as soon as possible.

Ownership has given volunteers and workers a voice in revitalization projects. There is hardly an office to be found in our buildings. People involved in the construction also benefit from the access-to-tools projects that locate in the buildings. Property ownership has deepened our community connections.

Re-Engaging Substantive Economics: The Ideas of Karl Polanyi

Historically, human communities organized much of their subsistent daily work through co-operative effort. The Iroquoian people, who in 1500 CE had settlements in present-day Waterloo Region, had as their principal aim of cultural life, the acquisition of wealth "to win affection and approval by sharing this wealth with others."[23] In the Iroquoian matriarchal society friendship was equated with hospitality, gift giving, and exchanges.

The Iroquoian evolved in a way similar to other Aboriginal cultures by integrating the social function of economic activity into everyday activities. Their daily work was embedded in social relationships. Tribal societies did not create a separate economic system for production and distribution. The rewards for producing and trading went to the whole community through the mechanism of "reciprocity" and "redistribution." People helped one another and in general, the group ensured all were looked after. Tasks were assigned so that giving and receiving roughly equalled out. Chiefs would provide gifts to the sick and ailing.[24]

In European society, up to 1700 CE, the exchange of goods was protected by local customs. Bartering, haggling, and local exchanges were regulated to ensure the peace of the community. It was important that the production and distribution of goods improve social relations. Karl Polanyi described these living arrangements, whether Aboriginal or European, as substantive economics, the way humans made a living, outside the dictates of scarcity, interacting with their social and cultural environment.[25]

How did land, labour and money become commodities? Polanyi called this *The Great Transformation*, the disembedding of the economy from the community, where it had formerly been submerged.[26] Polanyi describes the political effort of the upper-class movement to dislodge communally developed exchange relationships from the culture of the working class. The major break came through the Poor Law of 1834, which forced a new dependency on wage labour by restricting both communal land holdings and the parish system of subsidizing minimal wages with bread relief. Over the next 150 years, economists twisted and turned the workings of the economic system to emphasize that individuals should compete against each other to earn their daily bread, isolating them from forming community with each other. People were displaced from their social-cultural identity. This weakened the "matrix of human well-being, the bonds of social solidarity." The great transformation created rootlessness, loss of identity, and spiritual anomie.[27]

The new economic model known as the self-regulating market, which Polanyi describes as coming into its own in 1834, is given credit for the fantastic increase in wealth that has come to those societies which unhinged traditional culture from producing and selling. The dark shadow of unrestrained economic activity is the ongoing decimation of the natural environment, which is no small point, as it is the source of human existence! The second dark shadow is that communities are becoming ever more disconnected through fragmentation and self-interest.[28]

The Working Centre is focused on these dark shadows. How can we help people reinvent a sustaining culture by re-embedding economic activity into reciprocal relationships? We don't believe state welfare to be the complete answer, because it reproduces the anomie of disconnection by offering material support without creating community. Polanyi believed history will only change when people grasp tools to rebuild community and repair solidarity.

An important step is to create work that is not about personal profit, but about community well-being. Ethics reintegrated into economic relationships transforms people's consciousness. New matrices of social relationships grow from such efforts—circles of family, friends, and companions sharing a desire to produce meaningful work. In such circles, new social creativity relies on the agency of individuals and groups to develop cultural supports. This is how human communities can develop new services that change the landscape, that help people become more connected.[29]

One way The Working Centre attempts to rebuild reciprocal exchange is to generate circles of support that encourage community- and home-production initiatives. Many individuals told us about frustrated dreams of opening up small workshops like woodworking and industrial sewing. We have tried to promote small enterprise through the recovery of traditional virtues that shape pride of ownership, labour, and craft.[30] These initiatives resulted in projects like BarterWorks, community gardens, and support for Recycle Cycles. In early 2000, we experimented with Ernesto Sirolli's concept of business facilitation but this was a skill area where we had limited success.[31]

In March 2004, we received an invitation to establish a micro-business project called ASSETS (A Service for Self-Employment Training and Support), an initiative of the local chapter of the Mennonite Economic Development Associates (MEDA). The group had learned first-hand how ASSETS operated in urban centres like Toledo, Ohio, and Miami, Florida. With backing from local Mennonite entrepreneurs, this group wanted to support grassroots business development by establishing an ASSETS project in Waterloo Region.

The stumbling block was finding the resources to establish the project independently. ASSETS found its niche by nesting in The Working Centre's social infrastructure. With minimal start-up costs, this partnership fulfilled one of our original ideas of supporting small enterprise with a participant-centred approach.[32]

Waterloo Region ASSETS+ Project (WRAP) is a ten-week business-planning course that takes participants through the steps of writing a business plan. The course creates dialogue between participants as they debate and help each other with their plans. WRAP is not government funded and this ensures that people enrol because they are genuinely interested in pursuing their business idea, rather than being diverted through official channels. The process starts when the participant first meets a facilitator to propose a business idea. Together they ensure the idea has substance. The course work builds the idea into a business plan. After graduation, WRAP provides net-working, a local exchange website and office hours to support the graduates.[33]

It is a joy to attend a graduation night. After crafting a viable micro-business plan, the graduates, often surrounded by family and friends, talk about their business idea and accept their completion certificate. We have seen two hundred graduates with business ideas for graphic design, jewellery, food preparation, food retail, bookstores, high-end used goods, urban culture bed and breakfast, and herbal products. Between 10 and 20 per cent of the busi-nesses have a strong social focus, creating products or services that enhance co-operative living. Examples include affordable eco-friendly lodging, herbal products, children's books, selling fair-trade jewellery, and co-operative ser-vices such as a recording studio for musicians.

WRAP illustrates the potential of co-operative community development. When the skills and knowledge of entrepreneurial development are focused on revitalizing communities and people-centred development, new grass-roots development takes shape.

Re-Embedding Economic Relationships in Community

The bikes lined up in front of the job search resource centre reflected the fact that those not in the paid workforce could not afford to operate cars. Our interests in supporting bike culture led us to offer informal support to a cam-paign by ambitious university students to fix up old discarded bikes.[34] When two hundred bikes were dropped off in one weekend, the students had little choice but to organize a bike shop. They found a downtown Waterloo ware-house basement and started involving students and volunteers to repair old bikes and offer bike maintenance help.

Five years later, in 1998, Recycle Cycles lived in an unheated garage that only operated with a summer student grant. It needed a permanent home. Even before we started renovating the second floor of 43 Queen it was agreed that Recycle Cycles would relocate and that The Working Centre would be its custodian. In its new location the first step was to develop consistent hours and service. In the first year one hundred bikes were recycled and about three hundred people fixed their bike at the public stands. By our fourth year we were operating year round and we had doubled the bikes recycled and repaired. By our tenth year up to eight hundred bikes were being recycled and three thousand people were using the shop to repair their bikes with the help of over fifty volunteers. Recycle Cycles had become a successful self-sustain-ing community bike shop.

Recycle Cycles demonstrates how a community group can re-establish substantive economic practices, employing slow development from the bottom up. A project grows because of the commitment of the individuals involved. People shape their tools when there is ample opportunity to contribute and be helpful. Thousands of volunteer hours are committed to bike recycling and teaching bike maintenance. These efforts are a direct result of Recycle Cycles commitment to economic diversity, mutual aid, and the sharing of work. Recycle Cycles can be contrasted against Christopher Lasch's despair that "raw ambition counted more heavily, in distribution of worldly rewards, than devoted service to a calling."[35] Rather than minimal service or work that fails to build community, here we have a group organizing bike repair tools to be useful and productive.

In March 2000, there was a scramble to finish the second floor at 43 Queen. Hours were spent painting the exposed plumbing and sprinkler pipes, cleaning up the construction mess, and installing the lighting. As the finishing touches were being applied, people continued to question why we would locate a bike shop upstairs. It took five years to demonstrate that having the perfect location was not the most important aspect, but that a friendly, hospitable place could create access to tools no matter where it lived. On the second floor, this bike shop developed new economic and cultural structures rooted in social relationships, making possible a cultural matrix of solidarity. Recycle Cycles re-embeds work in social relations where people contribute through the new skills they have learned. In such places people experience economics as step-wise participatory decision making, where sharing is integral, inclusion is natural, and money stays local.

Conclusion: Transition to Common Work

When Joe walks into Worth a Second Look (WASL), Frank, the cashier, immediately greets him with his trademark call, "Don't worry about me, Joe!" Frank is a steady hand as cashier on Thursdays and Fridays, except during Oktoberfest, when he helps the Lion's Club run their beer tent. It was not long ago when people were institutionalized for developmental issues. Frank has spent many of his fifty years in such places, but not anymore. Frank has his own apartment and lives by his own rules. Every night he goes out to cafés, bars, and card-playing community events. Frank is a storehouse of gossip. He keeps track of everyone, and if someone has been arrested or in a fight, Frank will tell you the details. Frank is a fine cashier, proud of his contribution to the WASL community.

Janice also has a developmental disability. She has volunteered at WASL from its first days, working about twenty hours a week, sorting and displaying items and helping out on the front cash. Joe first met Janice's mother, Alice, in 1984 in uncomfortable circumstances, first by phone and then at her house. Joe sat in Alice's living room, asked to account for Bill's actions. Why did we allow Bill to live in our basement? Did we not know that he had a family? What about Janice, who has a developmental disability—who will help look after her? Joe was almost speechless in the face of the sadness of the broken relationships.

Bill had come to us; a former executive vice president with a drinking problem, he was eligible for a UI subsidized job and we put his managerial skills to work. But work was the least of Bill's concerns. He had lost his way and lost faith in himself. He had left his family and had taken up woodworking. We let him stay in the basement of our home for a few months in mid-1984. We loved the beautiful pine table that he made for us, but his life was not coming together. Joe was in Alice's living room because Bill had disappeared and the police had picked him up, running in the middle of Victoria Street.

Joe was trying to explain what kind of help he needed, but Alice was having none of it. She could not believe her husband had sunk so low. Was he not a successful executive?

Today, many years later, Alice is picking up Janice and she tells Joe about Bill's recent death. Janice has already told Joe about her father dying. His last days were in a long-term care facility because of a brain injury he sustained in an accident. Alice describes Bill's death as a story of rebirth. She had never divorced him. Bill had always been her first love, and she did not abandon him over these thirty years. She had kept her faith in Bill and in God. In his final moments, Bill had given Alice a deep look of love, of appreciation, of thankfulness for staying with him. It was a story of love and grace told in the midst of a thrift store with Janice looking on, proud of her mother's commitment to her father. Later, at home, as Joe relates this story, Stephanie remembers Bill cursing the baby gate over the stairs that he had to climb over to get to his basement bedroom.

This story reminds us of the indescribable emotions that are part of everyday living, the joys and the breakdowns of human relationships. What kind of society can support the building of community in ways that offer genuine supports, help a family deal with loss, and allow the stranger to find comfort while searching for connectedness? What is the role of work and employment in the building of community?

The Working Centre Community

The Working Centre's social infrastructure offers pathways to building community. Our projects are interwoven into the culture of downtown Kitchener and have high participation. Our goal has been to offer alternatives that respectfully integrate into the culture. People's ideas and actions have dynamically changed the way we do things. Inclusion and local democratic action have resulted in an evolving structure that draws people toward projects that express common values. People want to be part of projects where their labour is respected, where they can participate by shaping the tools they are using, and where their work helps others in useful ways.

The Working Centre creates access to tools in areas as diverse as bikes, bartering, fix-it shops, housing, renovations, cafés, medical clinics, showers, laundry facilities, filmmaking, arts and sewing spaces, community gardens, greenhouse production, and so on. Each of these community tools emphasizes teaching, learning, and serving. These are the building blocks of community. The result is an integrated community providing sustainable services using the skills and talents of a community.

The Working Centre gently draws people into its community. People want their work to be meaningful. Some want their labour to do no harm to the earth and not be exploitive of other people. There are those excluded from work—the injured, older workers with outdated skills, and people with limited skills. Those with different abilities may not find work in the regular job market, but their labour is appreciated in our community. There are those with mental health and anxiety issues who cannot function in high-stress environments. Others have addictions that make it impossible to keep a job. Others have been burned out by previous jobs and now search for lower-stress employment. Every month the job market eliminates thousands of jobs. Job seekers, both short-term and long-term, are searching to find their way in. We help people test out new skills like cooking, computer repair, and outreach. Job placements, career-path exploration, and retraining are options people work through. There are people who want into the labour market and there are many who are excluded from job opportunities.

The Trap of a Job for All

In Jane Jacob's final years, she despaired of the minimal commitment our society provides to families, and she could not fathom why our work culture avoided solving problems people face. Jacobs asks if it is necessary for everyone to have a job. She had little hope that people would recognize how dependent they are on self-serving private and public institutions that dominated resources, had few limits, and controlled the direction of planning. They claim their power by the benefits of the jobs they create, and Jacobs had no patience for this power grab at the expense of community. "As exalted cultural purposes of life go, a job for everyone is less brutal and deluded than most cultural ideals. But as my grandmother used to say, 'You can run anything into the ground.'"[1]

For thirty years there has been a jobs-at-all-cost policy without an understanding of where this will lead us. The dream of a job for all, or what is known as full employment, is an impossibility that promotes unlimited economic growth. Governments use full-employment as a way of getting elected. Politicians cater to job creation. The problem, as Thomas Homer Dixon has calculated, is that our economy needs 3% GDP growth just to maintain employment.[2] What is the environmental and social cost of the constant increase in GDP?

How can communities be inclusive and productive without a focus on the myth of full employment? Work can be creating naturalized urban landscapes to produce food, compost, and other materials. Instead of an uncritical embrace of technology, we can slow down and use bikes and more simple tools. Rather than an indifference to supporting local economies we can recreate urban and suburban life with shared housing, granny flats, greenhouses, fix-it shops, and workshops in backyards. For apartment dwellers, workshops with shared tools can model different ways of structuring work. These ideas create small personal work that strengthens local communities.

We may have no choice but to create this new culture, as it becomes increasingly evident that current economic models are reaching their limits. Thomas Homer Dixon predicts that growing population and consumption will keep rubbing up against energy shortages, environmental damage, global warming, and gaps between rich and poor. These will all work in combinations, like tectonic plates slowly colliding, unleashing unpredictable results on communities whether they are resilient or not.[3] Is it not reasonable to save some cultural, resource, and economic capital as protection to deal with these forces?

Thomas Berry asks us about the destruction of our habitat caused by waste heaps, polluted waters, and sterile soils. Even if we have conceived of industrial society as a way to escape our natural environment, it is clear that we have "violated the norms of limitations, so upset the chemical balance of the atmosphere, the soil, and the oceans, so exploited the Earth in our use of fossil fuels, that we are devastating the fertility of the planet and extinguishing many species of wildlife."[4] Can we recognize how the promotion of desires through the consumer economy is already beyond environmental limits? We now inhabit a limping planet that is overcome with greenhouse gases, climate change, chemical pollution, biodiversity loss, fresh-water constraints, threatened fish stocks, a rising food crisis, and insatiable energy demands. There is a limit to growth and a limit to the number of jobs we need. It seems to us that we have hit these limits.

Human culture is the life blood through which individuals learn the truly good things in life, through "wearing the harness of the social bond,"[5] the ability to nurture relationships rooted in places and spaces that give meaning. What will sustain us? Where do we get energy, spirit, and hope if not from linking to others, offering compassion, working at meaningful endeavours? Human community, more than anything, is the building of webs of enduring relationships. Solidarity is thinking critically about how to act toward our neighbours: How do I live responsibly? How do I live out the ethical call to love?

What Does Common Work Look Like?

The stories in this book demonstrate that small local economies can grow and prosper by boldly redefining new ways our cultures can integrate reciprocal relationships. At The Working Centre we celebrate when the virtues are integral to our development. We embraced a small-is-beautiful, producerist work ethic. We have sought to re-embed social relationships into daily work. Social inclusion is our method of community engagement. Our philosophy of community tools liberates us from bureaucratic overdevelopment. Our approach to salaries stresses equality and demonstrates that the virtues can be practically lived. We have sketched out a philosophy that integrates self-help and mutual-aid approaches. This common unity is what we call *common work*. It is not a Utopian dream. It is practical action, lived in the day-to-day by building connections between people, ideas, and projects that transform community living.

The Working Centre is an ensemble, rich in relationships, rooted in service to the community. It is a place to come when faced with hardship or when searching for community. People come when they lose their job or when they want to learn a craft. Some struggle with mental health issues while others deal with family and financial loss. Many seek thrifty ways of living, directly reducing their food expenses through sharing a free meal at St. John's Kitchen. Many struggle with limited income but learn new skills—whether new Canadians, recently retired, unemployed, volunteers, or students. All join in practical projects that combine supports and community.

Well over a thousand people a day travel through The Working Centre, carrying with them stories of, as Philip Hallie would say, good and evil, help and harm.[6] Humans thrive in the give and take of reciprocal relationships where, free of status, people work as equals. The flow of skills and the gifts offered are multiplied many times over.

The Working Centre offers pedestrian-scale living where services based on access to tools are all within walking distance. Places such as the Queen Street Commons Café offer the atmosphere of the local square, a place to meet and hang out, while the renovated buildings accentuate unique architecture and commitment to revitalized use.

Last year, fifty different groups from high schools, churches, unions, universities, community groups, and funders came by to learn about The Working Centre. The Queen Street tour can take an hour. A full tour that covers the Victoria Street projects, 37 Market Lane, and Hacienda Sarria Market Garden can take three to four hours. Our places are marked by colourfulness, open concept designs, and tidy functional work areas. Visitors see that each project is a beehive of people working actively together with an egalitarian spirit. It is difficult to tell who is a volunteer, who is staff, and who are the people using the service.

A CAW regional director who visited St. John's Kitchen after the CAW Social Justice Fund contributed a substantial sum toward renovations immediately understood St. John's Kitchen. "The place is like a café with conversation and characters," he observed. He could see that people came together not only to share a meal but for the daily experience of being part of a place. The bright, earthy, functional design of the open kitchen and dining area helps create a place of dignity and friendship. Over thirty years, a culture has rooted itself around the distribution of surplus food in a daily weekday meal, with a rhythm of service and assembly. When the doors open at 8:00 each morning, twenty to thirty people come in for a coffee, muffins, and an assortment of breads. Some help with preparing to serve the 250 to 350 people who come for lunch; others read the newspaper. There is much work to do at St. John's Kitchen—looking after coffee, sorting market produce, operating the dishwasher, and sorting clothes and other items for free distribution. Soon the medical clinic opens for drop-in visits.

When you visit St. John's Kitchen you witness hundreds of conversations. The outreach workers are listening to Jim as he tells them about the bedbugs in his apartment, and they recount the first time they helped him rid the bedbugs by bagging and washing his clothes. Tom asks if Jim needs help contacting his caseworker. Tom looks at Leslie and categorically states, "I hate bedbugs."

The Clean Team, two Job Café workers with distinctive lime green T-shirts, are talking about our contract with the Kitchener Downtown Business Improvement Area to sweep King Street twice a day between April and November. "We need more hours, we could be doing a better job if they expanded it."[7] Near the serving line, there is a photocopied sheet of paper that announces the passing of a thoughtful member of the St. John's Kitchen community who was a Job Café worker on the WASL truck.

On the other side of the building is the busy entrance to WASL. Along the way you will notice that there is a constant flow of people and cars in the laneway and the parking lot. Trucks are arriving to be loaded and unloaded continually. In the small warehouse buildings, recycled clothing is collected and sorted; there is a staging area for deliveries, a space for assembling Community Access Bikeshare bikes, and room for woodworking projects. WASL is a hub of activity, with over twenty volunteers a day.

Barb Crockard coordinates the Hospitality House; she has been thinking about Robert, the first resident of the house, who passed away unexpectedly.

"He was a towering, mostly gentle giant, with the bluest eyes, a shock of silvery hair, and a beard to match. He was a familiar face about town, having a very successful career panhandling, an astute financier amongst his peers."[8] His difficult life brought him to Hospitality House, where for two years, even while dealing with significant darkness, he wandered about the 97 Victoria campus always looking for change to buy his next lottery ticket. The Hospitality House adds a dimension of hospice care to our community.

In our early years there was tension with the Region of Waterloo (ROW), and we never seemed to speak the same language. Then a slow shift happened, first when ROW deeded a large house with five bedrooms to The Working Centre to provide transitional housing for woman. Another project was the reduced fare bus pass program (Transit for Reduced Income Program, or T.R.I.P.) that we manage for the ROW helping 1,600 individuals obtain a reduced monthly bus pass. At the same time the yearly support for Psychiatric Outreach Project made possible other support for this developmental project. The ROW contributes through its STEP Home program to our Downtown Outreach and Street to Housing workers. Over time these joint projects have contributed substantially to our Region.

On Queen Street South, people often feel like they have entered a different culture. "Does all this community really exist in downtown Kitchener?" "What have I been missing that I had no idea this was going on?" As a touring group gathers at the Queen Street Commons Café, a patron plays music on the piano, most of the tables are filled with people having conversations, and the café coolers are brimming with desserts and wholesome, affordable entrees and salads. Everyone would be happy to end the tour and sit down and have a coffee and relax with a friend. For ten years the highlight of the Queen Street tour was visiting Recycle Cycles on the second floor. This is now the office for the Mennonite Coalition for Refugee Support (MCRS), an independent project supporting refugees. MCRS has lived at The Working Centre for twenty-five years. The Commons Studio video-skills project also has space on the second floor. As we cross the street, we look back at 43 Queen, explaining how we used our own labour to renovate and build two transitional apartments with three bedrooms each on the third floor.

At the Job Search Resource Centre at 58 Queen, more than forty people sit at the café tables, gather at the front reception desk, and use the fax and public phone areas and the public access computers. During the renovations we opened a double door entrance between 58 and 66 Queen to extend our employment counselling space. The resource centre also hosts the Housing Help Desk, reduced-fair bus pass program, and the Money Matters Desk.

There is a cluster of projects for WRAP, BarterWorks, and the Local Exchange Help Desk for micro-business development. We briefly look in to see Maurita's Kitchen. Today in this well-equipped commercial kitchen, there are ten volunteers preparing entrees and desserts for the café and catering orders. It is a place for camaraderie and for learning to cook affordable home style vegetarian meals. The tour group moves aside as a volunteer passes with trays of homemade buns and muffins for the café. We take the stairs down to Computer Recycling, where volunteers are fixing and refurbishing computers. It is like the bike shop, except that volunteers are hunched over computers while a customer looks on, hoping his computer can be fixed.

Most of those who tour The Working Centre are not used to all this purposeful community. Western culture usually nurtures independence from others, the desire to be self-sufficient. The opposite is true at The Working Centre, where you find engaged conversation, people enlivened by opportunities to contribute, and a mix of productiveness and camaraderie.

The tour makes visible public spaces that integrate social relationships into economic projects. Belonging, attachment, and meaningful relationships grow through service to others and inclusion in the gritty work of project improvement. Urban environments thrive from conversations and common projects.

Public places need multiple activities. The Lancaster House provides alternative housing for interns, those in transition, and guests. One year when refugees were streaming to Kitchener we temporarily housed a hundred people; many were large families in transit. GROW Herbal uses the front and back yards for growing herbs and flowers. We built a garage where the herbal products are stored and produced. The attached greenhouse is used for growing seedlings and microgreens, tiny nutrient-dense young edible broccoli, radish, or arugula greens for salads and sandwiches. Presently we are experimenting with aquaponics and learning the nutrient ecology to make the system thrive. These projects, from shared housing, gardening, herb harvesting, and microgreens and seedling production, teach practical thrift skills.

The day Joe dropped off the first microgreen harvest to Maurita's Kitchen, a high school teacher was in the resource centre expressing his excitement about The Working Centre community that he had just encountered. He was teaching a course on Catholic social teachings and had already grasped the difference between charity and justice by breathing in the nooks, crannies, and open spaces of the projects. He had spent time at St. John's Kitchen and now was watching the salads and entrées being produced in the kitchen. Common work is "the sharing of goods and resources, from which authentic development proceeds … not guaranteed by merely technical progress and relationships of utility." We have learned that sharing as a lifestyle needs a philosophy of the virtues, which creates "the potential of love that overcomes evil with good, opening up the path toward reciprocity of consciences and liberties."[9]

The Working Centre community continues to develop projects. In 2011, we purchased a former horse barn that had been converted into a warehouse. It has a front entrance on Market Lane and another entrance down the lane off King Street. When it came up for sale, we decided that Recycle Cycles, which was already servicing four thousand bicycles annually on the second floor at 43 Queen, would thrive with main floor space. Recycle Cycle volunteers agreed and started participating in designing the new shop. On move-in day, twenty Recycle Cycle volunteers loaded five trucks and over eight hours emptied the old location and partially set up the new one.

The storefront on Market Lane was converted into The Green Door, a used clothing boutique, and on the third floor is the Green Door Arts project; together they operate under the slogan Recycle, Reuse, Repurpose. The clothes are collected and sorted at WASL with an eye toward creative repurposing. The third floor Arts space offers more retail space and five sewing machines. Volunteers teach sewing skills, soap making, herbal crafting, screen printing on repurposed T-shirts, and other crafts related to reusing and repurposing old clothing. The crafts are sold at the Green Door. It did not take long to revitalize the space and with the help of Job Café workers, all 7,500 square feet were occupied and bustling within four months.

In late June 2011, Ron Doyle, a local entrepreneur tracked us down to talk about establishing a market garden at the Hacienda Sarria, a repurposed 1905 sugar beet factory. "The Hacienda Sarria needs an orchard and prosperous gardens," Doyle explained. By that autumn we were already working together to build such a place. The garden now has eight thousand square feet of interlocking brick pathways, a cooler, a water tower, and an irrigation system. This past summer five interns were taught market gardening skills. In 2013 over thirteen thousand bags and bunches of lettuce, carrots, kale, beets, spinach, herbs, and more were sold through community shared agriculture projects and local markets. Doyle's experience walking the Camino de Santiago trail in Spain reinforced the art of slowly accomplishing a goal with labour that satisfies the soul. This is the path The Working Centre travels, building community while creating access to tools to give people the opportunity to shape their work.

Transition to Common Work

When Ivan Illich wrote *Tools for Conviviality* he saw that tools were increasingly monopolized by large institutions and that environmental and social destruction was mounting. His response was to encourage, "every one of us, and every group with which we live and work, [to] become the model of the era which we desire to create."[10] This is how The Working Centre understands the transition to common work, a model for this era, which needs to be created. This movement has gathered steam as the social economy grows, becoming more common as the concept of reciprocal relationships becomes ever more embedded in people's daily work.

The good society, we believe, combines individual creativity and autonomy, decentralized approaches, moderation and balance, and the search for fulfillment. It requires widespread efforts to provide real opportunities for people to participate in making communities better. "Loyalty, devotion, faith, and self-denial," remarks Wendell Berry, "are not ethereal virtues but concrete terms by which the possibilities of love are kept alive in this world."[11]

The Working Centre has shown it possible to integrate personal desires, spiritual well-being, communal pursuits, and a deeply rooted concern for the other with work that nourishes the natural environment. The heart of the Western crisis of overdevelopment is an environmental crisis and a crisis of faith in the potential of community. Both can be addressed together.

The Working Centre, even in its thirty-second year, continues to engage in the step-by-step process of dialogue about its structures. Our development has not happened by decree or osmosis. It is a constant challenge to create conditions that allow participation and inclusion to take root. It takes years to nurture trust and loyalty, and where formerly these virtues were ingrained in village and family patterns, they now find meaning in fair-minded community settings.

On a late afternoon in February 2014, eighty staff people gather at St. John's Kitchen to discuss our organizational structures. The theme of the discussion centred on how over thirty-two years each project has evolved a similar but different approach based on participation, frugality, hospitality, inclusion, and access to tools. Less obviously, but with the same positive energy, the board and the complimenting roles of administration and fundraising have been servants helping to support the main work of the projects. The gathering introduced the language of the common table. This is a new group for project coordinators to discuss organizational issues and create dialogue between the projects. Inter-project meetings and staff–volunteer coordination meetings also take a common table format.

It is especially significant that Margaret Nally has joined us at this meeting. She continues to offer spiritual and organizational support. She is enlivened by the spirit of young people who offer their talents to our growing community. She is there to participate in the group discussions listening and adding her own experiences. Patrice Reitzel (Thorn) is also there.[12] After fifteen years of teaching, she is now retired but is working part-time as an employment counsellor. In the meeting, Joe refers to the ideas of Ivan Illich and the mentoring of Ken Westhues, whose ideas on reciprocal relationships have anchored our thinking since the 1980s. The tradition of building solidarity and loyalty is integral to The Working Centre experiment. That evening Margaret and Bob invited us to a special Bruce Cockburn concert to celebrate Conrad Grebel University College's fiftieth anniversary. The soundtrack of the 1980s reminded us of a time of birthing and suspicion. "And I'm wondering where the lions are…" and "Got to kick at the darkness 'til it bleeds daylight."[13]

In 1982, we started without organizational baggage. We knew of the lions and the darkness, but we stayed committed to creating a cultural matrix of solidarity. People were searching for a society where virtue is integrated into the way tools are deployed and used. Today our communities share tools, engage in productive activities, intermingle the generations, and include those traditionally left out. Relationships of trust grow when we allow work to teach us about the other. Simple virtuous actions like listening, respecting, helping, and offering oneself to the betterment of the other concretely demonstrates love in action. This is how decentralized communities cohere and create pathways of support.

If you look hard you can see people walking away from frantic consumption. People are learning the practical arts. "Those seeking liberty eat slowly, travel locally, plant gardens, work ethically, build communities, share tools, and eschew bigness in economic and political life," says Andrew Nikiforuk.[14] People are choosing to live with grace. We find satisfaction walking around The Working Centre and witnessing the culture come alive in places and spaces where people are fixing bikes, recycling clothing and furniture, providing showers and laundry, fixing computers, renovating buildings, making housing available, cooking and serving redistributed food, helping people find jobs, helping people with their mental health, providing medical supports, walking with people for long distances, making crafts, redistributing furniture, shovelling snow, teaching organic gardening, cooking vegetarian meals together, and running a complex people's café. All this and more is done co-operatively, with a conscious effort to change the way work is accomplished to ensure we share the common wealth with dignity and by using our hands to do the work of community.

The transition to common work is practical work that emphasizes skill, craft, and friendship. It is old work wrapped in new garments. Common work is sustained through relationships integrated in volunteer work, community work, heavy work, light work, compassionate work, and paid and unpaid work. It seeks to solve real human problems while re-embedding reciprocal relationships into the heart of the work.

The transition to common work means teaching the skills of co-operation and enterprise. It means re-embedding economics in participatory, craft-centred, social relationships. It means small-scale decentralized models that naturally generate solidarity. It means creating structures that teach the meaning of work as fulfilling one's dignity and creative spirit. What we have learned is that it is joyful, hard work to help The Working Centre travel along this path.

Map of The Working Centre
Buildings and Projects

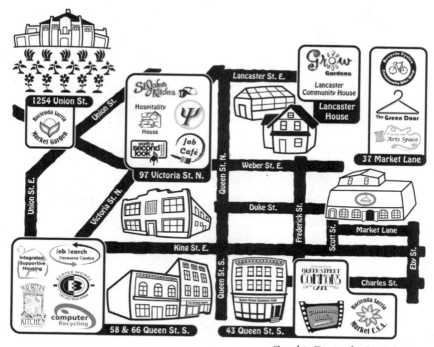

Graphic Design by Joe Johnson

Every month over 10, 000 people use Working Centre services and projects. The Working Centre is an integrated community where people can find assistance and supports like job searching, a daily meal, bicycle repair, public access computers, used furniture, and transitional housing. Communities of support grow from each project as people help each other through the struggles and opportunities they face.

Map of The Working Centre
Locations in Downtown Kitchener

The Working Centre

in Downtown Kitchener

Graphic Design by Kyle Murphy

1. 94A Queen Street South (First location)
2. 91 Queen Street South (Second location)
3. 58 Queen Street South (Main office)
4. 43 Queen Street South
5. 66 Queen Street South
6. 97 Victoria Street North
7. 91 Victoria Street North
8. 87 Victoria Street North
9. 83 Victoria Street North
10. 37 Market Lane

11. 79 Lancaster Street East
12. Queens Greens Community Garden
13. 256 King Street East
14. St. John the Evangelist Anglican Church
    (First location for St. John's Kitchen)
15. Hacienda Sarria Market Garden
16. Bridgeport Café, Waterloo
17. Tri-Tech Recycling, Waterloo
18. May Place Community Garden

A Thirty-Year Chronology of The Working Centre

1982 MARCH Ideas start developing to establish a centre that analyzes and acts on poverty and unemployment.

1982 MAY Monday May 2 is The Working Centre's first day. On May 17, a second-floor office at 94A Queen Street South above Global Community Centre is secured.

1983 JANUARY Unemployed Worker Centre's project opens in three locations: St. John the Evangelist Anglican Church, Knox Presbyterian Church, and Chicopee Community Centre.

1984 AUGUST Project funding ends for Unemployed Worker Centres.

1984 OCTOBER Planning for St. John's Kitchen begins.

1985 JANUARY St. John's Kitchen serves its first meal on January 15.

1985 SEPTEMBER Ted Schmitt invites The Working Centre to be part of the new Ontario Help Centre program.

1985 NOVEMBER 58 Queen Street South rented and renovations begin.

1986 JANUARY Ontario Help Centre funding commences with the opening of the new Job Search Resource Centre at 58 Queen Street South.

1988 FEBRUARY The first fundraising dinner recognizing Kitchener mayor Dominic Cardillo.

1988 NOVEMBER Tri-Tech Recycling public depot opens at Dotzert Court in a Waterloo industrial park.

1989 MARCH In the second year, the fundraising dinner is renamed The Mayor's Dinner. Jonas Bingeman is the guest of honour.

1991 MAY Tri-Tech Recycling winds down its operation

1991 MAY First plant-closing contract secured to provide job search support to laid-off Domtar workers.

1993 SEPTEMBER Job search support provided to one thousand laid-off rubber workers from the closed Uniroyal Strange Street factory.

1994 NOVEMBER 58 Queen Street South is purchased, and the apartments on the third floor are renovated and rented to volunteers needing housing.

1995 OCTOBER Ken Westhues's book *The Working Centre: Experiment in Social Change* is self-published. Over one thousand copies have since been printed and sold.

1996 JUNE Purchase of 79 Lancaster as a Working Centre community house.

1997 DECEMBER Major renovations of 58 Queen Street South expand and open up resource centre.

1998 FEBRUARY Purchase of 43 Queen Street South with plans for a major community renovation project.

1998 APRIL Seven hundred people at the tenth Mayor's Dinner recognize Ken Murray. The Queens Green Community Garden established.

2000 OCTOBER Open House celebrating the completion of 43 Queen, creating housing, a bike shop, arts space, computer recycling space, a crafts store and new job search resource area.

2002 JUNE Working with Kitchener Downtown Community Collaborative the first downtown outreach workers provide support to people who are homeless or at risk.

2003 JANUARY Purchase of 66 Queen Street South, the building next to 58 Queen that had been vacant for five years. CMHC awards The Working Centre a national affordable housing award for 43 Queen.

2005 MAY Purchase of 97 Victoria North and the immediate start of renovations to move St. John's Kitchen and establish a new furniture and housewares thrift store.

2005 OCTOBER Maurita's Kitchen is named in a ceremony for Maurita McCrystal, who had served as The Working Centre's board president for fifteen years before she passed away from cancer.

2005 DECEMBER Worth a Second Look Furniture and Housewares thrift store is opened on the main floor of 97 Victoria North.

2006 MAY Queen Street Commons Café and Maurita's Kitchen start operating. Employment services move from 43 Queen into the newly combined 58/66 Queen Street South resource centre.

2006 JULY St. John's Kitchen moves from the church into the newly renovated space on the second floor of 97 Victoria Street North.

2006 OCTOBER An open house celebrates the completion of 97 Victoria Street North.

2007 MARCH The Region of Waterloo deeds a large house with five bedrooms to The Working Centre to provide transitional housing for women.

2007 MAY The Working Centre celebrates its twenty-fifth anniversary with an Open House on Queen Street South, closing the street in the evening. Celebrations noted the renovations of the three buildings, the many projects, and the new housing.

MARCH 2008 Purchase of 87 and 91 Victoria North, two houses directly beside the 97 Victoria North building, to create a Hospitality House for homeless individuals who are acutely ill.

OCTOBER 2009 A garage and greenhouse is built in the back yard at Lancaster House for microgreen and seedling production.

MAY 2011 Purchase of 37 Market Lane to relocate Recycle Cycles Community Bike Shop and to establish the Green Door Clothing thrift store and the Green Door Arts Space.

OCTOBER 2011 Work begins on the two-acre market garden that will commence operations in April 2012.

APRIL 2012 Nine hundred people attend the twenty-fifth Mayors' Dinner recognizing The Working Centre's thirtieth anniversary with Margaret and Bob Nally as guests of honour.

MARCH 2013 Purchase of 83 Victoria North beside the Hospitality Houses for the purposes of establishing a Community Dental Clinic. Local dentists have joined a committee to guide the development of the project.

NOVEMBER 2013 The Hospitality House was recognized with an award by the Hospice of Waterloo Region for establishing this house for individuals who are homeless and at risk who are acutely ill.

SEPTEMBER 2014 Purchase of 256 King Street East, directly across from 37 Market Lane, with the purpose of establishing eight single-housing units on the top floor and project space on the main floor and basement.

NOVEMBER 2014 Joe and Stephanie Mancini are granted the Bene Merenti medal by Pope Francis in recognition of faithful service.

People of The Working Centre

Transition to Common Work speaks to the receptive nature of the Kitchener-Waterloo culture. We have been blessed by people who practise co-operation. There are hundreds of people who have contributed to The Working Centre story, who have shared in the journey as The Working Centre found roots. This section tries to capture many of the people and organizations we have remembered through the stories included in this book, and even so this list is but a small sampling of the many people who have journeyed with us.

The people of Global Community Centre, especially Margaret and Bob Nally and Patrice Thorn, Anna Hemmendinger and John Chamberlin, Hulene Montgomery, Michael Graham, Jane Reble, Ken Epps, Theron and Joy Kramer, and John and Peggy Lord.

The church community in Waterloo Region, including members of the Congregation of the Resurrection and the School Sisters of Notre Dame, St. John the Evangelist Anglican Church, and all the churches and faith groups who have provided workers, volunteers, and financial support. Bob Reid and Eugene McCarthy of the St. Vincent de Paul Society, who made possible the sale of 97 Victoria to establish a long-term home for St. John's Kitchen.

The labour movement of Waterloo Region has supported our work from the beginning—leaders like Wayne Samuelson, George Goebel, Bruce Davidson, Joyce and Bob Cruickshank, Sue Oberle, Tammy Heller, Jim Woods, and Tim Mitchell have carried a long tradition, many coming from CAW Local 1524. This same group made possible our annual golf tournament, with volunteers that include Rob Pyne, Paul Roeder, Janis Turenne, Frank Curnew, Steve Sachs, and UA Local 527 members Tom Crystal, John Germann, Steve Morrison, and Chris Riehl. Jim Woods started the conversation with the CAW Social Justice Fund about a $70,000 contribution toward the new home for St. John's Kitchen. When Tammy Heller died of cancer in 2010, we lost a dear friend who had put her gifted networking skills and energy into building the golf tournament.

The idea of a community kitchen started with Maria and Michael George, and was eventually supported by Martin Buhr and Brice Balmer at the House of Friendship, Anna Kaljas, Rev. Cy Ladds of St. John the Evangelist, and the Core Area Ministry Committee members, including John Wintermeyer, Gerhard Fischer, Florence Rosenburg, Ann Zettel, Judy Winter, and Ken Motts. St. John's Kitchen has been hosted by a number of dedicated people over the years, including Rose Uhrig, Arleen Macpherson, Gretchen Jones, Jennifer Mains, and many others who have served this project with compassion and respect. .

Eunice Valenzuela has guided the Mennonite Coalition for Refugee Support since the early 1990s and has intertwined MCRS with The Working Centre in mutually supporting ways.

We have had ongoing support from business and community people such as Jim Erb, Murray Haase, Jim and Sue Hallman, Jonas and Lawrence Bingeman, Fred Walker, Jim Beingessner, Neil Aitchison, Bob and Dennis of Strassburger Windows, Robert Dyck, Ted and Bruce Wright, Greg Fritz, Ron Doyle, Fr. Bob Liddy, Fr. Toby Collins, Wendy Czarny, Don Roth, Kelly Anthony, Paul Born, Rosemary Smith, Cathy Brothers, Megan Conway, Sally Lerner, Irene O'Toole, Kaye Crawford, Rev. Christopher Pratt, Barb Chrysler, Rob Davis, and Bob Shantz, who have all been crucial supporters.

Over the years we have worked with federal, provincial, and municipal staff who are truly committed to community service. These include Lesley Baresh, Ted Schmidt, Sara Rans, Laura Hamilton, Ray Gormley, Dick Parker, Linda Snyder, David Dirks, Sue Turner, Susan Kulczycki, Marie Morrision, Mike Schuster, Nancy Burnett, and Sue Forrester. We have also worked with many municipal, provincial and federal politicians. Ken Seiling as Region of Waterloo Chair for thirty years and Carl Zehr as Kitchener Mayor for seventeen years have had the longest service and offered numerous opportunities for support. We will always appreciate the early support in 1982 of Kitchener Mayor Dominic Cardillo.

A special thanks to Rita Levato who served on the board for ten years and with her father-in-law, Merv Villemaire, looked after many legal issues related to purchasing our buildings. Through Sorbara Law, Merv interested Gary Keller to continue to provide legal support.

There is no adequate way of thanking all the volunteers over these thirty years. Just last year we addressed five hundred Christmas cards to regular volunteers. There are people who stand out, such as Don Allen, Larry Crawford, Lynn Kroetsch and Ramsay Simmons, Jim Fischer, Carol Murdock, Rose Ronzio, Nan, Mae, Norm, Gerry, Kathy, John Smith, Marlene Paulter, George Ashcroft, Caroline Pratt, Brian and Margaret Hendley, Lorraine Green, Charley Mini, Suzanne Galloway, David Oppenheimer, Kaitlin Powers, Greg Meadows, Stephen, Frank, Delores, Diane and Shawneen, Chris Aagaard, Barb Hannigan, Debbie, Deborah Evans, Ray, Paul, Tony, Sr. Shirley Morris, and Margaret Maika. All those working at St. John's Kitchen, the Job Search Resource Centre, Recycle Cycles, Commons Studio, Worth a Second Look, Computer Training, Money Matters, Maurita's Kitchen, Queen Street Commons Café, Computer Recycling, and all our various construction projects have made giant contributions to building community.

Audrey Rietzel, Michael Graham, and Theron Kramer each loaned Tri-Tech Recycling $5,000 as a personal investment in community recycling. There were no strings on this personal contribution, just an expectation that we would work to make this venture successful. Dave Dawson, Tri-Tech Recycling's shop manager, had been laid off from a plant closing and was keen to learn the recycling industry from the bottom up. Hundreds worked behind the scenes to try and make Tri-Tech successful.

We wish to thank the people that made downtown outreach possible, including Marty Schreiter, Karen Kwiatkowski, Julie Dean, Shelley Adams, Jennifer Mains, the core of outreach workers, the Hospitality House staff, and the Psychiatric Outreach Project doctors and nurses, and all those who work within our Integrated Supportive Housing.

The Job Search Resource Centre grew from Maria George, Janet Wilson, and Lynn Osborne-Way to Chris Mockler, Val Girodat, Jan Stroh, Mary Lou Emburg, David Vickery, Sandy Kuhl, Janet Ferguson, Lisa McKinnon, Joanne Martin, Dave Bright, and Marlene Henderson. After that point it becomes difficult to name all the people who brought a commitment and compassion to supporting each person who walked through our doors, a person at a time. A few names must be mentioned who helped us to explore the ways our work expanded to meet growing numbers of unemployed without losing our core philosophy: Christa Van Daele, Jason Spencer, Michael Bernhard, and many others who continue to work with us through these challenges.

The workers committed to Community Tools projects form a list of creative, innovative and dedicated individuals who helped to practise how Community Tools projects welcome people from all walks of life in these creative ventures—shaping the ideas and involving people in the work. A few people to mention include Sara Macdonald and Greg Newton, who established the Queens Greens Community Garden, Joan Rawski, Rob MacIntyre, and Gretchen Jones who established the Petersburg SJK garden; Diane Heisler and Ed Bennett brought us strong connections with Milverton Amish and Old Order Mennonite farmers, and Susan Gallagher found land donated by Herb and Barbara Quickfall for the GROW Herbal and St. John's Kitchen garden. Karin Kliewer, Amaryah DeGroot, Angie Koch, Angie Freeman, Adam Kramer, Kim Knowles, Jesse Robertson, Kari Kokko, Charles McColm, Greg Roberts, Misha Gingerich, Kayli Kinnear, Margaret O'Shea-Bonner all hold or have held project building roles.

Over the years many have worked behind the scenes, holding the administration and fundraising commitments, our relationships with funders, keeping our spaces clean and in good repair, and holding on to all the details that make this work possible. Our present Common Table Group includes Don Gingerich, Jennifer Mains, Jen Smerdon, Kara Peters Unrau, Rebecca Mancini, Nathan Stretch, Jesse Robertson, and Joe Bauman.

Many people have had a major impact on the development of the Mayors' Dinner, including Dominic Cardillo, Richard Christy, Carl Zehr, Lynne Woolstencroft, Herb Epp, Brenda Halloran, Murray Haase, Margaret Motz, Dave Kropf, Joyce Stankiewicz, Neil Aitchison, Lawrence Bingeman, Fred Walker, Jim Hallman, Steve and Eve Menich, Don Allen, Roman Dubinski, Lorna van Mossel, Hulene Montgomery, Arleen Macpherson, and Chloe Callendar.

These lists cannot adequately include all of the people who have contributed in immense ways over thirty-three years. We know that there have been over five hundred people who have worked at The Working Centre and over fifteen hundred volunteers. What everyone who has journeyed with us has in common is a commitment to making their community a better place. We are deeply grateful for all the ways people have shared their engaged presence and diverse skills to build The Working Centre community.

Notes

NOTES TO CHAPTER ONE

1. Sir Albert Howard, *An Agricultural Testament* (London: Oxford University Press, 1940), 1.

2. We have integrated six virtues into our culture: *work as gift, living simply, serving others, rejecting status, building community*, and *creating community tools*. These virtues are practical and crucial ways of acting. See chapter 4 a description of the virtues and how we adopted them for our work.

3. We searched out community development practitioners who generated conditions for expressing generosity; for example, Fr. Moses Coady called it "The Intangibles of Cooperation" in *Alexander Laidlaw: The Man from Margaree, Writings and Speeches of M.M. Coady* (Toronto: McClelland and Stewart, 1971), 106; and since the 1960s Jean Vanier has described how to eschew material prosperity in order to give generously. See Jean Vanier, *Becoming Human* (Toronto: House of Anansi, 1998), 109.

4. Wendell Berry, "Off Your Horse, Out of Your Car," in *Sex, Economy Freedom, and Community* (New York: Pantheon, 1992).

5. The documentary "Freedom 95" aired on CBC Radio's *The Sunday Edition* on November 3, 2013. You can listen to it at http://www.cbc.ca/thesundayedition/documentaries/2013/11/03/documentary-7/.

6. The Job Café offers short-term, casual labour for individuals who are unable to work full-time. We assist people to earn additional income and to contribute to the community in a variety of ways.

7. On The Working Centre website we provide a full description of how these authors and activists have influenced our thinking and approaches. http://www.theworkingcentre.org/influential-thinkers/552.

8. We adopted the definition of producerism found in Christopher Lasch, *The True and Only Heaven: Progress and Its Critics* (New York: Norton, 1991), which reflects a producer ethic, supporting small producers—farmers, artisans, master craftsmen, journeymen—who were squeezed by capitalists who had more money,

state support, and growing market share. Workers were increasingly hired by large capitalist or state enterprises that consequently marginalized those who sought to generate their own work with their own hands.

9. In the 1980s, we understood the insidious effects of consumerism as an integral part of our economic system. E. F. Schumacher (*Good Work* [New York: Harper & Row, 1979]), Juliet B. Schor (*The Overworked American* [New York: Basic Books, 1991]), and Tim Kasser (*The High Cost of Materialism* [Cambridge: MIT Press, 2002]) defined how the work–spend cycle and an obsessive focus on material goods led to reduced community connections and marginalize wider social goals.

NOTES TO CHAPTER TWO

1. Philip Cross and Philippe Bergevin, *Commentary no. 366: Turning Points: Business Cycles in Canada since 1929* (Toronto: CD Howe Institute, 2012). http://www.cdhowe.org/pdf/Commentary_366.pdf.
2. Goran Hyden, *Beyond Ujamaa in Tanzania: Underdevelopment and an Uncaptured Peasantry* (Berkeley: University of California Press, 1980).
3. Julius Nyerere, *Freedom and Development* (London: Oxford University Press, 1973), 67.
4. Hyden, *Beyond Ujamaa in Tanzania*.
5. The Nestle boycott continues to this day. http://www.infactcanada.ca/nestle_boycott.htm.
6. PLURA (Presbyterian, Lutheran, United, Roman Catholic, and Anglican) was a social justice coalition that offered small grants to grassroots organizations committed to justice.
7. The pastoral circle is described in detail in chapter 4.
8. John Paul II, Laborem Exercens: Encyclical Letter on Human Work on the ninetieth anniversary of Rerum Novarum, September 1981. http://www.vatican.va/holy_father/john_paul_ii/encyclicals/documents/hf_jp-ii_enc_14091981_laborem-exercens_en.html.
9. We called our organizing group The Working Group and it was made up of Margaret and Bob Nally, Patrice Reitzel, Anna Hemmendinger, and Leo MacNeil, an unemployed rubber worker. The owner of the building, Chris Mustakas, was open to our ideas and offered friendly terms. Thirty-two years later his son Alex (Drayton Entertainment) was guest of honour at the 27th Mayors' Dinner.
10. Grindstone Island was a lodge owned by a group of Quakers and was used for nonviolence training and co-operative conferences.
11. When we got to Central Park the atmosphere was like that of a carnival with speeches and music in the distance. An estimated one million people listened to Bruce Springsteen, James Taylor, Joan Baez, and Jackson Browne.
12. We built on Global Community Centre's links to labour.
13. Joe Mancini, *Leisure Time? The Final Report of the Unemployed Worker's Centre* (Kitchener, ON: Working Centre Publications, 1984).

14. Canadian Conference of Catholic Bishops. *Ethical Reflections on the Economic Crisis* (Ottawa: CCCB Publication Services, 1983). While this statement made headlines for critically questioning the priorities of the Canadian economy, it reinforced for The Working Centre our grassroots work to integrate ethics into the economy.

15. The Core Area Ministry Committee (CAMC) was an initiative lead by Rev. Brice Balmer, minister at First Mennonite, who convinced the downtown churches to appoint members to analyze and act on downtown poverty issues.

16. Between February and May 1984, Fr. Andrew Naud, a priest of the Old Catholic Church, established a free meal and lodging in a house near Weber and Water streets. The twenty-four-hour days were demanding. He abruptly left on a walk to North Bay to raise money, and ended up doing similar work in the North.

17. In September 1985, The Working Centre was located in a second-floor strip mall (91 Queen Street South), reflecting our dire straits. We had a small grant for a couple of staff to work with volunteers to provide job-search services.

18. The majority were from cities with large labour councils. Windsor established their Unemployed Help Centres (UHC) in 1976, and others were established after 1983.

NOTES TO CHAPTER THREE

1. Leopold Kohr, *The Overdeveloped Nations: The Diseconomies of Scale* (London: C. Davies, 1977); Joe Mancini, "Alternatives to the Overdeveloped Society," *Good Work News 94* (September 2008), 1.

2. E.F. Schumacher, *Small Is Beautiful: Economics as if People Mattered* (New York: Harper & Row, 1975).

3. We have been deeply concerned by the habitat and ecosystem devastation caused by exponential resource use. Sentimentality for the beauty of the earth contrasts with the economics of consumer society. Rich countries have a rapacious demand for an ever greater share of non-renewable energy resources, fresh water, arable land, forests and fisheries to support a rich standard of living. This is done through large-scale agriculture organized by giant corporations or the burning of immense amounts of carbon for fertilizers, increased production of consumer goods and transportation. The poor, 30 per cent of the world's population, living on a dollar or two a day, do not participate in this system. In rich societies, corporations and governments assure the public that consumption is the national duty that keeps the economy going. This carbon-burning industrial system is at odds with the earth's natural systems and is inflicting harsh and irreversible damage. The Working Centre has tried to respond by integrating practices that teach and model alternatives in the broad areas of food, technology, getting around, education, community tools, and decentralized work.

4. Kenneth Westhues, *First Sociology* (New York: McGraw Hill, 1982), 429–69.

5. Ibid., 455.

6. Ibid., 452.

7. Ibid., 464.

8. See chapter 9 for a full explanation of Community Tools.

9. Ibid.

10. Scrappies collect metal (some of it of high value) that nobody wants, and they turn it into cash by selling to recyclers.

11. Kenneth Westhues, *The Working Centre: Experiment in Social Change* (Kitchener, ON: Working Centre Publications, 1995), 27.

12. David Cayley, *Conversations with Ivan Illich* (Toronto: House of Anansi, 1992). After we read this book we subsequently began a twenty-year dialogue with David and his wife, Jutta Mason. We talked, among other things, about her work at the Dufferin Grove Park.

13. Elizabeth Lemmerer, "Examining a Sample of the American-Mexican Scientific Cooperation in the 1960s: A Social Network Analysis of the CIDOC Network," Mag Phil diss., University of Vienna, 2009. http://othes.univie.ac.at/6734/1/2009-09-24_0305546.pdf.

14. Ivan Illich, *Celebration of Awareness: A Call for Institutional Revolution* (San Francisco: Heyday Books, 1969), 16.

15. Kenneth Westhues, "Joseph P. Fitzpatrick: God's Spoiled Child," paper presented at the Annual meeting of the Association for the Sociology of Religion, Washington, DC, 1995. http://www.kwesthues.com/fitzpatrick.htm.

16. Ivan Illich, *Tools for Conviviality* (London: Fontana, 1975).

17. We started adopting terms that people were unfamiliar with. *Counterproductivity* is when institutions of modern society undermine their own stated aims. Illich's book *Tools for Conviviality* provides a compendium of examples of this phenomenon. *Access to Tools* was a phrase used by *The Whole Earth Catalogue* an American counter-cultural magazine that published between 1968 and 1972 and then periodically up to 1996; we adopted it, using Illich's idea of not only access but recognizing that people need the freedom to shape their tools and "put then to use in caring for and about others." Illich, *Tools for Conviviality*, 11. Producerism is described in chapter 1, footnote 8.

18. Eric Fromm, *The Essential Fromm: Life Between Having and Being* (New York: Continuum, 1998).

19. Paul Goodman, *Growing Up Absurd* (New York: Vintage, 1960).

20. Anders Hayden, *Sharing the Work, Sharing the Planet: Work Time, Consumption & Ecology* (Toronto: Between the Lines, 1999), 47.

21. Ibid., 48.

22. John Kenneth Galbraith, *The Affluent Society* (New York: New Mentor Book, 1958), 275.

23. Juliet B. Schor, *The Overworked American*, 107–38.

24. Leopold Kohr, *The Overdeveloped Nations: The Diseconomies of Scale* (London: C. Davies, 1977), 28.

25. Ibid.

26. Henry Mintzberg, *The Canadian Condition* (Toronto: Stoddart, 1995), 56–57. Mintzberg is a Canadian management theorist who understands how emergent ideas and process can easily be stifled by imposed bureaucratic structures in both the public or private sector.

27. Leopold Kohr, *The Breakdown of Nations* (London: Routledge & Paul, 1957), xviii.

28. Cayley, *Conversations with Ivan Illich*, 82. John Papworth (ed.), *A Pair of Cranks: A Compendium of Essays by Two of the Most Influential and Challenging Authors of the 20th Century* (London: New European Publications, 2003).

29. Jim Lotz, *The Lichen Factor* (Sydney, NS: UCCB Press, 1998), 47–54.

30. Christopher Hedges, *Death of the Liberal Class* (New York: Random House, 2010), 11.

31. Kohr, *The Breakdown of Nations*.

32. See Chapter 6, Note 5 for a full list of plant closings for which we provided job search services.

33. Our first Tools for Living group had seventeen people who explored alternative work options.

34. Andy Macpherson's art is on the cover of this book and inside it, and can also be found in issues of our newsletter, *Good Work News*.

35. Kenneth Westhues, *The Working Centre: Experiment in Social Change* (Kitchener, ON: Working Centre Publications, 1995).

NOTES TO CHAPTER FOUR

1. Peter Maurin, *Catholic Radicalism: Phrased Essays for the Green Revolution* (New York: Catholic Worker Books, 1949), 93.

2. "A philosophy which regards the freedom and dignity of each person ... moving away from self-centred individualism toward the good of the other. This is done by taking personal responsibility for changing the conditions, rather than looking to the state or other institutions to provide impersonal charity." From *The Aims and Means of The Catholic Worker* found at http://www.catholicworker.org/aims andmeanstext.cfm?Number=5.

3. The Working Centre salary policy is addressed in chapter 8.

4. Westhues, *The Working Centre*, 29–31.

5. David Schwartz, *Who Cares? Rediscovering Community* (New York: Perseus Books, 1997), 38.

6. Common tables are what we call our meetings. The concept is discussed further in chapter 11.

7. Jane Jacobs, *The Nature of Economies* (New York: Random House, 2000), 46.

8. Ibid.

9. Robert Ellsberg, ed., *The Duty of Delight: The Diaries of Dorothy Day* (Milwaukee: Marquette University Press, 2008).

10. See note 6 in chapter 2.
11. From Peter Maurin's essay about personalism: "A personalist is a go-giver, not a go-getter" (see the epigraph for this chapter).
12. After retiring in 1999, Arleen became a member of Working Centre Board of Directors and was elected president in June 2013.
13. Arleen Macpherson, "Ten Years at St. John's Kitchen," *Good Work News* 39 (December 1994): 1.
14. Kenneth Westhues's first version of "Building Relationships Where People Are Real" was published in *Economic Justice Newsletter*, 24 (December 1990): 1–8. A rewritten version appeared in *Good Work News* 54 (September 1998): 1, 4–5.
15. Kenneth Westhues, "Building Relationships Where People Are Real," *Good Work News*, 1.
16. Ibid 4, 5.
17. In a special ceremony with Maurita's family we named the 68 Queen commercial kitchen for Maurita.
18. Stephanie Mancini, "Maurita McCrystal: Friend and Mentor," *Good Work News* 77 (June 2004): 1.
19. Simone Weil, *The Need for Roots* (London: Routledge, 1997), 44.
20. William Christian and Sheila Grant, *The George Grant Reader* (Toronto: University of Toronto Press, 1998), 135.
21. Carl Honoré, *In Praise of Slow, How the Worldwide Movement Is Challenging the Cult of Speed* (Toronto: Vintage Canada, 2004), 277.
22. Cayley, *Conversations with Ivan Illich;* Ivan Illich, Declaration on Soil, a joint statement drafted in Hebenshausen, Germany, December 6, 1990, in collaboration with Sigmar Groeneveld, Lee Hoinacki, and other friends.
23. Alasdair MacIntyre, *After Virtue* (South Bend: University of Notre Dame Press, 1984), 263.

NOTES TO CHAPTER FIVE

1. Committee representatives included Rev. Cy Ladds and Judy Winters from St. John's Anglican Church, Dick Parker from Regional Social Services, Brice Balmer from the House of Friendship and the Downtown Ministerial Committee, and Joan Brown from the John Howard Society. Kay Rempel attended our first meeting as staff from Ministry of Community and Social Services.
2. Urie Bender, *The Lyle Hallman Story* (Kitchener: self-published, 1993).
3. Ferne Burkhardt, *A Mighty Flood: The House of Friendship Story* (Kitchener: House of Friendship, 1989).
4. Louisa D'Amato, "Soup Kitchen Helps Poor Fight for Survival," *Kitchener-Waterloo Record*, January 13, 1986.
5. Brian Caldwell, "Soup Kitchen Hungry for Funds: 250 People a Day Can't Get Along Without the Help" *Kitchener-Waterloo Record*, June 8, 1990.

6. Arleen Macpherson, "Hope in Small Daily Happenings," *Good Work News* 52 (March 1998): 2.

7. Arleen Macpherson, "10 Years at St. John's Kitchen," *Good Work News* 39 (December 1994): 1.

8. Worth a Second Look (WASL), the furniture and housewares thrift store, was quickly blessed with over fifty volunteers, many offering hundreds of hours to launch the store in December 2005. Proceeds from WASL helped fund the renovations in the first year when thousands of goods were picked up, delivered, sorted, fixed, priced, and sold.

9. Gretchen Jones, "The Daily Work of St. John's Kitchen," *Good Work News* 75 (December 2003): 3.

10. Leslie Morgenson, "A Profound Community," *Good Work News* 68 (March 2002): 3.

11. Dave Conzani, "Give Us This Day Our Daily Bread," *Good Work News* 47 (December 1996): 1; Dave Conzani, "The Miracle on Park Street," *Good Work News* 43 (December 1995): 1.

12. Dave Conzani, "Miracle on Duke Street," *Good Work News* 39 (December 1994): 5. Reprinted in Westhues, *The Working Centre, Experiment in Social Change*, 79–85.

13. Jim Lotz, *The Lichen Factor: The Quest for Community Development in Canada* (Sydney, NS: UCCB Press, 1998), 111.

14. Jim Lotz and Michael J. Welton, *Father Jimmy: The Life and Times of Jimmy Tompkins* (Sydney, NS: Breton Books, 1997), 96.

15. Bruce K. Alexander, *The Globalization of Addictions: A Study in Poverty of Spirit* (London: Oxford University Press, 2008).

16. Unpublished interview

17. Jennifer Mains, "Seeking Beauty," *Good Work News* 111 (December 2012): 3.

18. Dr. George Berrigan, "Health Community Healthy Minds," *Good Work News* 111 (December 2012): 6.

19. As Downtown Outreach developed initially, the Region of Waterloo (ROW) was not involved, but soon after, with the establishment of a planning division focused on reducing homelessness, ROW became an active partner. Together, along with other groups, we have worked co-operatively on a philosophy of service for STEP Home (Steps to End Persistent Homelessness), ensuring that new regional support dollars are directed toward walking with individuals, thereby giving them the freedom to search for solutions. In a separate form of support, for six years ROW contributed $60,000 to the Psychiatric Outreach Project, which was the kind of flexible support necessary for developing this crucial service.

20. The LHINS (Local Health Integration Network) are corporations established by the Ontario government to determine regional health service priorities.

21. Unpublished interview.

NOTES TO CHAPTER SIX

1. Luisa D' Amato, "Waste of Money: Region's $312,000 Plan to Counsel Jobless Just Duplication," *Kitchener-Waterloo Record*, November 18, 1987; Luisa D'Amato, "Grassroots Aid to Jobless Backed; Regional Plan Stalled," *Kitchener-Waterloo Record*, December 10, 1987. When we met with the provincial officials to negotiate the grant, they questioned the region's original proposal as there was only $100,000 to allocate.

2. Henry Mintzberg, *The Canadian Condition* (Toronto: Stoddart, 1995), 56–57.

3. This paragraph reflects a critical perspective of how bureaucracies operate and the way they spend money. We have drawn from social critics who consider modern institutions counterproductive and overdeveloped (see chapter 3, 36–39). We have especially relied on Leopold Kohr *The Overdeveloped Nations: The Diseconomies of Scale* (Swansea: 1977); Jane Jacobs, *Dark Age Ahead* (New York: 2002); and Ivan Illich, *Tools for Conviviality* (Berkeley: 1973). Robert Frank *Falling Behind: How Rising Inequality Harms the Middle Class* (Berkley, CA: University of California Press, 2007) considers the "welfare losses" in society when more resources go toward individual wage competition instead of other priorities (see chapter 8, page 120).

4. "What Is the Minimum Wage?" *Economic Justice* Newsletter 13 (March 1988), 1–3.

5. "St. John's Kitchen," *Economic Justice* Newsletter 14 (June 1988), 6.

6. The following is a list of companies that closed their doors and whose employees we provided job search services to: Domtar, Stillmeadow Farms in Elora, Hoffman Meats, Epton Manufacturing, Murphy's Potato Chips, Electro-Porcelain, Bonnie Stewart Shoes, Easy Heat, Uniroyal, B.F. Goodrich, Waterloo Manufacturing, Labatts, Lear, Kaufman Rubber, Kitchener Frame, MTD, VSA, La-Z-Boy, NCR, IAC, Custom Trim, Diemaco, Zettel, and more.

7. Ryan Flanagan, "Laid-off Factory Workers Report Less Income, More Stress: CAW Study," *Kitchener Post*, September 27, 2012.

8. This story was covered by Jason Zeidenberg, who explored the experience of high unemployment in Waterloo Region for *THIS Magazine* 28(5): 33–37, and subsequently gave The Working Centre permission to republish the article; Jason Zeidenberg, "Lost in the Technology Triangle," *Good Work News* 40 (March 1995), 1.

9. Andrea M. Noack and Leah F. Vosko, *Precarious Jobs in Ontario: Mapping Dimensions of Labour Market Insecurity by Workers' Social Location and Context* (Toronto: Law Commission of Canada, 2012); Leah F. Vosko, Cynthia J. Cranford, and Nancy Zukewich, "The Gender of Precarious Employment in Canada," *Industrial Relations* 58, no. 3 (2003) 454–82.

10. Ottawa Economic Development Corporation, *The Hidden Workforce* (Ottawa: OEDC Publication, 1998).

11. Benedict XVI, Caritas in Veritate: On Integral Development in Charity and Truth. Section 77, 2009.

12. Maurita's Kitchen is a productive kitchen that uses a co-operative volunteer and training model.
13. Dorothy Day, "Peter's Program," *The Catholic Worker*, May 1955, http://www .catholicworker.org/dorothyday/Reprint2.cfm?TextID=176.
14. Tom Moore, "Suitcase Full of Broken Dreams," *Good Work News* 50 (September 1997), 5.
15. Clive Crook, "The Height of Inequality," *Atlantic Monthly*, September 1, 2006. See also Jan Pen, Income Distribution (London: Penguin Press, 1971).
16. See chapter 10, "Small Is Beautiful" for a description of ASSETS: A Service for Self Employment and Training Supports.
17. See two excellent Canadian books: Charles Long, *How to Live Without a Salary* (Michigan: Warwick Press, 1982); Wayne Roberts, *Get a Life: How to Make a Good Buck, Dance Around the Dinosaurs and Save the World* (Toronto: Get a Life Publishing, 1995).
18. Bill McKibben, *Deep Economy: The Wealth of Communities and the Durable Future* (New York: Holt Paperbacks, New York, 2008), 105.
19. Wendell Berry, "Conserving Communities," in *Another Turn of the Crank* (New York: Counterpoint Books 1995), 21.
20. Some recent countries of origin include India, Pakistan, Turkey, Colombia, China, Syria, Egypt, Sudan, Mexico, Cameroon, Iran, El Salvador, Nicaragua, Peru, Ethiopia, Eritrea, Kenya, Sudan and South Sudan, Somalia, Uganda, and Iraq.
21. During the last five years, we have hired employment counsellors from countries as diverse as Pakistan, India, Turkey, China, Cameroon, Nigeria, Kenya, Colombia, Mexico, and Germany.
22. To publicize the plight of older workers we worked with CBC *Radio National News* to produce a twenty-minute documentary on older workers, which we called "Freedom 95." It aired to a national audience on *The Sunday Edition* with Michael Enright and *The World at 6*. Maureen Brosnahan, "Freedom 95," *The Sunday Edition*, CBC Radio One, November 2, 2013.

    We also held an Older Worker's Forum that attracted 130 workers and municipal, provincial, and federal politicians. We think this national publicity caught the attention of the federal government.
23. Bill Curry, "Government Spends Millions on Ads for 'Economic Action Plan' That Ended Two Years Ago," *Globe and Mail*, January 25, 2014; "Wanted: Policy Analyst. Experience Necessary," Editorial, *Globe and Mail*, January 16, 2014.
24. Waterloo Region ASSETS+ Project (see chapter 10 for a more detailed explanation of this project).

NOTES TO CHAPTER SEVEN

1. Information about the Queens Green Community Garden can be found at http://www.theworkingcentre.org/queensgreen-community-garden/528.

2. The handbook that describes the community bake oven building process can be found at http://www.theworkingcentre.org/community-bake-oven/530.

3. GROW Herbal was started by Sue Gallagher as a project of Achievement in Motion (AIM) to establish therapeutic gardens for people who have experienced mental health issues. She used donated land for the herbal gardens and found a grant for a plastic-covered greenhouse. Sue was a friend through her work providing supports at St. John's Kitchen. The original idea for GROW was partly inspired by the Working Centre volunteers who kept the front window at 58 Queen filled with exotic plants. When AIM ran into financial difficulties we were asked to help keep the project operating.

4. Karin Kliewer, "St. John's Kitchen Garden Community," *Good Work News 79* (December 2004), 3.

5. Sue Gallagher, "Garden Imagery," *Good Work News 80* (March 2005), 4.

6. Microgreens are two-to-three-week-old young greens that are eaten for their dense nutrition. Seeds such as radish, arugula, basil, and kale become flavourful microgreens.

7. The transformation of a vacant lot into the Hacienda Sarria Market Garden is documented in "From Vacant Land to Vibrant Garden," *Good Work News 110* (September 2012), 4–5.

8. For more information about SPIN see their website at http://spinfarming.com/creators/.

9. Ken Westhues, "Building Relationships where People Are Real," *Economic Justice Newsletter 24* (December 1990), 6.

10. Alexis de Tocqueville, *Democracy in America*, Translation Harvey C. Mansfield and Delba Winthrop (Chicago: University of Chicago Press, 2000), lxviii–lxix.

11. Steve Johnson, *Future Perfect: The Case for Progress in a Networked Age* (New York: Penguin, 2012), 30.

12. Archives of Working Centre publications can be found at http://www.theworkingcentre.org/previous-publications/553.

13. Will Ferguson (1954–2011) was a pugnacious labour politician who was a hero in his St. Mary's ward and came close to becoming mayor. He had the good fortune of running for the New Democratic Party in 1990 when Bob Rae led the party to power in Ontario. Will was making a name for himself as minister of energy, but a series of events ended his political career.

14. For a tribute see: Joe Mancini, "Dominic Cardillo 1930–2013," *Good Work News 113* (June 2013), 3.

15. Sue was the Treasurer for Canadian Auto Workers (CAW) Local 1524 and in her role joined The Working Centre Board and was a strong advocate for our work. It was Sue's determination and ability to connect with CAW leadership and locals that enabled this fledgling idea to develop into a successful long-running annual fundraising event.

16. The golf tournament has raised on average about $17,000 or more a year.
17. Jim Lotz, *The Moral Equivalent of War: The New Role of Social Entrepreneurship* (Kitchener: Working Centre Publications, 2012), 52.
18. Unpublished letter submitted by Gordon Crosby.
19. Jeremy Rifkin, *Age of Access: The New Culture of Hypercapitalism Where All of Life Is a Paid-for Experience* (New York: Putnam, 2000), 59.
20. We are not aware of research that compares the franchise model of development (as described by Rifkin) with the way that large governmental or private organizations impose controls on NGOs in the field. This paragraph is written from experience, reflecting how larger entities write the rules and NGOs must follow. Over thirty years these rules have become tighter and more restrictive. This results in NGOs that are encouraged to be less creative and more rule responsive.
21. Bob Nally, "A Beehive of Social Innovation or a Celtic Weave," *Good Work News* 109 (June 2012), 4.
22. Louisa D'Amato, "Soup Kitchen Helps Poor Fight for Survival," *Kitchener-Waterloo Record*, January 13, 1986.

NOTES TO CHAPTER EIGHT

1. In this group of workers, the atmosphere was tense as people were realizing that a list of check marks could determine their salary.
2. The Working Centre Salary Policy can be found online at http://www.theworkingcentre.org/sites/default/files/salary-policy.pdf.
3. Richard Layard, *Happiness: Lessons for a New Science* (New York: Penguin Press, 2005), 128.
4. Layard, *Happiness*, 95–108.
5. Ibid., 152.
6. Robert Frank is an economics professor at Cornell University and author with US Federal Reserve chairman, Ben Bernanke, of *Principles of Economics* (New York: McGraw-Hill 2003). His other books, *The Winner-Take-All Society* (with Philip J. Cook; New York: Martin Kessler Books at The Free Press, 1995), *Luxury Fever* (Princeton: Princeton University Press, 2000), and *Falling Behind: How Rising Inequality Harms the Middle Class* (Berkeley: University of California Press, 2007) demonstrate a concern for how society distorts seemingly reasonable choices.
7. Ibid.
8. Westhues, *The Working Centre Experiment in Social Change*, 3, 32.
9. Layard, *Happiness*, 51.
10. Layard, *Happiness*, 159–60. "No sensible employer takes the tastes of his employees as given. He tries to develop their pride in work, and their willingness to help each other.... If we want a better workplace, we should teach our children that job satisfaction comes from work well done and not from getting ahead."

11. Calculated by rising gross domestic product and the price of housing.
12. James Oliver, *Selfish Capitalist* (New York: Random House, 2008), 236–37; R. Wilkinson and K. Pickett, *The Spirit Level: Why Equality is Better for Everyone* (New York: Penguin, 2009), 63–72. The study that Wilkinson and Pickett used to calculate the Canadian rate for mental illness comes from WHO International Consortium in Psychiatric Epidemiology, "Cross-international comparisons of the prevalence and correlates of mental disorders," *Bulletin of the World Health Organization* 78, no. 3 (2000): 413–26. It can be accessed at http://www.who.int/bulletin/archives/78%284%29413.pdf?ua=1.
13. Layard, *Happiness*, 35.
14. Daniel H. Pink, *Drive: The Surprising Truth about What Motivates Us* (New York: Penguin, 2009), 59.
15. de Tocqueville, *Democracy in America*, lxix.
16. Dorothy Day, *Loaves and Fishes: The Inspiring Story of the Catholic Worker Movement* (New York: Orbis Books, 1997), 17.
17. Illich, *Tools for Conviviality*, 22.
18. Joe Mancini, "Diploma in Local Democracy," *Good Work News* 114 (September 2013), 3.
19. Peter Maurin's "Better or Better Off," one of his "easy essays," can be found at http://www.catholicworker.org/roundtable/easyessays.cfm#Better Or Better Off; quoted in Westhues, *The Working Centre Experiment in Social Change*, 59.
20. Layard, *Happiness*, 38.
21. See our website for more information about E.F. Schumacher: http://www.theworkingcentre.org/influential-thinkers/2501-ef-schumacher.

NOTES TO CHAPTER NINE
1. More information about LETS and the history of BarterWorks can be found at http://www.theworkingcentre.org/barterworks-history/664.
2. Illich, *Tools for Conviviality*, 11.
3. Andrew Nikiforuk, *The Energy of Slaves: Oil and the New Servitude* (Vancouver: Greystone Books, 2012); Ivan Illich, *Energy and Equity* (New York: Harper & Row, 1974).
4. Illich, *Tools for Conviviality*, 10.
5. Jane Jacobs, *The Economy of Cities* (New York: Random House, 1969), 49–84.
6. Other community tools projects include The Sewing Space, 2nd Floor Craft Space, Paperkraft, Public Access Showers and Laundry at St. John's Kitchen, Public Access Computers, Self-Directed Computer Training, Community Voice Mail, GROW Herbal Gardens, Queen's Green Community Garden, Queen's Green Bake Oven, The Front Window, Job Café, the Urban Agriculture Project, the Good Food Box, the Commons Market, Multicultural Cinema Club, and recently the Local Exchange and Community Access Bikeshare.

7. Lotz, *The Lichen Factor*, 11.

8. This description was from a humorous email recounting some daily events.

9. John Maier, "WASL: More Than a Thrift Store," *Good Work News* 88 (March 2007), 6.

10. Our model of Integrated Supportive Housing invites people during a time of transition into shared housing and offers relationship-based support within the web of Working Centre and other community services.

11. Christopher Lasch, "Conversations and the Civic Arts" in *The Revolt of the Elites and the Betrayal of Democracy* (New York: W.W. Norton, 1995), 117.

12. Lasch, "Conversations and the Civic Arts," 121.

13. Oldenburg, Ray, *Great Good Place: Cafes, Coffee Shops, Bookstores, Bars, Hair Salons and Other Hangouts at the Heart of a Community* (Cambridge, MA: Marlowe & Company, 1999).

14. All the food is prepared in Maurita's Kitchen, which is a lively and productive community tool.

15. Geeta Vaidyanathan, "Housing as if People Mattered," *Good Work News* 72 (March 2003).

16. Benedict XVI, Caritas in Veritate, 120.

17. Richard Heinberg, *The End of Growth* (Gabriola Island: New Society Press 2011), 280. The Working Centre is listed with seven other groups in the USA and Britain each described as local multi-function hubs that help citizens solve practical problems arising from a no-growth economy.

18. Margaret Maika, "Our Sewing Space," *Good Work News* 51 (December 1997), 7.

19. Jacobs, *The Economy of Cities*, 60.

20. Ibid., 48–80.

NOTES TO CHAPTER TEN

1. Mary Follett Parker, "Community Is a Process," *Philosophical Review* XXVIII (1919), 576–88. Available at http://economics.arawakcity.org/node/95.

2. Ibid.

3. The writings of Jane Jacobs, Wendell Berry, Ken Westhues, Ivan Illich, Jean Vanier, Jane Addams, and Moses Coady are all examples of describing the life-world through street-level transactions.

4. Kenneth Westhues, "Joseph P. Fitzpatrick: God's Spoiled Child" (paper presented at the Annual meeting of the Association for the Sociology of Religion, Washington, DC, 1995).

5. This is the project description of the Diploma in Local Democracy project. For more information see http://www.theworkingcentre.org/diploma-local-democracy/188. It is a description put together by Ken Westhues and Joe Mancini and then illustrated by Andy Macpherson for a Waterloo School for Community Development graphic.

6. Palmer Parker, *Healing the Heart of Democracy: The Courage to Create a Politics Worthy of the Human Spirit* (San Francisco: Jossey-Bass, 2011), 43–46.

7. Francis, Apostolic Exhortation: The Joy of the Gospel, Section 54, 2013.

8. Kenneth Westhues, "Producerism: A Real-Life Example," *Good Work News* 54 (March 1999), 4.

9. Schumacher, *Small Is Beautiful*. Like Ivan Illich, Schumacher lived through the Second World War and worked as an economist with J. K. Galbraith on the reconstruction of Europe.

10. Geeta Vaidyanathan, "Housing as if People Mattered," *Good Work News* 72 (March 2003), 1.

11. Schumacher, *Small Is Beautiful*, 53–62.

12. Jim Lotz, *Understanding Canada: Regional and Community Development in a New Nation* (Toronto: NC Press, 1977). Republished by The Working Centre, it can be accessed at http://www.theworkingcentre.org/sites/default/files/understanding-canada.pdf. This is a treasure of a book, documenting first-hand Canadian community development during the 1960s and 1970s.

13. Lotz, *Understanding Canada*, 3.

14. Gregory Baum, "Foreword" in Westhues, *The Working Centre Experiment in Social Change*, vi.

15. Christopher Lasch, *The True and Only Heaven: Progress and Its Critics* (New York: Norton, 1991), 205.

16. Ibid., 31–34.

17. Bernard Murchland, "On the Moral Vision of Democracy: A Conversation with Christopher Lasch," *Civic Arts Review* 4 (Fall 1991). http://car.owu.edu/pdfs/1991-4-4.pdf.

18. Lasch, *Revolt of the Elites and the Betrayal of Democracy*, 7.

19. Mark and Louise Zwick, G. K. Chesterton and Dorothy Day on Economics: Neither Socialism nor Capitalism (Distributism), 2001. A talk given at the American Chesterton Society annual conference in St. Paul, Minnesota, in June 2001. http://cjd.org/2001/10/01/g-k-chesterton-and-dorothy-day-on-economics-neither-socialism-nor-capitalism-distributism/.

20. G. K. Chesterton, *What's Wrong with the World* (New York: Dover Edition, 2007), 35.

21. Dorothy Day, *From Union Square to Rome* (New York: Orbis Books, 2006), 149.

22. Day, *Loaves and Fishes*, 187–199.

23. Bruce Trigger, *The Huron Farmers of the North* (Texas: Harcourt Brace Jonanovich, 1990), 48–49. For a specific discussion on the ethnic origins of the pre-1600 aboriginal settlements along the Grand River, see Charles Garrad, *Petun to Wyandot: The Ontario Petun from the Sixteenth Century*, ed. Jean-Luc Pilon and William Fox (Ottawa: Canadian Museum of History and University of Ottawa Press, 2014), 44–45, 136–53. For further discussion on Iroquois and northern Iroquois culture, see Daniel K. Richter, *The Ordeal of the Longhouse: The Peoples of the Iroquois League in the Era of European Colonization* (Chapel Hill: University of North Carolina Press, 1992).

24. Trigger, *The Huron Farmers of the North.*

25. Gregory Baum, *Karl Polanyi on Ethics and Economics* (Montreal: McGill-Queen's University Press, 1996), 13–14.

26. Karl Polanyi, *The Great Transformation: The Political and Economic Origins of Our Times* (Boston: Beacon Press, 1957).

27. Baum, *Karl Polanyi on Ethics and Economics,* 42.

28. Thomas Berry, *The Dream of the Earth* (San Francisco: Sierra Club, 1988); Thomas Homer-Dixon, *The Upside of Down: Catastrophe, Creativity, and the Renewal of Civilization* (Toronto: Knopf Canada, 2006); Lasch, *Revolt of the Elites and the Betrayal of Democracy,* 25–49.

29. Gregory Baum, *Religion and Alienation* (Toronto: Novalis, 2006), 238–39.

30. Joe Mancini, "Home Production, Recovering Traditional Virtues: Part Common Sense—Part Small Enterprise," *Economic Justice Newsletter* 34 (September 1993), 4–5; Joe Mancini, "Relearning How to Produce for Ourselves" and "The Fun and Joy of Small-Scale Capitalism," *Economic Justice Newsletter* 32 (March 1993), 1–7.

31. Ernesto Sirolli, *Ripples from the Zambezi* (Gabriola Island: New Society Press, 1999).

32. The Waterloo Region ASSETS Project (WRAP) began in June of 2006 with consultation support from the Lancaster Pennsylvania MEDA head office.

33. For more information about WRAP see http://www.waterlooregionassets.org/.

34. This campaign resulted in Recycle Cycles, which was started by a group of University of Waterloo students involved with the Waterloo Public Interest Research Group (WPIRG) in 1993.

35. Christopher Lasch, *The True and Only Heaven: Progress and Its Critics* (New York: Norton, 1991), 33.

NOTES TO CHAPTER ELEVEN

1. Jane Jacobs, *Dark Age Ahead* (New York: Random House, 2002), 60.

2. Thomas Homer-Dixon, *The Upside of Down: Catastrophe, Creativity, and the Renewal of Civilization* (Toronto: Knopf Canada, 2006), 189–205.

3. Homer-Dixon, *The Upside of Down,* 9–30.

4. Thomas Berry, *The Dream of the Earth* (San Francisco: Sierra Club, 1988), 11.

5. Kenneth Westhues, "The Twinkling of American Catholic Sociology," in *Essays in Memory of Werner Stark, 1910–1985,* ed. Eileen Leonard, Hermann Strasser, and Kenneth Westhues, 220–44 (New York: Fordham University Press, 1993), 224.

6. Philip Hallie, *Tales of Good and Evil, Help and Harm* (New York: Harper, 1999).

7. Over ten years, with the goal of involving people not regularly in the labour market, we have developed different street-cleaning models with the Kitchener Downtown Business Improvement Area.

8. Barb Crockard, "Robert Will Be Missed," *Good Work News* 105 (June 2011), 6.

9. Benedict XVI, Caritas in Veritate: On Integral Development in Charity and Truth, Section 9, 2009.

10. Ivan Illich, *Celebration of Awareness: The Call for Institutional Revolution* (San Francisco: Heyday Books, 1969), 15.
11. Wendell Berry, *A Continuous Harmony: Essays Cultural and Agricultural* (New York: Counterpoint Press, 1972), 158.
12. See the "People of the Working Centre" section at the back of the book for a note about people like Margaret and Bob Nally and Patrice Reitzel who supported The Working Centre in its early days.
13. Bruce Cockburn, "Wondering Where the Lions Are," from *Dancing in the Dragon's Jaws* (True North Records, 1979); "Lovers in a Dangerous Time," from *Stealing Fire* (True North Records, 1984).
14. Andrew Nikiforuk, *The Energy of Slaves*, 249.

Selected Bibliography

Alexander, Bruce. *The Globalization of Addiction: A Study in Poverty of the Spirit.* Oxford: Oxford University Press, 2008.

Alinsky, Saul. *Rules for Radicals: A Pragmatic Primer for Realistic Radicals.* New York: Random House, 1971.

Baum Gregory. *Compassion and Solidarity: The Church for Others.* Toronto: House of Anansi, 1987.

———. *Karl Polanyi on Ethics and Economics.* Montreal: McGill-Queen's University Press, 1996.

———. *Priority of Labour: A Commentary on Laborem Exercens, Encyclical Letter of Pope John Paul II.* New York: Paulist Press, 1982.

———. *Religion and Alienation.* Toronto: Novalis, 2006.

———. *Signs of the Times: Religious Pluralism and Economic Injustice.* Toronto: Novalis, 2007.

Benedict XVI. Caritas in Veritate: Encyclical Letter on Integral Development in Charity and Truth. June 2009. http://www.vatican.va/holy_father/benedict_xvi/encyclicals/documentshf_ben-xvi_enc_20090629_caritas-in-veritate_en.html.

Berry, Thomas. *The Dream of the Earth.* San Francisco: Sierra Club, 1988.

———. *The Great Work: Our Way into the Future.* New York: Bell Tower, 1999.

Berry, Wendell. *Another Turn of the Crank.* Washington, DC: Counterpoint Books, 1995.

———. *A Continuous Harmony: Essays Cultural and Agricultural.* Berkeley: Counterpoint Press, 1972.

———. *Sex, Economy Freedom, and Community.* New York: Pantheon, 1992.

———. *The Unsettling of America: Culture and Agriculture.* San Francisco: Sierra Club, 1976.

Bornstein, David. *How to Change the World: Social Entrepreneurs and the Power of New Ideas.* New York: Oxford University Press, 2007.

Burkhardt, Ferne. *A Mighty Flood: The House of Friendship Story.* Kitchener, ON: House of Friendship, 1989.

Canadian Conference of Catholic Bishops. *Ethical Reflections on the Economic Crisis.* Ottawa: CCCB Publication Services, 1983.

———. *Unemployment, The Human Cost.* Ottawa: CCCB Publication Services, 1980.

Cayley, David. *Conversations with Ivan Illich.* Toronto: House of Anansi, 1992.

———. *Rivers North of the Future: The Testament of Ivan Illich.* Toronto: House of Anansi, 2005.

Christian, William, and Sheila Grant Sheila, eds. *The George Grant Reader.* Toronto: University of Toronto Press, 1998.

Coady, Moses. *The Man from Margaree.* Edited by Alexander F. Laidlaw. Toronto: McClelland and Stewart, 1971.

Crook, Clive. "The Height of Inequality." *Atlantic Monthly* (September 1, 2006).

Diamond, Jared. *Guns, Germs and Steel: The Fates of Human Societies.* New York: W. W. Norton, 1997.

Homer-Dixon, Thomas. *The Upside of Down: Catastrophe, Creativity, and the Renewal of Civilization.* Toronto: Knopf Canada, 2006.

Day, Dorothy. *From Union Square to Rome.* New York: Orbis Books, 2006.

———. *Loaves and Fishes: The Inspiring Story of the Catholic Worker Movement.* New York: Orbis Books, 1997.

———. *The Long Loneliness.* New York: Harper & Brothers, 1952.

Day, Dorothy, and Francis J. Sicius. *Peter Maurin: Apostle to the World.* New York: Orbis Books, 2004

Economic Justice Newsletter. Working Centre Publications, Issues 1–36 (1984–1994).

Ehrenfeld, David. *Becoming Good Ancestors: How We Balance Nature, Community, and Technology.* Oxford: Oxford University Press, 2009.

Ellis, Marc. *A Year at The Catholic Worker.* New York: Paulist Press, 1978.

———. *Peter Maurin: Profit in the Twentieth Century.* New York: Paulist Press, 1981.

Ellsberg, Robert, ed. *The Duty of Delight: The Diaries of Dorothy Day.* Milwaukee, WI: Marquette University Press, 2008.

Francis. Apostolic Exhortation: The Joy of the Gospel. February 2014. http:// w2.vatican.va/content/francesco/en/apost_exhortations/documents/papa -francesco_esortazione-ap_20131124_evangelii-gaudium.html.

Frank, Robert H. *Falling Behind: How Rising Inequality Harms the Middle Class.* Berkley, CA: University of California Press, 2007.

———. *Luxury Fever: Why Money Fails to Satisfy in an Era of Excess.* New York: Free Press, 1999.

Frank, Robert H., and Philip J. Cook. *The Winner Take All Society: Why the Few at the Top Get So Much More Than the Rest of Us.* New York: Penguin Books, 1995.

Follett, Mary Parker. "Community as Process." *Philosophical Review* 28, no. 6 (1919): 576–88.

Fromm, Erich. Introduction to *Celebration of Awareness: A Call for Institutional Revolution,* by Ivan Illich. London: Calder & Boyas, 1971.

————. *The Essential Fromm: Life Between Having and Being*. New York: Continuum, 1998.

Galbraith, John Kenneth. *The Affluent Society*. Boston: New Mentor Books, 1958.

Gonick, Cy. *Out of Work: Why There Is So Much Unemployment and Why It's Getting Worse*. Toronto: James Lorimer & Company, 1978.

Good Work News. Working Centre Publications, Issues 37–119 (1994–2014).

Goodman, Paul. *Communitas: Means of Livelihood and Ways of Life*. New York: Vintage, 1960.

————. *Growing Up Absurd: Problems of Youth in the Organized Society*. New York: Vintage, 1960.

————. *New Reformation: Notes of a Neolithic Conservative*. New York: Random House, 1970

Hallie, Philip. *Tales of Good and Evil, Help and Harm*. New York: Harper, 1999.

Hayden, Anders. *Sharing the Work, Sharing the Planet: Work Time, Consumption & Ecology*. Toronto: Between the Lines, 1999.

Hedges, Chris. *Death of the Liberal Class*. Toronto and New York: Random House, 2012.

Heinberg, Richard. *The End of Growth: Adapting to Our New Economic Reality*. Gabriola Island, BC: New Society Press, 2011.

Honoré, Carl. *In Praise of Slow: How a Worldwide Movement Is Challenging the Cult of Speed*. Toronto: Vintage Canada, 2004.

Illich, Ivan. *Celebration of Awareness: A Call for Institutional Revolution*. Berkeley: Heyday Books, 1969.

————. *Deschooling Society*. New York: Harper & Row, 1972.

————. *The Right to Useful Unemployment and Its Professional Enemies*. London: Marion Boyars Publishers, 1996.

————. *Tools for Conviviality*. Berkeley: Heyday Books, 1973.

Illich, Ivan, John McKnight, and Harley Shaiken. *Disabling Professions*. London: Marion Boyars Publishers, 1977.

Jacobs, Jane. *Dark Age Ahead*. New York: Random House, 2002.

————. *The Death and Life of Great American Cities*. New York: Knopf, Doubleday Publishing Group, 1961.

————. *The Economy of Cities*. New York: Random House, 1969.

————. *The Nature of Economies*. New York: Random House, 2000.

John Paul II. Laborem Exercens: Encyclical Letter on Human Work on the ninetieth anniversary of Rerum Novarum. September 1981. http://www.vatican.va/holy_father/john_paul_ii/encyclicals/documents/hf_jp-ii_enc_14091981_laborem-exercens_en.html.

Johnson, Leo. *Poverty in Wealth: The Capitalist Labour Market and Income Distribution in Canada*. Toronto: New Hogtown Press, 1974.

Johnson, Steve. *Future Perfect: The Case for Progress in a Networked Age*. New York: Penguin Books, 2012.

Kasser, Tim. *The High Price of Materialism*. Cambridge, MA: MIT Press, 2002.

Kohr, Leopold. *The Breakdown of Nations*. London: Routledge & Paul, 1957.

———. *Development Without Aid*. Swansea: C. Davies, 1973.

———. *The Overdeveloped Nations: The Diseconomies of Scale*. Swansea: C. Davies, 1977.

Kotler, Neil G., and Joseph Dahms. *Neighborhood Economic Enterprises: An Analysis, Survey, and Guide to Resources in Starting Up Neighborhood Enterprises*. Dayton, OH: Charles F. Kettering Foundation, 1978.

Kropotkin, Petr Alekseevich. *Fields, Factories, and Workshops*. London: T. Nelson, 1912.

———. *Mutual Aid: A Factor of Evolution*. New York: McClure, Philips & Company, 1902.

Lasch, Christopher. *Haven in a Heartless World: The Family Besieged*. New York: Harper 1977

———. *The Revolt of the Elites and the Betrayal of Democracy*. New York: W.W. Norton, 1995.

———. *The True and Only Heaven: Progress and Its Critics*. New York: W.W. Norton, 1991.

Layard, Richard. *Happiness: Lessons for a New Science*. New York: Penguin Books, 2006.

Long, Charles. *How to Live Without a Salary*. Toronto: Warwick Press, 1982.

Lotz, Jim. *The Humble Giant: Moses Coady, Canada's Rural Revolutionary*. Toronto: Novalis, 2005.

———. *The Lichen Factor: The Quest for Community Development in Canada*. Sydney, NS: Cape Breton University Press, 1998.

———. *The Moral Equivalent of War: The New Role of Social Entrepreneurship*. Kitchener: Working Centre Publications, 2012.

———. *Understanding Canada: Regional and Community Development in a New Nation*. Kitchener, ON: Working Centre Publications, 2010 edition.

Lotz, Jim, and Michael Welton. *Father Jimmy: The Life and Times of Jimmy Tompkins*. Sydney, NS: Breton Books, 1997.

Maurin, Peter. *Catholic Radicalism: Phrased Essays for the Green Revolution*. New York: Catholic Worker Books, 1949.

McIntyre, Alasdair. *After Virtue: A Study in Moral Theory*. London: Duckworth, 1981.

McKibbon, Bill. *Deep Economy: The Wealth of Communities and a Durable Future*. New York: Holt Paperback, 2007.

Mintzberg, Henry. *The Canadian Condition: Reflections on a "Pure Cotton."* Toronto: Stoddart, 1995.

Moore Lappé, Frances. *Food First: Beyond the Myth of Scarcity*. Boston: Houghton Mifflin, 1977.

Nikiforuk, Andrew. *The Energy of Slaves: Oil and the New Servitude*. Vancouver: Greystone Books, 2012.

Noack, Andrea M., and Leah Vosko. *Precarious Jobs in Ontario: Mapping Dimensions of Labour Market Insecurity by Workers' Social Location and Context.* Toronto: Law Commission of Canada, 2012.

Nyerere. Julius. *Freedom and Development.* London: Oxford University Press, 1973.

Oldenberg, Ray. *The Great Good Place: Cafes, Coffee Shops, Bookstores, Bars, Hair Salons, and Other Hangouts at the Heart of a Community.* Cambridge, MA: Da Capo Press, 1997.

Oliver, James. *Selfish Capitalist.* London: Random House, 2008.

Ottawa Economic Development Corporation. *Ottawa's Hidden Workforce.* Ottawa: OEDC Publication, 1998.

Papworth, John, ed. *A Pair of Cranks: A Compendium of Essays by Two of the Most Influential and Challenging Authors of the 20th Century.* London: New European Publications, 2003.

Parker, Palmer. *Healing the Heart of Democracy: The Courage to Create a Politics Worthy of the Human Spirit.* San Francisco: Jossey-Bass, 2011.

Pen, Jan. *Income Distribution.* London: Penguin Books, 1971.

Pink, Daniel H. *Drive: The Surprising Truth about What Motivates Us.* New York: Penguin Books, 2009.

Polanyi, Karl. *The Great Transformation: The Political and Economic Origins of Our Times.* Boston: Beacon Press, 1957.

Putnam, Robert. *Making Democracy Work: Civic Traditions in Modern Italy.* Princeton, NJ: Princeton University Press, 1993.

Rifkin, Jeremy. *The Age of Access: The New Culture of Hypercapitalism Where All of Life Is a Paid-For Experience.* New York: Putnam, 2000.

———. *The Empathic Civilization: The Race to Global Consciousness in a World in Crisis.* New York: Jeremy P. Tarcher/Penguin Group, 2009.

———. *The End of Work: The Decline of the Global Labor Force and the Dawn of the Post-Market Era.* New York: G. P. Putnam's Sons, 1995.

Roberts, Wayne. *Get a Life: How to Make a Good Buck, Dance Around the Dinosaurs and Save the World.* Toronto: Get a Life Publishing, 1995.

Schor, Juliet. *The Overworked American: The Unexpected Decline of Leisure.* New York: Basic Books, 1991.

Schumacher, E. F. *Good Work.* New York: Harper & Row, 1979.

———. *Small Is Beautiful: A Study of Economics as if People Mattered.* New York: Harper & Row, 1975.

Schwartz, David. *Who Cares? Rediscovering Community.* Boulder, CO: Perseus Books, 1997

Sirolli, Ernesto. *Ripples from the Zambezi.* Gabriola Island, BC: New Society Press, 1999.

Stapleton, John. "Zero Dollar Linda": A Meditation on Malcolm Gladwell's 'Million Dollar Murray,' The Linda Chamberlain Rule, and the Auditor General of Ontario." Toronto: Metcalf Foundation, 2010.

de Tocqueville, Alexis. *Democracy in America*. Translated and edited by Harvey C. Mansfield and Delba Winthrop. Chicago: University of Chicago Press, 2000.

Trigger, Bruce. *The Huron Farmers of the North*. Texas: Harcourt Brace Jovanovich, 1990.

Turner, John F. C. *Housing by People: Towards Autonomy in Building Environments*. New York: Pantheon Books, 1977.

Tyagi, Amelia Warren, and Elizabeth Warren. *The Two-Income Trap: Why Middle-Class Parents Are Going Broke*. New York: Basic Books, 2004

Vanier, Jean. *Be Not Afraid*. New York: Paulist Press, 1975.

———. *Becoming Human*. Toronto: House of Anansi, 1998.

———. *Community and Growth*. New York: Paulist Press, 1989.

———. *Made for Happiness: Discovering the Meaning of Life with Aristotle*. Toronto: House of Anansi, 2001.

Verberg, Norine. "The Kitchener-Waterloo Working Centre: A Verstehen Study of a Canadian Social Justice Response to Unemployment in the Eighties." Unpublished M.A. thesis, University of Waterloo, 1988.

Vosko, Leah F., Cynthia J. Cranford, and Nancy Zukewich, "The Gender of Precarious Employment in Canada." *Industrial Relations* 58, no. 3 (2003): 454–82.

Weil, Simone. *The Need for Roots*. London, Routledge, 1997.

Wesley, Frances, Brenda Zimmerman, and Michael Patton. *Getting to Maybe: How the World Is Changed*. Toronto: Vintage Canada, 2007.

Westhues, Kenneth. *First Sociology*. New York: McGraw-Hill, 1982.

———. "The Twinkling of American Catholic Sociology." In *Essays in Memory of Werner Stark, 1910–1985,* edited by Eileen Leonard, Hermann Strasser, and Kenneth Westhues, 220–44. New York: Fordham University Press, 1993.

———. *The Working Centre: Experiment in Social Change*. Kitchener, ON: Working Centre Publications, 1995.

Wilkinson, Richard G., and Kate Pickett. *The Spirit Level: Why Greater Equality Makes Societies Stronger*. London: Penguin Books, 2009.

Zwick, Mark, and Louise Zwick. *The Catholic Worker Movement: Intellectual and Spiritual Origins*. New York: Paulist Press, 2005.